# Indigent Records in Sonoma County California

1878 to 1926

## Volume 1
## The Indigents

Sonoma County
Genealogical Society, Inc.

HERITAGE BOOKS
2006

# HERITAGE BOOKS
*AN IMPRINT OF HERITAGE BOOKS, INC.*

**Books, CDs, and more    Worldwide**

For our listing of thousands of titles see our website
at
www.HeritageBooks.com

Published 2006 by
HERITAGE BOOKS, INC.
Publishing Division
65 East Main Street
Westminster, Maryland 21157-5026

Copyright ' 2006 Sonoma County Genealogical Society, Inc.

Other books by the author:

CD: *Sonoma County [California] Records, Volume 1*

*Early School Attendance Records of Sonoma County, California, Beginning 1858*

*Index to Naturalization Records in Sonoma County, California, Volume 1: 1841-1906*

*Index to* The Sonoma Searcher: *Volume 16, No. 1 to Volume 28, No. 3*
*(Including Index to* The Sonoma Searcher: *Volume 1, No. 1 to Volume 15, No. 4, SCGS, August 1993)*

*Index to Vital Data in Local Newspapers of Sonoma County, California, Volume I: 1855-1875*

*Index to Vital Data in Local Newspapers of Sonoma County, California, Volume II: 1876-1880*

*Index to Vital Data in Local Newspapers of Sonoma County, California, Volume III: 1881-1885*

*Index to Vital Data in Local Newspapers of Sonoma County, California, Volume IV: 1886-1890*

*Militia Lists of Sonoma County, California, 1846 to 1900*

*Naturalization Records in Sonoma County, California, Volume II: 1906-1930*

*Santa Rosa Rural Cemetery, 1853-1997*

*Sonoma County, California Cemetery Records, 1846-1921, Third Edition*

*Sonoma County, California Death Records, 1873-1905, Second Edition*

*The 1930 School Census of Sonoma County, California*

All rights reserved.  No part of this book may be reproduced or transmitted in any form or by any means, electronic or mechanical, including photocopying, recording or by any information storage and retrieval system without written permission from the author, except for the inclusion of brief quotations in a review.

International Standard Book Number: 978-0-7884-4135-3

# Contents

|  |  | Page |
|---|---|---|
| Indigent Lists of Sonoma County, California: 1878 to 1926 | | iii |
| | Arrangement and Recording of Data | viii |
| | Problems and Conventions | ix |
| | A Substitute Census | x |
| | Taxpayer Notables | x |
| | Sonoma County Townships | xi |
| | State Codes | xii |
| | International Codes | xii |
| | Acknowledgments | xiv |
| Part I | surname, given name, township, sex, residence, marital status, number of children, age of applicant, nativity of applicant | 1-45 |
| Part II | surname, given name, children's names, children's ages, children's birthplaces, lives with whom, relationship | 47-98 |
| Part III | surname, given name, reason for application, property owned, habits of sobriety, source of income, amount of money requested, date of request (day, month, year), amount of award/comments | 99-176 |
| Part IV | Demographics: Filing Status, Marital Status, Townships, Number of Children, Nationality, Awards | 177-178 |

# Indigent Lists of Sonoma County, California
# 1878 to 1926

The earliest records for persons seeking financial aid from Sonoma County are found in the Sonoma County Archives dated 1878 and span the years up to 1926.

Over that period of time, the document forms varied considerably in content and detail. The earliest applications consisted of no more than a few words scribbled on a scrap of paper. After 1900, most applications were on a standard form which required the signatures of at least ten taxpayers who knew the applicant. Generally, the taxpayers lived in the same township as the applicant. After printed forms were used, the information varied from time to time, but most of them asked for the indigent's place of residence, marital status, number of children, ages of children, who the applicant lived with, reason for asking for support, property owned, sources of income, and sobriety. In some years, information on age and nativity of the applicant, birthplace of children, and relationship of person(s) the applicant lived with was also included.

The format for data presentation is in two volumes. Volume I gives information about the applicant, his or her family, and circumstances of the request. Volume II gives a listing of the taxpayers who supported the applicant on his/her request for county funds. The signatures found on the applications are original signatures.

Figures 1a and 1b give an example of one of the earliest application forms; Figures 2a and 2b show an example of the later forms.

Samples of documents follow. Figures 1a and 1b, dated 5 May 1890, are fairly representative of the earliest requests made for financial support. Figures 2a and 2b are typical of the applications after forms were designed, although there was variation in the form throughout the time period until 1926. When the forms were designed, they required the signatures of at least ten taxpayers who swore to the following:

> The undersigned hereby certify that we have investigated in regard to the above named person and are satisfied that [he/she] should be place on the indigent list.

The data recovered from the Sonoma County Archives includes over 1,200 applications. Some persons applied more than once, and there were a few that applied as many as four or five times. Most applicants had the ten required signatures of taxpayers, some exceeded the required number, and one applicant obtained the signatures of 142 taxpayers! Several others obtained the signatures of at least 50 taxpayers.

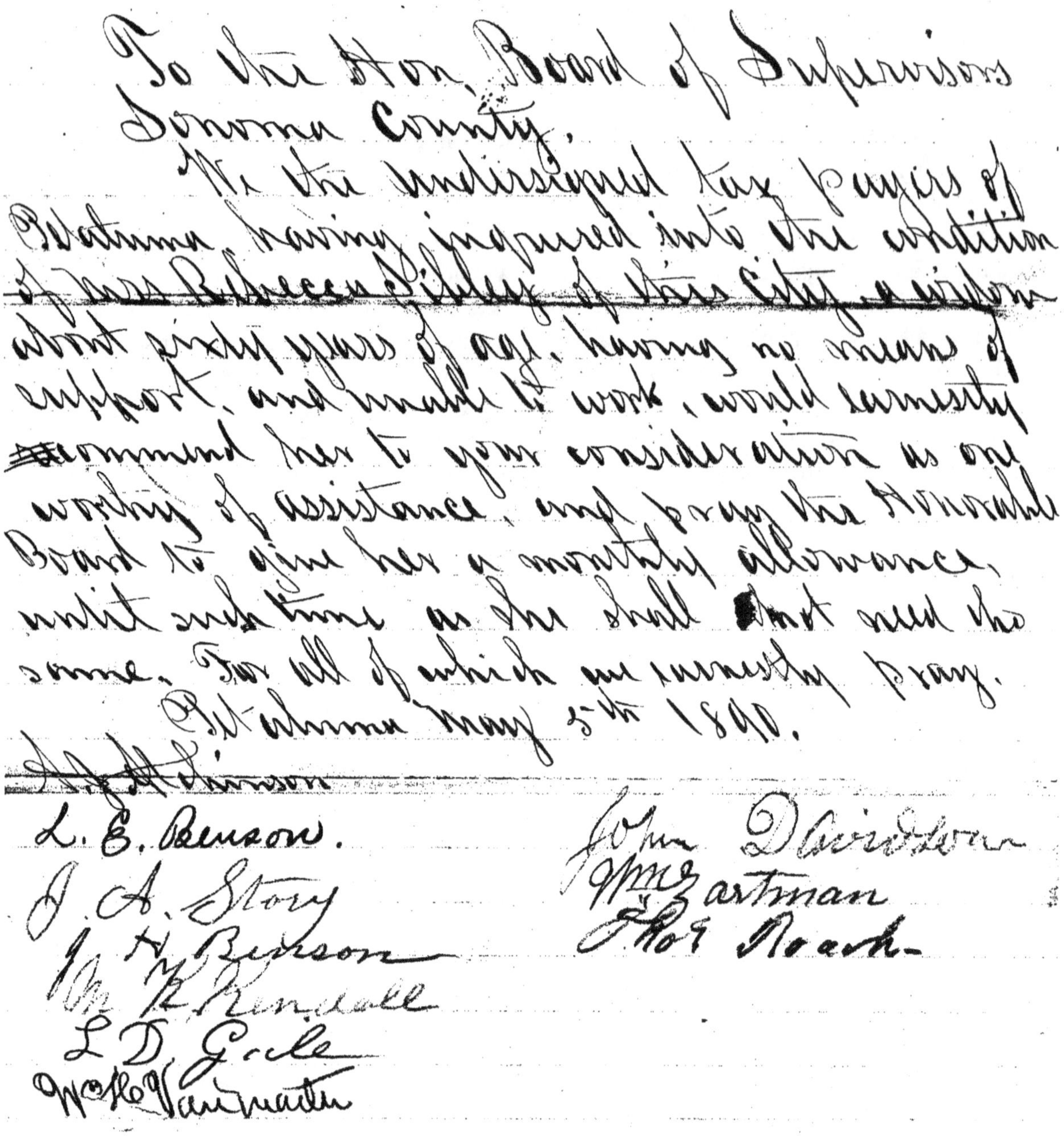

To the Hon. Board of Supervisors
Sonoma County,

We the undersigned tax payers of Petaluma having inquired into the condition of Mrs Rebecca Riley of this city, a widow about sixty years of age, having no means of support, and unable to work, would earnestly recommend her to your consideration as one worthy of assistance, and pray the Honorable Board to give her a monthly allowance, until such time as she shall not need the same. For all of which we earnestly pray.

Petaluma May 5th 1890.

L. E. Benson.
J. A. Story
J. H. Benson
Wm. K. Kendall
L. D. Gale
W. H. Vanmater

John Davidson
Wm Hartman
Thos Roach

Figure 1a: Sample of application letter dated 5 May 1890.

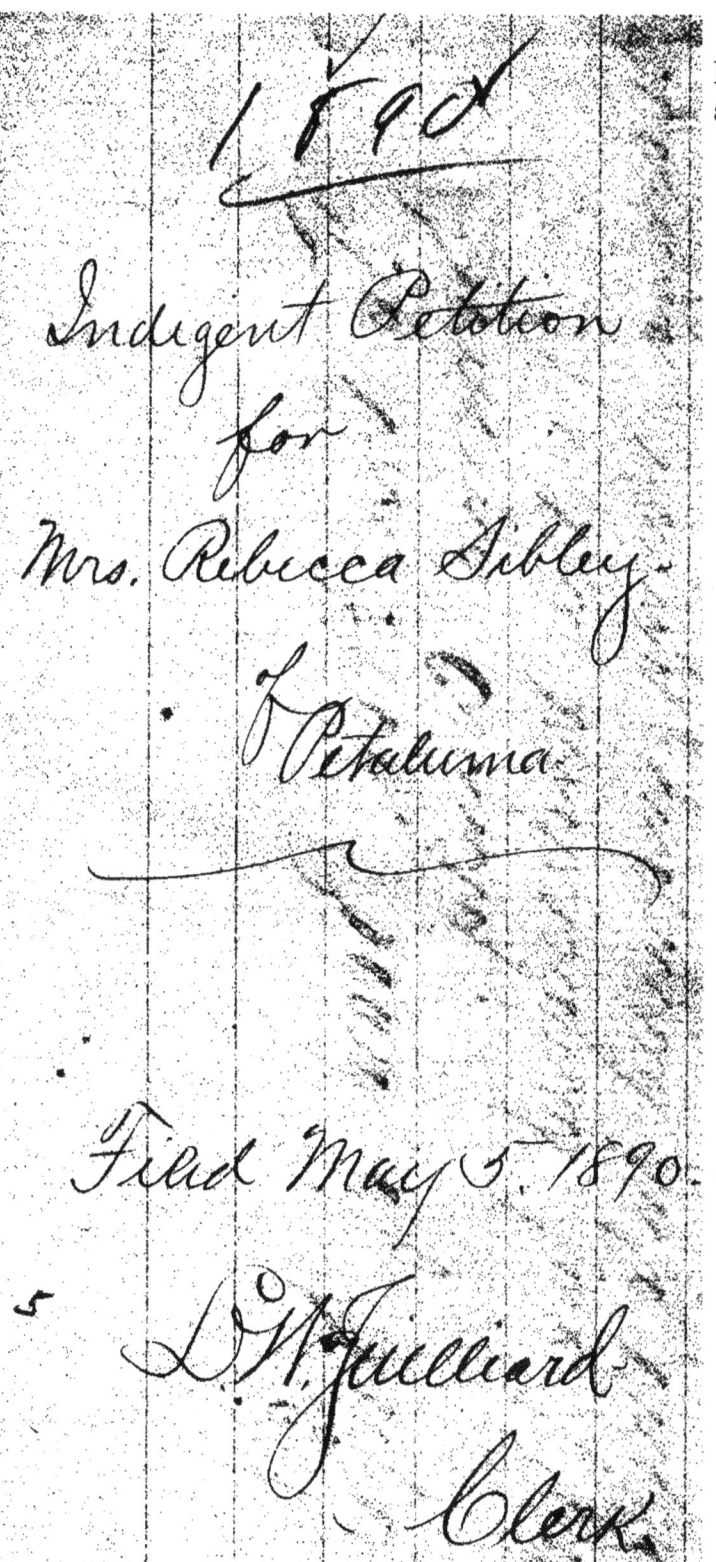

Figure 1b: Reverse side of sample application 1a.

# Petition to Be Placed on the Indigent List

To the Honorable Board of Supervisors of Sonoma County, State of California:

Gentlemen – The undersigned residents and taxpayers of _____ Township, in said Sonoma County, respectfully represent that the following-named person is one properly to be placed on the Indigent list of this County:

a. Name _Frederick Parsler_ Sex _male_

b. Residence No. _____ Street
_Glen Ellen_

c. Married or single _Single_; widow or widower _____

1. Have _3_ Children, Names and Ages of each. Give names of children ~~that are orphans or half-orphans~~
_Fred Parsler_ ⎫
_Edwin Parsler_ ⎬ all non-residents & none have contributed to my support.
_Lily Belle Parsler_ ⎭

2. Age of each _47; 43; 41._

3. Place of birth of each child _____

4. Name of persons with whom petitioner lives _no one_

5. Where said persons reside _____

6. Are children relatives of persons with whom they reside? If so, what relationship?

7. Petitioner asks to be placed on the Indigent list for the following reasons, viz:
_old age (76 years) & consequent inability to earn a livelihood_

8. Property or estate _none_

9. Habits of sobriety _good_

10. Money received by petitioner from other sources than County _x_

We therefore petition your honorable body to place the said _Frederick Parsler_ on the Indigent list of Sonoma County at a monthly allowance of at least $ _8.00_ per month, and your petitioners will ever pray, etc.

Figure 2a: Sample of form used in 1916 showing basic information about indigent applicant.

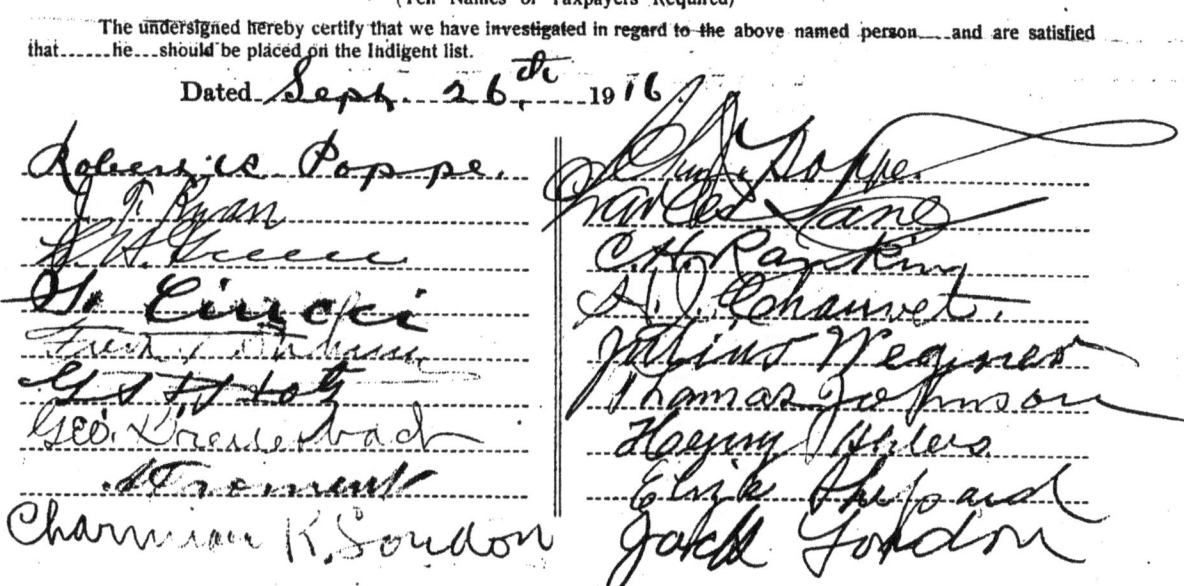

Figure 2b: Sample of signatures appearing at bottom of indigent's application. Note Jack London and his wife, Charmian, were signers on this application.

## Arrangement and Recording of Data

| Variable | | Comments |
|---|---|---|
| Surname | 1 | See Problems and Conventions following. |
| Given name | 2 | When given |
| Township | 3 | There were sixteen townships in Sonoma County during this period of time. These included Analy, Bodega, Cazadero, Cloverdale, Glen Ellen, Knights Valley, Mendocino, Ocean, Petaluma, Redwood, Russian River, Salt Point, Santa Rosa, Sonoma, Vallejo, and Washington. Some towns also carried the township name; these include Bodega, Cazadero, Cloverdale, Glen Ellen, Petaluma, Santa Rosa, and Sonoma. |
| Sex | 4 | m=male; f=female |
| Residence | 5 | Response may be as specific as street address or as general as town or township. Note also Problems and Conventions following.. |
| Marital status | 6 | s=single; m=married; d=divorced; w=widowed; a=abandoned; ds=deserted |
| No. children | 7 | When given |
| Age of applicant | 8 | When given |
| Nativity of applicant | 9 | When given, most locations are coded by state or country. A few entries may have more specific designations such as city or county. |
| Children's names | 10 | Only the given and middle names of children are given unless the surname of the child differs from the parent. |
| Children's ages | 11 | When given; some birth dates given |
| Children's birthplaces | 12 | Birthplace of children may be as specific as town/city or as general as county, state, or country. If a town is given and no county or state specified, that town is in Sonoma County. If a county is given and no state specified, that county is in California. Otherwise state and country codes are given. |
| Lives with whom | 13 | When given |
| Relationship | 14 | When given |
| Reason | 15 | The vast majority of applications are made because of old age and illness. However, some of the younger applicants have been abandoned by their husbands, or husbands have been incarcerated or died, leaving the young family without support. |
| Property | 16 | Most applicants have no or very little property. |
| Sobriety | 17 | All applicants state they have good habits of sobriety. |
| Money source | 18 | Most applicants have little or no other source of support. |
| Allowance Requested (col. R on data sheets) | 19 | After forms were instituted, a place was provided for amount of funds requested. |
| Petition date | 20 21 22 | After forms were instituted, a place for the presentation date of the petition is always included. In addition, there is usually a filing date for the petition and sometimes a date when the determination of amount of award was made. Usually these dates are from a few days to a week or two apart. A few petitions have no date at all. |
| Amount Awarded/ Comments | 23 | If an award was made, the amount is recorded in the comments column. This column is also used for other useful information not recorded elsewhere. |

**Problems and Conventions**

Legibility proved to be a problem in many cases as can been seen from examples on Figure 1a and Figure 2b. All names were read by at least two persons (the person who entered the data and one of the two persons who proofread the data) and if legibility was a particular problem, a third person attempted to resolve the problem. Still, some names proved to be totally illegible. If a name could be partially read, blanks were sometime inserted to indicate illegible letters, or a question mark was used to indicate the uncertainty of the name.

In transcribing these records it became obvious that there were problems that could not be resolved by the transcribers. Sometimes the spelling of an indigent surname varied in the case of several applications for the same individual. For example, Ferguson, Fergusson, and Furguson obviously referred to the same person. We have presented the names as transcribed from the records. Sometimes conflicting information on a single application could not be reconciled and was recorded as presented. In the case of an individual making several applications, the information might not agree. For example, one person with four applications was listed as female, twice male, and one blank. Occasionally a relative or an official filed an application for indigent children, so no parent was listed. It was found that the resident township of the indigent certifiers (taxpayers) was usually the same as the indigent applicant, but this was not always true.

To assure consistency the following conventions are used for addresses. If the street address is given, in a town named for the township, only the street address is shown. For example, 241 Edith St., Petaluma Township will not have Petaluma written after the street address. However, 425 Piper St. Healdsburg, will carry the town name because Healdsburg is in Mendocino Township. Also, San Francisco will be abbreviated as SF. In addition, the following abbreviations are used:

| bet. = between | w = widow(er) |
| --- | --- |
| cor. = corner | m = married |
| nr. = near | s = single |
| dau. = daughter | d = divorced |

If no state is given in the place of birth, assume Sonoma County, except for San Francisco and Sacramento.

An attempt was made to complete addresses, but that was not possible in all cases.

In addition, some entries contain bits of humor that were left intact, such as:
    *Money Source*—"eggs of 50 chickens";
    *Sobriety*—"medium"; "but little—"; "quiet old hermit";
    *Marital Status*—"deserted";
    *Comments*—"dejected."

**A Substitute Census**
More than 16,000 signatures, over 8,000 of which were included in the time period 1881 to 1909, provide a good index of persons living in Sonoma County during the period for which only a substitute 1890 census is available. However, these are not 8,000 unique individuals since many taxpayers signed more than one application. Never-the-less, this information is considered of enough value that Volume II of this publication is devoted to an index of the taxpayers who vouched for these early indigents.

**Taxpayer Notables**
A number of persons who helped shape Sonoma County history are found among the persons who signed in support of the applicants. Perhaps most notable was General Mariano Guadalupe Vallejo, who was Commander of the Presidio at San Francisco when California was under Mexican rule. In 1834 he was sent to Sonoma as Military Commander and Director of Colonization of the Northern Frontier. He was to take charge of the Mission San Francisco Solano de Sonoma, the northernmost mission in California.[1] Vallejo signed the petition for Matilda VanGeldern of Sonoma in 1887. Not far behind Vallejo in prestige was author Jack London and his wife, Charmian, who signed for Frederick Parker of Glen Ellen on 26 September 1916 (see Figure 2b, page vii). Luther Burbank, plant wizard, signed for eight different applicants between 1911 and 1915. Others who were notable in early Sonoma County history include Col. James B. Armstrong, Lizzie Armstrong Jones, Harrison M. LeBaron, George McNear, William McKay Stewart, and Henry J. Poehlmann.

---

[1] *A Unit of the California State Park System* (Sacramento, Calif.: Department of Parks and Recreation), pamphlet.

Sonoma County, California
Townships
Map — Circa 1896-1897

| | |
|---|---|
| Analy | Petaluma |
| Bodega | Redwood |
| Cazadero | Russian River |
| Cloverdale | Salt Point |
| Glen Ellen | Santa Rosa |
| Knights Valley | Sonoma |
| Mendocino | Vallejo |
| Ocean | Washington |

**State Codes**

| Alabama | AL |
|---|---|
| Alaska | AK |
| Arizona | AZ |
| Arkansas | AR |
| California | CA |
| Colorado | CO |
| Connecticut | CT |
| Delaware | DE |
| District of Columbia | DC |
| Florida | FL |
| Georgia | GA |
| Guam | GU |
| Hawaii | HI |
| Idaho | ID |
| Illinois | IL |
| Indiana | IN |
| Iowa | IA |
| Kansas | KS |

| Kentucky | KY |
|---|---|
| Louisiana | LA |
| Maine | ME |
| Maryland | MD |
| Massachusetts | MA |
| Michigan | MI |
| Minnesota | MN |
| Mississippi | MS |
| Missouri | MO |
| Montana | MT |
| Nebraska | NE |
| Nevada | NV |
| New Hampshire | NH |
| New Jersey | NJ |
| New Mexico | NM |
| New York | NY |
| North Carolina | NC |
| North Dakota | ND |
| Ohio | OH |

| Oklahoma | OK |
|---|---|
| Oregon | OR |
| Pennsylvania | PA |
| Puerto Rico | PR |
| Rhode Island | RI |
| South Carolina | SC |
| South Dakota | SD |
| Tennessee | TN |
| Texas | TX |
| Utah | UT |
| Vermont | VT |
| Virginia | VA |
| Virgin Islands | VI |
| Washington | WA |
| West Virginia | WV |
| Wisconsin | WI |
| Wyoming | WY |

**International Codes**

| AFG | Afghanistan |
|---|---|
| AFR | Africa |
| ALS | Alsace-Lorraine |
| ARG | Argentina |
| AUS | Austria |
| AUT | Australia |
| AZR | Azores |
| BAR | Barbados |
| BAV | Bavaria |
| BER | Bermuda |
| BHS | Bahamas |
| BLG | Belgium |
| BOH | Bohemia |
| BOL | Bolivia |
| BOR | Borneo |
| BRA | Brazil |
| BRG | British Guiana |

| BUL | Bulgaria |
|---|---|
| BUR | Burma |
| BWI | British West Indies |
| CHL | Chile |
| CHN | China |
| CLB | Colombia |
| CLZ | Canal Zone |
| CND | Canada |
| COR | Costa Rica |
| CRT | Croatia |
| CUB | Cuba |
| CZH | Czechoslovakia |
| DEI | Dutch East Indies |
| DMR | Dominican Republic |
| DNK | Denmark |
| ELS | El Salvador |
| ENG | England |

| ESI | East India |
|---|---|
| EUR | Europe |
| FIN | Finland |
| FR CND | French Canadian |
| FRN | France |
| FRP | French Polynesia |
| GAM | Guam |
| GBR | Great Britain |
| GER | Germany |
| GIB | Gibraltar |
| GRC | Greece |
| GUA | Guatemala |
| HAI | Haiti |
| HIN | Hindustan |
| HLD | Holland |
| HND | Honduras |

| | | | | | | | |
|---|---|---|---|---|---|---|---|
| HUN | Hungary | | NRY | Norway | | SEA | (born at sea) |
| HWI | Hawaii | | NSC | Nova Scotia | | SGP | Singapore |
| ICE | Iceland | | NTH | Netherlands | | SIB | Siberia |
| IDA | India | | NZD | New Zealand | | SLO | Slovakia |
| IND | Indonesia | | OTT | Ottoman Empire | | SPN | Spain |
| IOM | Isle of Man | | PAL | Palestine | | SRB | Serbia |
| IRL | Ireland | | PAN | Panama | | SWD | Sweden |
| ISR | Israel | | PER | Persia | | SWI | Sandwich Islands |
| ITL | Italy | | PHL | Philippines | | SWT | Switzerland |
| JAM | Jamaica | | PLD | Poland | | SYR | Syria |
| JPN | Japan | | PRS | Prussia | | TRK | Turkey |
| JVA | Java | | PRT | Portugal | | URG | Uruguay |
| KOR | Korea | | PRU | Peru | | VEN | Venezuela |
| LAT | Latvia | | PUR | Puerto Rico | | VIE | Vietnam |
| LEB | Lebanon | | ROM | Romania | | VRI | Virgin Islands |
| LIT | Lithuania | | RUS | Russia | | WIN | West Indies |
| LUX | Luxembourg | | SAF | South Africa | | WLS | Wales |
| MEX | Mexico | | SAM | South America | | WTS | Western Islands |
| MLT | Malta | | SAX | Saxony | | YUG | Yugoslavia |
| NAM | North America | | SCT | Scotland | | | |
| NBW | New Brunswick | | | | | | |

# Acknowledgments

This publication was made possible through the volunteer efforts of members of the Sonoma County Genealogical Society.

**Project Director**
Carmen J. Finley

**Project Coordinator**
Anna Conley

**Project Technician**
Joe Panaro

**Historian**
Ray Owen

**Data Entry**
Anna Conley
Muriel Morrow
Lois Nimmo
Joe Panaro

**Proofreaders**
Doris Dickenson
Carmen Finley
Lois Nimmo

**Editor**
Doris Dickenson

**Camera Ready Copy**
Carmen J. Finley

Special recognition is also given to Anthony Hoskins, History, Genealogy, and Archives Librarian, Sonoma County Library, for providing the documents and the use of the facilities of the History and Genealogy Library. The library is located at 3rd and E Streets, Santa Rosa, California 95404, 707/545-0831, ext. 562.

# Part I

surname, given name, township, sex, residence, marital status, number of children, age of applicant, nativity of applicant

| 1 | 2 | 3 | 4 | 5 | 6 | 7 | 8 | 9 |
|---|---|---|---|---|---|---|---|---|
| SURNAME | GIVEN NAME | TOWNSHIP | SEX | RESIDENCE | MAR. | NO. CHILDREN | AGE | NATIVITY |
| Abino | Rosania | Petaluma | f | Liberty School Dist. | w | 5 | 45 | PRT |
| Adams | J. W. | Santa Rosa | m | | m | 2 | | |
| Adams | Melissa, Mrs. | Santa Rosa | f | 311 Santa Rosa Ave. | w | | 55 | WI |
| Adams | W. J. | Santa Rosa | m | | m | 1 | | |
| Adams | W. J. | Santa Rosa | m | bet. Beaver & King Sts. | m | 2 | | |
| Albertson | Iver | Santa Rosa | m | 629 Sonoma Ave. | m | 2 | | |
| Alexander | Ada Lue, Mrs. | Petaluma | f | 674 Edith St. | w | 4 | 35 | CA |
| Alexander | Lou Humphreys, Mrs. | Petaluma | f | 329 Edith St. | w | 4 | | |
| Allan | Maude, Mrs. | Petaluma | f | R.F.D. 5 | w | 2 | | |
| Allen | Bessie May | Mendocino | f | Healdsburg | | | > 7 | |
| Allen | W. H. | Santa Rosa | m | De Turk St. | w | | | |
| Alsved | Louisa, Mrs. | Sonoma | f | Glen Ellen | m | 2 | 43 | FIN |
| Alway | Abby, Mrs. | Sonoma | f | Napa St. | w | | 75 | |
| Amwell(e) | Letta | Mendocino | f | 528 Brown St., Healdsburg | m | 3 | | |
| Andersen | Thomas & wife | Petaluma | m/f | 319 Pleasent St. | m | | 65+ | |
| Anderson | John P. | Russian River | m | | m | | 83 | NC |
| Anderson | Louisa | Santa Rosa | f | | | | | |
| Anderson | Mary | Russian River | f | | m | | 87 | NC |
| Andrews | Carrie | Petaluma | f | 314 Fifth St. | m | 2 | | |
| Andrews | Elizabeth, Mrs. | Santa Rosa | f | Santa Rosa | | 4 | 26 | |
| Anker | Erik | Santa Rosa | m | 424 Sebastopol Ave. | m | | | |
| Anker | Peter & wife | Cloverdale | m/f | Washington St. | m | | | |
| Anker | Peter & wife | Cloverdale | m/f | Washington St. | m | 1 | | |
| Antone | Peter | Ocean | m | mouth of Russian River | m | 2 | | |
| Archer | N. A., Mrs. | Santa Rosa | f | Elliott Ave. | m | 2 | | |
| Archer | N. A., Mrs. | Santa Rosa | f | Santa Rosa | w | 2 | | |
| Arnett | Alice | Analy | f | Sebastopol | w | 4 | | |
| Arnett | John H. | Russian River | m | Windsor | | | | |
| Arnold | Joe, Mrs. | Santa Rosa | f | Seventh St. | m | | abt. | |

-1-

| 1 | 2 | 3 | 4 | 5 | 6 | 7 | 8 | 9 |
|---|---|---|---|---|---|---|---|---|
| SURNAME | GIVEN NAME | TOWNSHIP | SEX | RESIDENCE | MAR. | NO. CHILD-REN | AGE | NATIVITY |
| Arnold | T. J., Mrs. | Santa Rosa | f | Second St. | w | | 50 | |
| Arnold | Temassah | Ocean | f | Kidd Creek School Dist. | w | 5 | | |
| Ash | Arethusa, Mrs. | Santa Rosa | f | 215 Orange St. | | 2 | 54; 70 | USA |
| Asman | Louis, Mrs. | Santa Rosa | f | 1007 Cleveland Ave. | m | 3 | | |
| Asman | Louise | Santa Rosa | f | 137 Tenth St. | d | 3 | | |
| Asmussen | Alfred, Mrs. | Santa Rosa | f | 742 Wilson St. | m | 6 | | |
| Azevedo | Manuel | Analy | m | Sebastopol | s | | | |
| Badgley | Edgar Jasper | Analy | m | R.F.D. 4, Sebastopol | m | 6 | | |
| Bailey | James | Petaluma | m | Keller St. | m | | 78 | |
| Bailey | Samuel H. | Bodega | m | Camp Meeker | w | | | |
| Bailey | William | Bodega | m | Bodega Bay | | | 80+ | |
| Bain | Mrs. | Sonoma | f | Sonoma | w | 3 | 50+ | |
| Bainbridge | Benj. | Santa Rosa | m | College Ave. & Lincoln St. | | 4 | | |
| Baker | Elvira J. | Russian River | f | Windsor | w | 3 | | |
| Balzari | Rosa | Petaluma | f | 241 Edith St. | w | 1 | | |
| Burnes | J. R., Mrs. | Santa Rosa | f | Decoe St. off West Third St. | w | | | |
| Barker | John | Mendocino | m | Dry Creek Valley | s | | | |
| Barnes | Peggy | Petaluma | f | | | | 80+ | |
| Barnes | Peggy | Petaluma | f | | | | 90+ | |
| Barnes | Wm. | Santa Rosa | m | | | | | |
| Barry | Anna | Petaluma | f | 1007 Third St. | w | 4 | 37 | CA |
| Bartlow | Emma, Mrs. | Mendocino | f | West St., Healdsburg | w | 2 | | |
| Bartow | Helen, Mrs. | Mendocino | f | West St., Healdsburg | d | 3 | | |
| Battaglia | Mary | Santa Rosa | f | West Seventh St. | d | 1 | | |
| Batten | Christina | Santa Rosa | f | 105 Tracy St. | w | | 80 | |
| Batten | Cora | Santa Rosa | f | Santa Rosa | w | 2 | | |
| Batten | Cora | Santa Rosa | f | 739 Mendocino Ave. | w | 2 | | |

| 1 SURNAME | 2 GIVEN NAME | 3 TOWNSHIP | 4 SEX | 5 RESIDENCE | 6 MAR. | 7 NO. CHILDREN | 8 AGE | 9 NATIVITY |
|---|---|---|---|---|---|---|---|---|
| Baxman | Lewis | Salt Point | m | Timber Cove | | several | | |
| Beansford | Ida B. | Santa Rosa | f | 421 King St. | s | | | |
| Beckett | Mrs. | Russian River | f | Windsor | | 5 | | |
| Bee | Alice, Mrs. | Redwood | f | Guerneville | | 4 | | |
| Bee | Alice, Mrs. | Redwood | f | Guerneville | | | | |
| Bee | Mary A. | Redwood | f | Third St., Guerneville | m | 5 | 54 | |
| Bee | Mary A. | Redwood | f | Guerneville | m | 5 | | |
| Bee | Mary, Mrs. | Redwood | f | | m | 3 | | |
| Beebe | T. J. | Santa Rosa | m | Temple St. | s | | 64 | MO |
| Beebe | Thomas J. | Santa Rosa | m | 413 Brown St. | s | | 75 | |
| Bell | Mary | Mendocino | f | Healdsburg | w | 3 | | |
| Bell | Peter & Clara E. | Analy | m/f | McKinley St., Sebastopol | m | | 76; 70 | |
| Bemiss | Sam | Santa Rosa | m | Roberts Ave. | s | | 69 | |
| Bemiss | Samuel | Santa Rosa | m | Roberts Ave. | s | | 69 | |
| Bemiss | Samuel | Santa Rosa | m | Roberts Ave. | s | | | |
| Bemiss | Samuel | Santa Rosa | m | Dohn place just outside city limits | s | | 67 | |
| Bemiss | Samuel | Santa Rosa | m | 721 First St. | s | | 65 | |
| Benson | Mathis Charles | Cloverdale | m | Champlain Ave. | m | 2 | | |
| Bentel | Bertha | Santa Rosa | f | Santa Rosa | w | 2 | | |
| Berlin | David & Agnes | Cloverdale | m/f | Cloverdale | m | | 82 | |
| Berry | (children) | Analy | f | Sebastopol | | 4 | | |
| Berry | Emma, Mrs. | Analy | f | | w | 5 | | |
| Berryessa | Jacinto | Mendocino | m | Dry Creek | m | 1 | | |
| Berryessa | Jacinto | Washington | m | Alexander Valley | m | | | |
| Berwert | Frank | Sonoma | m | Third St. West | s | | | |
| Betrix | Emile | Cloverdale | m | | m | | | |
| Bilow | Anna, Mrs. | Santa Rosa | f | Davis St. | w | 1 | 44 | GER |

| 1 SURNAME | 2 GIVEN NAME | 3 TOWNSHIP | 4 SEX | 5 RESIDENCE | 6 MAR. | 7 NO. CHILDREN | 8 AGE | 9 NATIVITY |
|---|---|---|---|---|---|---|---|---|
| Binder | Charles | Russian River | m | Windsor | | | | |
| Binegar | W. L. | Russian River | m | Greeley Ranch, Healdsburg | s | 1 | 62 | |
| Biret | Grace | Santa Rosa | f | 219 Second St. | w | 1 | | |
| Birkhoff | C. | Santa Rosa | m | Fourth St. | m | 5 | | |
| Bish | Abraham | Santa Rosa | m | 534 Mendocino Ave. | m | 8 | 80 | VA |
| Bishop | George W. | Russian River | m | on Mark West Springs Rd. | w | 2 | 80 | VA |
| Bishop | Mattie | Petaluma | f | 567 First St. | w | | 65 | ENG |
| Black | Sarah | Mendocino | f | 129 North St., Healdsburg | w | | 62 | |
| Blair | John | Redwood | m | Guerneville | | | 88 | |
| Blake | E. M., Mrs. | Petaluma | f | 13 E. Washington St. | w | 1 | | |
| Blank | Cord, Mrs. | Santa Rosa | f | | w | 6 | | |
| Blank | Cord, Mrs. | Santa Rosa | f | | w | 5 | | |
| Bledsoe | Thomas | Mendocino | m | 129 North St., Healdsburg | s | | 73 | |
| Blele | Christian O. | Santa Rosa | m | 804 Second St. | w | | | |
| Boids | Erminia | Santa Rosa | f | 110 Seventh St. | m | | | |
| Borgwardt | A. | Santa Rosa | m | Santa Rosa | | | | |
| Bowman | Francis J. | Santa Rosa | f | 316 Sixth St. | w | 3 | | |
| Boyd | Ben, Mrs. | Santa Rosa | f | | m | | | |
| Boyd | W. M., Mrs. | Petaluma | f | 732 Third St. | m | 8 | | |
| Bradford | Herbert | Mendocino | m | | m | 2 | | |
| Bransford | Ida | Santa Rosa | f | 421 King St. | s | | 50 | |
| Bray | E. C. | Santa Rosa | m | Santa Rosa | | | 70 | |
| Bray | Elisha G. | Santa Rosa | m | 424 Eighth St. | s | | 77 | OH |
| Breaks | Charles H. | Santa Rosa | m | Fulton | m | 5 | 44 | ENG |
| Bremer | Caroline | Cloverdale | f | Cloverdale | s | | 70 | GER |
| Breshear | Clara | Russian River | f | Windsor | m | 2 | | |
| Brimigian | Samuel | Ocean | m | Cazadero | w | | | |
| Broomhall | John | Santa Rosa | m | South Park Addition | w | 3 | 68 | |
| Brown | Amanda, Mrs. | Santa Rosa | f | Santa Rosa | w | 3 | 65 | OH |

-4-

| 1 SURNAME | 2 GIVEN NAME | 3 TOWNSHIP | 4 SEX | 5 RESIDENCE | 6 MAR. | 7 NO. CHILDREN | 8 AGE | 9 NATIVITY |
|---|---|---|---|---|---|---|---|---|
| Brown | Charlotte | Santa Rosa | f | 409 Mendocino St. | w | | 77 | |
| Brown | Charlotte, Mrs. | Santa Rosa | f | 621 Humbodt St. | w | | 75 | |
| Brown | F. L., Mrs. | Santa Rosa | f | 626 Charles St. | w | 1 | | SF |
| Brown | Fanny, Mrs. | Cloverdale | f | Cloverdale | | 2 | | |
| Brown | M., Mrs. | Petaluma | f | 212 Baker St. | | 4 | | |
| Brown | Nancy | Santa Rosa | f | 714 Third St. | w | | 72 | |
| Browning | Tandy | Petaluma | m | Petaluma | s | | 75 | KY |
| Bruce | Florence I. | Analy | f | nr. Cadwell Station | w | 4 | | |
| Brunk | Margaret, Miss | Santa Rosa | f | 671 King St. | s | | 60 | MO |
| Bryant | Rachael | Mendocino | f | Healdsburg | w | | | |
| Bryant | Rachel J., Mrs. | Mendocino | f | 434 Piper St., Healdsburg | w | 1 grand-child | 62 | |
| Buckland | Mary J., Mrs. | Santa Rosa | f | 533 First St. | w | 1 | 70 | KY |
| Buckner | Mary J. | Mendocino | f | Healdsburg | | | abt. 63 | |
| Buckner | Mary J., Mrs. | Mendocino | f | Healdsburg | | | 63 | |
| Buckner | Mary Jane | Santa Rosa | f | Santa Rosa | | | abt. 63 | KY |
| Buell | Lillian | Petaluma | f | Cunningham Station | w | 3 | | |
| Bulotti | James | Santa Rosa | m | 1 Sixth St. | s | | | |
| Burke | (children) | Santa Rosa | m | Wilson St. | | 8 | | |
| Burkhardt | Joseph & Margaret | | m/f | | m | | 73; 59 | |
| Bums | John J. | Bodega | m | Freestone | w | | | |
| Burns | Sarah | Petaluma | f | | w | 5 | 42 | USA |
| Burns | Thomas | Sonoma | m | Sonoma | w | | 79 | IRL |
| Bush | J. J., Mrs. | Mendocino | f | 146 North St., Healdsburg | w | 4 | 71 | |
| Butler | A. M. | Petaluma | m | 419 Third St. | w | | | |
| Butler | Bettie | Santa Rosa | f | | | | abt. | |

| 1 SURNAME | 2 GIVEN NAME | 3 TOWNSHIP | 4 SEX | 5 RESIDENCE | 6 MAR. | 7 NO. CHILDREN | 8 AGE | 9 NATIVITY |
|---|---|---|---|---|---|---|---|---|
| Butler | Mr. & Mrs. | Petaluma | m/f | Bremin St. | m | | 16 | |
| Butts | John W. | Santa Rosa | m | Fulton | m | 3 | 64; 72 | |
| Byrnes | Jennie | Santa Rosa | f | 333 Second St. | w | | | |
| Cadd | Edwin | Mendocino | m | Dry Creek Valley | m | | | |
| Cadden | Thomas | Santa Rosa | m | Rincon Valley | m | | | |
| Cain | Robert M. | Salt Point | m | Stewarts Point | s | | | |
| Camario | Fernando | Analy | m | Vine Hill Dist., Sebastopol | w | | | |
| Cambra | M. J. & family | Santa Rosa | m | | m | 7 | | |
| Camenzina | Joseph | Sonoma | m | El Verano | m | 6 | | |
| Cameron | Douglas | Santa Rosa | m | College Ave. | s | 4 | | |
| Cameron | Mary | Santa Rosa | f | 407 Seventh St. | m | 5 | | |
| Campbell | Mary E. | Santa Rosa | f | Santa Rosa | w | 1 | | |
| Campbell | T. T., Mrs. | Santa Rosa | f | | | | | |
| Capell | Susan Francis | Mendocino | f | Dry Creek Valley | s | 2 | 61 | MO |
| Capell | Susan Francis | Mendocino | f | Dry Creek Valley | w | | 60 | USA |
| Capponi | Elena | Santa Rosa | f | 222 W. Seventh St. | w | | 72 | ITL |
| Capponi | Elena | Santa Rosa | f | 222 W. Seventh St. | w | | | |
| Capponi | Enrico & wife | Santa Rosa | m/f | 222 W. Seventh St. | m | | 71; 71 | |
| Capri | Rosa | Santa Rosa | f | 21 Seventh St. | w | 1 | | |
| Capri | Rosa | Santa Rosa? | f | 21 Seventh St. | w | 1 | | |
| Capucci | Marie Gianpietri | Santa Rosa | f | 307 Hewitt St. | m | 1 | | |
| Capucci | Mary | Santa Rosa | f | 205 Seventh St. | m | 1 | | |
| Capucci | Mary, Mrs. | Santa Rosa | f | 129 W. Seventh St. | m | 2 | | |
| Caretto | Peter | Santa Rosa | m | 427 Orange St. | m | 1 | | |
| Carillo | Vincento | Sonoma | m | El Verano | w | 2 | 110 | CA |
| Carlson | John | Bodega | m | Ludalff's Ranch, Sebastopol | s | | | |

| 1 SURNAME | 2 GIVEN NAME | 3 TOWNSHIP | 4 SEX | 5 RESIDENCE | 6 MAR. | 7 NO. CHILDREN | 8 AGE | 9 NATIVITY |
|---|---|---|---|---|---|---|---|---|
| Carlson | John | Bodega | m | Sebastopol | s | | | |
| Carr | James | Santa Rosa | m | | | | 71 | Co.Meath, IRL |
| Carrell | Ethel, Mrs. | Santa Rosa | f | 343 W. Eighth | m | 7 | | |
| Carriger | Elizabeth, Mrs. | Santa Rosa | f | Santa Rosa | | 4 | | |
| Carrillo | Joaquin | Santa Rosa | m | Santa Rosa | m | 6 | abt. 70 | |
| Carrillo | Joaquin | Santa Rosa | m | Santa Rosa | | 5 | 72 | |
| Carstensen | Henry | Petaluma | m | 108 Third St. | m | 3 | | |
| Carstensen | Henry & wife | Mendocino | m/f | East St, Healdsburg | m | 3 | | |
| Casares | Laura, Mrs. | Bodega | f | Occidental | | 2 | | |
| Caton | Anna | Petaluma | f | Petaluma | w | 1 | 65 | PRT |
| Cavalli | Irene, Mrs. | Petaluma | f | 31 Keller St. | m | 4 | 26 | |
| Chaffee | Homer H. | Santa Rosa | m | 218 Boyce St. | s | 1 | | |
| Chaffee | Jarvis | Santa Rosa | m | W. Eighth St. | m | 3 | 66 | NY |
| Charity | John | Santa Rosa | m | 715 Madison St | w | | | |
| Charles | M. L. | Sonoma | m | Sonoma | | | 71 | NC |
| Charles | M. L. | Sonoma | m | Sonoma | | | 71 | |
| Charles | Martin Luther | Sonoma | m | Napa St. | w | | 79 | NC |
| Chase | N. G., Mrs. | Santa Rosa | f | 434 A St. | w | 2 | | |
| Chicca | Americo | Santa Rosa | m | | m | 2 | | |
| Childres | Ruann, Mrs. | Santa Rosa | f | 2000 King St. | w | 4 | 69 | |
| Christensen | Anna M. | Cloverdale | f | Railroad Ave. | m | 6 | | |
| Christensen | C. P. | Santa Rosa | m | 326 South E St. | d | 2 | 71 | |
| Clanton | Rose Velmer | Petaluma | f | 327 Bassett St. | s | 1 | | |
| Clapp | Florence | Santa Rosa | f | 222 Second St. | m | | | |
| Clark | Ellena, Mrs. | Santa Rosa | f | Santa Rosa | | | 32 | |
| Clark | J. H., Mr. & Mrs. | Mendocino | m/f | Second St., Healdsburg | m | | 70; 64 | USA |

| 1 SURNAME | 2 GIVEN NAME | 3 TOWNSHIP | 4 SEX | 5 RESIDENCE | 6 MAR. | 7 NO. CHILDREN | 8 AGE | 9 NATIVITY |
|---|---|---|---|---|---|---|---|---|
| Clay | Ann, Mrs. | Santa Rosa | f | Santa Rosa | | | | |
| Clay | Annie, Mrs. | Santa Rosa | f | Santa Rosa | w | 3 | 25 | |
| Clements | Maria | Sonoma | f | First St. East | w | 1 | 80 | |
| Clements | Mary | Sonoma | f | Sonoma | w | 1 | 82 | |
| Clinesmith | Mary | Santa Rosa | f | 315 Sixth St. | m | 2 | | |
| Cloer | Sarah | Santa Rosa | f | | m | 2 | | |
| Cloer | Sarah C. | Analy | f | 234 Petaluma Ave., Sebastopol | w | 7 | | |
| Coburn | Lulu, Mrs. | Redwood | f | Guerneville | w | 2 | 34 | CA |
| Cody | Thomas Michle | Analy | m | Sebastopol | w | | | |
| Coffer | E. M., Mrs. | Santa Rosa | f | 616 Charles St. | w | 2 | | |
| Coffey | Clara Bell - see H. C. Kirpatrick | Santa Rosa | f | | | | | |
| Collins | Charles T. | Analy | m | Sebastopol | w | 5 | 40 | |
| Combs | Robert R. | Mendocino | m | Healdsburg | m | | | |
| Comstock | B. F. | Santa Rosa | | 631 Fourth St. | s | | 60 | NY |
| Conklin | I., Mrs. | Analy | f | Forestville | w | 2 | | |
| Conkling | Fannie | Petaluma | f | 506 Third St. | w | 4 | | |
| Conners | Thomas | Petaluma | m | 201 Third St. | w | | | |
| Connor | Thomas | Petaluma | m | 201 Third St. | w | | | |
| Cook | Ella | Redwood | f | Guerneville | m | 2 | 40 | USA |
| Cook | Ella, Mrs. | Santa Rosa | f | 328 Second St. | m | | 39 | IL |
| Cook | Jesse | Santa Rosa | f | Grand Ave. & Ware St. | m | | | |
| Cook | Madelia | Santa Rosa | f | 131 Ninth St. | m | 5 | | |
| Cook | Solome, Mrs. | Santa Rosa | f | Santa Rosa | w | 3 | 37 or 38 | |
| Cooper | Robert F. | Santa Rosa | m | 225 Eighth St. | m | 8 | 42 | IL |
| Cornett | Agnes, Mrs. | Mendocino | f | Healdsburg | | 3 | | |
| Cornwall | Henrietta | Petaluma | f | Eleventh & F Sts. | m | | 40 | |
| Corri | Joquin | Analy | m | | m | 2 | abt. | PRT |

| 1 SURNAME | 2 GIVEN NAME | 3 TOWNSHIP | 4 SEX | 5 RESIDENCE | 6 MAR. | 7 NO. CHILDREN | 8 AGE | 9 NATIVITY |
|---|---|---|---|---|---|---|---|---|
| Cotrell | (family) | Mendocino | m/f | Healdsburg | | | 30 | |
| Cottey | Annie L. | Petaluma | f | 542 Main St. | m | 5 | | |
| Cotty | A., Mrs. | Mendocino | f | Healdsburg | m | 3 | | |
| Coulson | Lucinda | Petaluma | f | 759 Howard St. | m | 3 | | |
| Cox | Ann E. | Santa Rosa | f | 410 Henley St. | w | | | |
| Cox | J. J. | Cazadero | m | Cazadero | s | | | |
| Cox | William | Santa Rosa | m | 410 Hendley St. | m | 2 | 70 | |
| Coyle | Michael, Mrs. | Petaluma | f | Petaluma | w | 5 | | |
| Crampton | Eugene R. | Petaluma | m | 15 Spring St. | m | 2 | | |
| Crealy | George | Santa Rosa | m | | s | | | |
| Cromwell | Rebecca, Mrs. | Analy | f | Sebastopol | | | 76 | |
| Cromwell | William T. | Analy | m | Sebastopol | | | 72 | TN |
| Crozier | P. B., Mrs. | Mendocino | f | University St., Healdsburg | w | | | |
| Culbertson | Alex | Santa Rosa | m | 408 Charles St. | s | | | |
| Culbertson | Alexander | Ocean | m | Duncans Mills | s | | 64 | PA |
| Culbertson | Alexander | Santa Rosa | m | 711 First St. | s | | 78 | |
| Culken | C. | Petaluma | m | 207 E St. | m | 1 | | |
| Cunningham | Mrs. | Santa Rosa | f | Santa Rosa | | | 80 | |
| Cunningham | Nettie | Santa Rosa | f | 614 Charles St. | w | | | |
| Cunningham | Nettie | Santa Rosa | f | no permanent street address | w | | 65 | |
| Cunningham | W. A. & J. | Santa Rosa | m/f | | m | | 83; 77 | NC |
| Curry | Patrick | Analy | m | Bloomfield | | | | |
| Curry | Patrick | Analy | m | Bloomfield | | | | |
| Curry | Patrick | Analy | m | Bloomfield | m | 2 | 76 | IRL |
| Curry | Patrick | Analy | m | Bloomfield | m | 2 | | |
| Curry | Patrick & family | Analy | m | Bloomfield | m | 2 | | |
| Damerell | Rebecca, Mrs. | Sonoma | f | Cherry St. | w | 6 | 35 | MO |

| 1 SURNAME | 2 GIVEN NAME | 3 TOWNSHIP | 4 SEX | 5 RESIDENCE | 6 MAR. | 7 NO. CHILDREN | 8 AGE | 9 NATIVITY |
|---|---|---|---|---|---|---|---|---|
| Damrell | R., Mrs. | Santa Rosa | f | 822 Cherry St. | w | 6 | 40 | MO |
| Darden | George | Santa Rosa | m | county hospital | w | 1 | 82 | TN |
| Dart | L., Mrs. | Santa Rosa | f | Carrington St. | m | | | |
| Dart | L., Mrs. | Santa Rosa | f | Carrington St. | m | | | |
| Darwell | J. M. | Knights Valley | m | camping out, Franz Valley | m | | | |
| Davidson | Augustus W. | Santa Rosa | m | Sebastopol Rd. | m | | 73 | KY |
| Davis | C. H., Mrs. | Petaluma | f | D St. | m | 1 | | |
| Davis | Grace | Santa Rosa | f | 933 Bush St. | w | 3 | | |
| Davis | J., Mrs. | Santa Rosa | f | Santa Rosa | | | 60 | |
| Davis | Manuel | Analy | m | nr. Forestville | w | 4 | 70 | |
| Davis | Mary | Redwood | f | Fourth & Mill, Guerneville | m | 3 | 30 | |
| Davis | Minnie | Cloverdale | f | Champlain Ave. | d | 3 | | |
| Davison | H. W. | Santa Rosa | m | Santa Rosa | | | 74 | GA |
| Davison | Henry W. | Santa Rosa | m | | | | over 75 | |
| Davison | Henry W. | Santa Rosa | m | | | | | |
| Davison | Henry W. | Santa Rosa | m | Santa Rosa | | | | |
| Davison | John William | Santa Rosa | m | 914 Beaver Lane | m | 5 | | |
| Deal | George | Redwood | m | Guerneville | | | | |
| Dean | Edwin B. | Analy | m | Bloomfield | s | | | |
| deBendeleben | Oufried | Santa Rosa | | First & B Sts. | s | 1 | 63 | GER |
| DeCeveness | Nicholas | Santa Rosa | m | R R #4 | s | | 83 | |
| deMooy | Ella Palmer, Mrs. | Analy | f | Halberg Bldg, Graton | w | 1 | | |
| Denny | C., Mrs. | Santa Rosa | f | Duncan's Mills | d | 2 | 35 | CA |
| Derrickson | J. W. | Ocean | m | Duncan's Mills | m | 1 | | |
| Deskin | E. | Analy | m | Harrison St., Sebastopol | m | 6 | | |
| Devereaux | R. E. | Santa Rosa | m | 428 Fourth St. | w | 3 | | |
| Devine | Mary E. | Santa Rosa | f | 42A Seventh St. | w | | | |
| Dicks | Margaret, Mrs. | Santa Rosa | f | 14 College Ave. | w | | 70 | OH |

| SURNAME | GIVEN NAME | TOWNSHIP | SEX | RESIDENCE | MAR. | NO. CHILDREN | AGE | NATIVITY |
|---|---|---|---|---|---|---|---|---|
| Dinucci | Isabella | Santa Rosa | f | 114 Ninth St. | w | 2 | | |
| Divers | Caroline | Bodega | f | Occidental | | | | |
| Divers | Edward, Mrs. | Bodega | f | Camp Meeker | w | | | |
| Dixon | William | Sonoma | m | United States St. | s | | 76 | |
| Dodson | M. J., Mrs. | Cloverdale | f | | | 3 | | |
| Doggett | Vida Mc L. | Santa Rosa | f | 1000 Fourth St. | d | 4 | | |
| Dohrman | Mrs. | Sonoma | f | | | | | |
| Doidge | Mary L. | Mendocino | f | Healdsburg | m | 1 | 52 | ENG |
| Doidge | Richard | Mendocino | m | Healdsburg | m | 1 | 77 | ENG |
| Doidge | Richard | Russian River | m | nr. Healdsburg | m | 1 | 78 | ENG |
| Doidge | Richard | Mendocino | m | Healdsburg | m | 1 | 77 | ENG |
| Doidge | Richard | Mendocino | m | University St., Healdsburg | m | | 89 | |
| Doidge | Richard | Mendocino | m | nr. Healdsburg | m | 1 | 74 | ENG |
| Dolan | Andrew | Bodega | m | Freestone | s | | 64 | CND |
| Dolan | Andrew | Bodega | m | Freestone | s | | | |
| Dolan | Andrew | Bodega | m | Freestone | s | | | |
| Donnolly | Bridget | Petaluma | f | 507 Prospect | w | | 83 | IRL |
| Donnolly | M., Mrs. | Petaluma | f | | w | 5 | | |
| Dorman | Louise, Mrs. | Sonoma | f | | w | | | |
| Doss | Seth B. | Mendocino | m | 127 Tucker St., Healdsburg | m | 11 | 73; 63 | |
| Dotterer | Minnie | Santa Rosa | f | Santa Rosa | | 2 | | |
| Dowd | Z. Z., Mr. | Mendocino | m | Healdsburg | m | 6 | | |
| Dower | James | Cloverdale | m | Lincoln School Dist. | s | | | |
| Doyle | M., Mrs. | Santa Rosa | f | 133 Seventh St. | m | 2 | | |
| Drake | Mabel Flora | Petaluma | f | 203 Liberty St. | m | 3 | | |
| Drake | S. G. | Salt Point | m | on J. A. Patchett's land | | | 77 | NH |
| Drake | S. G. | Salt Point | m | on J. A. Patchett's land | | | 82 | |
| Duarte | Sarah | Santa Rosa | f | Santa Rosa | | 3 | | |

| 1 SURNAME | 2 GIVEN NAME | 3 TOWNSHIP | 4 SEX | 5 RESIDENCE | 6 MAR. | 7 NO. CHILDREN | 8 AGE | 9 NATIVITY |
|---|---|---|---|---|---|---|---|---|
| Duarte | Sarah | Santa Rosa | f | Santa Rosa | m | 1 | | |
| Dudley | Mrs. | Santa Rosa | f | Santa Rosa | | | | |
| Dudley | Nellie, Mrs. | Santa Rosa | f | | w | 1 | | |
| Dudley | Nellie, Mrs. | Santa Rosa | f | Santa Rosa | | 1 | | |
| Dudley | Nellie, Mrs. | Santa Rosa | f | | | | | |
| Dudly | Mrs. | Santa Rosa | f | Santa Rosa | w | 1 | | |
| Duke | Catherine | Bodega | f | Camp Meeker | w | | 83 | |
| Duke | Catherine | Bodega | f | Camp Meeker | w | | 84 | |
| Dunbar | Haln Killigrew | Santa Rosa | m | 905 Fourth St. | | | 77 | ENG |
| Dunbar | Haln, K. | Santa Rosa | | 533 First St. | s | | 80 | IRL |
| Duncan | Charlotte, Mrs. | Santa Rosa | f | Santa Rosa | m | 3 | | |
| Dunham | Cora | Santa Rosa | f | 516 Humboldt St. | m | 4 | | |
| Dyer | Louie | Analy | m | Burnside | s | | 78 | |
| Eby | Sophia Elgin | Mendocino | f | 632 Johnson St., Healdsburg | w | 1 | | |
| Edwards | L., Mrs. | Santa Rosa | f | 534 First St. | w | 1 | | |
| Edwards | Leavina | Santa Rosa | f | 534 First St. | w | 1 | | |
| Elkerton | E. D. | Russian River | m | Windsor | m | 7 | | |
| Elliott | Charles, Mrs. | Santa Rosa | f | | m | 5 | | |
| Elliott | Chas., Mrs. | Santa Rosa | f | 922 Benton St. | m | 5 | | |
| Elliott | W. N. | Analy | m | Sebastopol | w | | 68 | |
| Elliott | William N. | Analy | m | Eastside Brown Ave. & McKinley St., Sebastopol | w | | | |
| Ellis | William J. | Sonoma | m | Sonoma | | | 72 | |
| Ellison | Minnie, Mrs. | Ocean | f | Cazadero St. | w | 6 | 38 | IA |
| Ellison | Minnie, Mrs. | Redwood | f | Guerneville | w | 2 | | |
| Elshio | Antonio F. | Petaluma | m | Petaluma | m | 8 | 48 | AZR |
| Emerson | Henry | Petaluma | m | Petaluma | | | 83 | KY |
| Entrena | Filomena | Santa Rosa | f | 231 Boys [Boyce/Boyd] St. | w | 2 | | |
| Eprosen | Felix | Washington | m | Geyserville | s | | | |

-12-

| 1 SURNAME | 2 GIVEN NAME | 3 TOWNSHIP | 4 SEX | 5 RESIDENCE | 6 MAR. | 7 NO. CHILDREN | 8 AGE | 9 NATIVITY |
|---|---|---|---|---|---|---|---|---|
| Evans | James A. | Cloverdale | m | | m | 6 | | |
| Fadigan | Edward | Santa Rosa | m | | s | | 77 | IRL |
| Fancher | John A. | Santa Rosa | m | 143 Scott St. | w | 6 | | |
| Fawcett | Mary | Santa Rosa | f | Creek St. | w | | | |
| Faylor | Mary, Mrs. | Redwood | f | Mercury | w | 5 | 74 | |
| Felitz | Mary | Santa Rosa | f | Santa Rosa | | large family | | |
| Fergeson | Levi | Analy | m | Pleasent Hill | s | | 83 | |
| Ferguson | Levi | Analy | m | Pleasant Hill | s | | 69 | USA |
| Fergusson | Levi | Analy | m | Pleasant Hill | s | | 70 | VA |
| Finley | Carrie Ann | Santa Rosa | f | Santa Rosa | w | 5 | | |
| Finley | N., Mrs. | Redwood | f | Guerneville | w | 2 | | |
| Finley | Nancy, Mrs. | Redwood | f | Guerneville | w | 2 | | |
| Fish | Mary, Mrs. | Santa Rosa | f | | | 8 | | |
| Fisher | L. F., Mrs. | Mendocino | f | Dry Creek Valley | m | 6 | | |
| Fisher | T. L. | Cloverdale | m | Leraux Ranch | m | 6 | | |
| Fitch | R. J. | Santa Rosa | m | 867 Second St. | m | 7 | | |
| Fitzpatrick | Mrs. | Petaluma | f | | w | | | |
| Flanigan | Richard | Santa Rosa | m | 316 Boyce St. | m | | | |
| Fletcher | Charles H. | Bodega | m | Camp Meeker | | | 70 | |
| Fletcher | Charles H. | Bodega | m | cabin on Barbier's property, Camp Meeker | s | | | |
| Fletcher | Chas. H. | Bodega | m | Camp Meeker | s | | 79 | |
| Flood | Lena, Mrs. | Petaluma | f | 11 Hinman St. | w | 1 | | |
| Fochetti | Bernardo | Sonoma | m | Sonoma | s | | 68 | SWT |
| Ford | Benjamin F. | Glen Ellen | m | Glen Ellen | m | 2 | | |
| Forpeilha | Rosa T. | Mendocino | f | | m | 4 | | |
| Foster | Augusta C., Mrs. | Petaluma | f | | | | | |
| Foster | G. H., Mrs. | Mendocino | f | Healdsburg | s | | 38 | KS |

-13-

| 1 | 2 | 3 | 4 | 5 | 6 | 7 | 8 | 9 |
|---|---|---|---|---|---|---|---|---|
| SURNAME | GIVEN NAME | TOWNSHIP | SEX | RESIDENCE | MAR. | NO. CHILDREN | AGE | NATIVITY |
| Fouder | Elizabeth | Santa Rosa | f | Third St. | w | 3 | | |
| Fouts | Elizabeth | Santa Rosa | f | Mark West Creek | w | 2 | 60 | SWT |
| Fowler | Cinfoliana | Santa Rosa | f | 120 Sixth St. | m | | 67 | MEX |
| Fowzer | William J. | | m | | | | 65 | PA |
| Francisco | A. | Analy | m | Occidental Rd. | m | 4 | 70+ | |
| Francisco | Antone | Vallejo | m | | m | | | |
| Franklin | Ann, Mrs. | Petaluma | f | | | | 69 | |
| Franklin | Ann, Mrs. | Petaluma | f | Petaluma | | | | |
| Fraser | A. F. | Santa Rosa | m | Rt. 6 Box 119 | w | | 77 | |
| Frederickson | Annie | Petaluma | f | Petaluma | m | 3 | 42 | ENG |
| Frediani | Caterina | Analy | f | Cosmo Ct., Forestville | m | 2 | | |
| Friend | Robert & Carline | Santa Rosa | m/f | 143 Scott St. | m | | both 80+ | |
| Frugoli | Francisco | Santa Rosa | m | Morgan St. | m | 3 | | |
| Frugoli | Francisco | Santa Rosa | m | 738 Wilson St. | m | 3 | | |
| Funk | L., Mrs. | Santa Rosa | f | 536 First St. | w | 1 | | |
| Funk | Louise, Mrs. | Santa Rosa | f | Temple St. | w | 1 | 49 | |
| Furia | Lazzaro | Santa Rosa | m | 413 First St. | m | 2 | | |
| Furia | Lazzaro | Santa Rosa | m | 413 First St. | m | 3 | | |
| Furlong | Thos. | Bodega | m | | m | | | |
| Futterer | Conrad | Sonoma | m | Napa St. | m | | 75; 68 | |
| Futterer | Conrad | Sonoma | m | Spain St. | m | | 73 | |
| Futterer | Conrad & Louisa | Sonoma | m/f | Spain St. | | | 80; 71 | |
| Gager | George G. | Santa Rosa | m | Stevenson St. | w | | 86 | |
| Gallaudett | E. J., Mrs. | Petaluma | f | 308 Walnut St. | w | | | |
| Gamboggi | Rosa | Santa Rosa | f | 1918 Deturk St. | m | | | |
| Ganyard | G. L., Mrs. | Petaluma | f | 516 F St. | m | 5 | | |

| 1 SURNAME | 2 GIVEN NAME | 3 TOWNSHIP | 4 SEX | 5 RESIDENCE | 6 MAR. | 7 NO. CHILDREN | 8 AGE | 9 NATIVITY |
|---|---|---|---|---|---|---|---|---|
| Garnero | Mary | Santa Rosa | f | 209 Seventh St. | m | 1 | | |
| German | Kate | Redwood | f | | m | 1 | | |
| German | Katie, Mrs. | Analy | f | Forestville | d | 3 | | |
| Gerrick | Ella | Sonoma | f | Broadway St. | m | 4 | 41 | MI |
| Giauque | Elizabeth | Santa Rosa | f | 413 First St. | w | 2 | 69 | OH |
| Giauque | Elizabeth | Santa Rosa | f | South Park Addition | w | 2 | | |
| Gibson | G. W. | Santa Rosa | m | 407 Riley St. | m | 5 | | |
| Gibson | G. W. | Santa Rosa | m | 407 Riley St. | m | | | |
| Gilcrist | Mrs. | Petaluma | f | 20 Washington St. | w | 1 | 69 | |
| Glidden | Charles & Esther | Analy | m/f | Sebastopol | m | | | |
| Gober | Elizabeth | Knights Valley | f | Knights Valley | w | 5 | 39 | MO |
| Goetjen | C. & wife | Petaluma | m/f | 215 English St. | m | 5 | | |
| Goetjen | C., Mr. & Mrs. | Petaluma | m/f | 215 English St. | m | 5 | | |
| Golett | Jane | Ocean | f | Markham | w | | 68 | IN |
| Gould | Mollie B. | Santa Rosa | f | 518 Henly St. | w | 2 | 36 | USA |
| Gounsky | Fannie, Mrs. | Petaluma | f | Petaluma | m | 4 | | |
| Gounsky | J., Mrs. | Petaluma | f | | | 5 | | |
| Gounsky | Mrs. | Petaluma | f | Petaluma | | 5 | | |
| Grace | Anne | Santa Rosa | f | | | | 60+ | |
| Grace | Annie, Mrs. | Santa Rosa | f | Santa Rosa | | | 64 | |
| Gray | Olive | Analy | f | Forestville | w | 4 | | |
| Green | Charles | Santa Rosa | m | | m | | | |
| Green | Hannah, Mrs. | Santa Rosa | f | First St. bet. B & Main Sts. | w | 3 | | |
| Green | Nellie M. | Santa Rosa | f | 703 Tupper St. | d | 2 | | |
| Green | Richard | Santa Rosa | m | | | | | |
| Greening | S. J., Mrs. | Santa Rosa | f | 14 Hewits addition Monroe St. | w | 3 | 58 | USA |
| Greenleaf | T., Mrs. | Petaluma | f | D St. | m | 6 | 36 | CA |
| Greenleaf | T., Mrs. | Petaluma | f | | m | 6 | 36 | CA |
| Gregory | Charles M. | Mendocino | m | Healdsburg | s | | | |

-15-

| 1 SURNAME | 2 GIVEN NAME | 3 TOWNSHIP | 4 SEX | 5 RESIDENCE | 6 MAR. | 7 NO. CHILDREN | 8 AGE | 9 NATIVITY |
|---|---|---|---|---|---|---|---|---|
| Griffin | J. M. | Santa Rosa | m | | | | 72 | |
| Griggs | Arthur Odell | Santa Rosa | m | 762 Wilson St. | m | 5 | | |
| Grube | Joseph | Santa Rosa | m | McDonald Ave. | w | | nearly 80 | |
| Guerin | Frank Merritt | Analy | m | Rt 4 Box 102, Sebastopol | s | | | |
| Guilfoyle | Mary | Sonoma | f | Spain St. | w | 7 | 71 | AUT |
| Gussman | Santo | Redwood | m | Mercury | w | 3 | 78 | |
| Gustavsen | Gus | Santa Rosa | m | 434 A St. | s | | | |
| Hale | Ada | Cloverdale | f | | w | | | |
| Hale | Ada E. | Cloverdale | f | Cloverdale | w | | | |
| Hall | Roxania | Mendocino | f | Centre St., Healdsburg | s | | | |
| Hall | William | Mendocino | m | Healdsburg | s | 2 | 85 | NY |
| Hall | William | Mendocino | m | Healdsburg | | | abt. 75 | |
| Hamele | Anna | Santa Rosa | f | Pierce St. | w | | | |
| Hamlin | Chas. J. | Vallejo | m | Cotati | m | 1 | | |
| Hammele | Anne | Santa Rosa | f | Pierson St. | w | | | |
| Handfest | George | Bodega | m | Occidental | s | | 72 | GER |
| Hanford | John | Sonoma | m | Baines Ranch, El Verano | s | | 79 | ENG |
| Hansen | A., Mrs. | Petaluma | f | Petaluma | w | | 74 | DNK |
| Hansen | Euchtho | Petaluma | f | Petaluma | w | | 72 | DNK |
| Hansen | Peter | Analy | m | Slotterback Tract, Sebastopol | m | 2 | | |
| Hansen | Peter | Santa Rosa | m | Lincoln & Sebastopol Sts. | m | 2 | | |
| Happy | J. H., Mrs. | Redwood | f | Guerneville | | | 64 | |
| Harbine | Charles | Santa Rosa | m | 931 Washington St. | m | 1 | 66 | |
| Harbine | Chas. | Santa Rosa | m | 583 Mendocino Ave. | w | | 72 | OH |
| Harbine | Chas. E. | Santa Rosa | m | 931 Washington St. | m | 1 | 67 | |
| Hardin | Amelia, Mrs. | Petaluma | f | cor. Third & H St. | m | | 70 | GER |
| Hardin | Mr. & Mrs. | Petaluma | m/f | Petaluma | m | | | |

| 1 | 2 | 3 | 4 | 5 | 6 | 7 | 8 | 9 |
|---|---|---|---|---|---|---|---|---|
| SURNAME | GIVEN NAME | TOWNSHIP | SEX | RESIDENCE | MAR. | NO. CHILDREN | AGE | NATIVITY |
| Harding | Anna M., Mrs. | Sonoma | f | Sonoma | w | | 73 | |
| Hardt | Augusta, Mrs. | Analy | f | Bloomfield | w | 6 | | |
| Hardy | Rebecca | Mendocino | f | Healdsburg | s | | 47 | OH |
| Harman | Albert M. | Cloverdale | m | Cloverdale | s | | 67 | WV |
| Harmon | Charles | Santa Rosa | m | 337 Bertha St. | w | | | |
| Harmon | Lizzie, Mrs. | Santa Rosa | f | 808 Spencer St. | w | | | |
| Harrison | N., Mrs. | Santa Rosa | f | | | | | |
| Harrison | Nannie, Mrs. | Santa Rosa | f | Santa Rosa | | | | |
| Hart | Joseph | Mendocino | m | Healdsburg | | | 59 | |
| Hasting | F. D. | Santa Rosa | m | King St. & McConnel Ave. | m | 6 | 80 | |
| Hasting(s) | F. D. | Santa Rosa | m | King St. | m | 5 | 82 | |
| Hastings | Edward & Mary | | m/f | SF | m | | | |
| Hastings | Emily | Santa Rosa | f | Wright St. | m | | 68 | |
| Hauser | A., Mrs. | Petaluma | f | 409 Third St. | w | 2 | | |
| Hauskneckt | Henry | Knights Valley | m | Knights Valley | m | 7 | 47 | GER |
| Hawley | Delia Ann | Santa Rosa | f | 42A W. Seventh St. | w | | | |
| Hawley | Delia, Mrs. | Santa Rosa | f | 914 Cleveland Ave. | w | | 69 | |
| Hayhurst | William | Analy | m | Vine Hill District | m | | | |
| Haynes | W. R. | Mendocino | m | Griffith residence, Vine Hill Dist. | m | 2 | | |
| Heinsen | Maggie | Petaluma | f | cor. F & Eighth St. | d | 4 | 29 | Que., CND |
| Heiss | Edwin, Mrs. | Santa Rosa | f | King St.& Spencer Ave. | w | 1 | | |
| Hekeler | Philip H. | Cloverdale | m | Second St. | s | | | |
| Hekeler | Philip Henry | Cloverdale | m | Washington St. | s | | 69 | |
| Henderson | J. H. | Knights Valley | m | Alexander Valley | s | | | |
| Henley | Daniel | Santa Rosa | m | McDonald Ave. | w | | 73 | MO |
| Herford | Thomas | Bodega | m | Freestone | w | 4 | | |
| Heryford | Nick | Santa Rosa | m | 439 First St. | m | 3 | 49 | IA |
| Hesse | Louisa, Mrs. | Cloverdale | f | | | | | |

| 1 SURNAME | 2 GIVEN NAME | 3 TOWNSHIP | 4 SEX | 5 RESIDENCE | 6 MAR. | 7 NO. CHILDREN | 8 AGE | 9 NATIVITY |
|---|---|---|---|---|---|---|---|---|
| Hesse | Louisa, Mrs. | Cloverdale | f | | | 3 | 49 | |
| Hester | Clara | Santa Rosa | f | 507 S. Davis St. | m | 4 | | |
| Hester | Clara, Mrs. | Santa Rosa | f | 507 S. Davis St. | m | 4 | | |
| Hester | Clara, Mrs. | Santa Rosa | f | 507 S. Davis St. | m | 4 | | |
| Hetzel | C. F. | Redwood | m | Guerneville | w | 9 | | |
| Hetzel | C. F. | Redwood | m | Guerneville | w | 9 | | |
| Hetzel | Carl | Redwood | m | Fourth St., Guerneville | m | 9 | | |
| Hevel | E. L. | Santa Rosa | m | Willow St. | m | | | |
| Hillbrant | Ethel | Mendocino | f | Lytton Springs | w | 4 | | |
| Hinkley | Eleanor | Santa Rosa | f | 605 Mendocino St. | s | | 86 | |
| Hinkley | Eleanor, Miss | Santa Rosa | f | 229 Third St. | s | | 84 | |
| Hinrichsen | John W. | Petaluma | m | | | | | |
| Hinrichsen | Therese | Petaluma | f | 465 Western Ave | m | 5 | 31 | GER |
| Hofer | George | Analy | m | Bloomfield | w | | 73 | |
| Hoffman | E. E., Mrs. | Petaluma | f | 319 B St. | m | 2 | | |
| Hofmann | Carl C. | Santa Rosa | m | 419 First St. | w | | 80 | GER |
| Holbrock | William | Glen Ellen | m | Glen Ellen | s | | 78 | |
| Holmes | Clara L. | Santa Rosa | f | 947 Sonoma Ave. | s | | | |
| Hopper | Harlow | Analy | m | Graton | s | | | |
| Horgan | Kate, Mrs. | Ocean | f | Willow Creek | w | 8 | | |
| Horgan | Mrs. | Bodega | f | Freestone | w | 8 | | |
| Houx | John W. & wife | Cloverdale | m/f | | m | | 75; 69 | |
| Howard | Amy M. | Santa Rosa | f | 345 W. Eighth St. | w | 3 | | |
| Howard | Amy, Mrs. | Santa Rosa | f | 346 W. Eighth St. | w | 6 | | |
| Howard | J. G. | Santa Rosa | m | Roberts Ave. | w | | | |
| Howard | J. G. | Santa Rosa | m | Roberts Ave. | w | | 71 | |
| Howard | Jas. G. | Santa Rosa | m | 711 Madison St. | w | 3 | 73 | |
| Howard | John C. | Santa Rosa | m | Santa Rosa | m | 3 | 72 | KY |

| 1 SURNAME | 2 GIVEN NAME | 3 TOWNSHIP | 4 SEX | 5 RESIDENCE | 6 MAR. | 7 NO. CHILDREN | 8 AGE | 9 NATIVITY |
|---|---|---|---|---|---|---|---|---|
| Howard | John C. | Santa Rosa | m | in a tent | | 3 + 2 orphans | | |
| Howard | John C. | Santa Rosa | m | camped south Santa Rosa Creek | m | 2 | 73 | USA |
| Howe | H. | Santa Rosa | m | 114 Ninth St. | w | 2 | | |
| Howe | Julia | Santa Rosa | f | 137 Tenth St. | m | 2 | | |
| Howeth | Mary | Santa Rosa | f | Santa Rosa | w | 6 | | |
| Hoyt | Charles | Analy | m | Route 1, Sebastopol | s | | | |
| Hughes | David W. | Cazadero | m | Cazadero | s | | 71 | ENG |
| Humphreys | W. F. | Petaluma | m | Sixth St. | m | | abt. 70 | ENG |
| Humphries | Charles | Petaluma | m | 674 Edith | m | | 78 | VA |
| Humphries | Emma, Mrs. | Petaluma | f | | m | 3 | | |
| Hurd | Marcus | Bodega | m | Occidental | | | 70 | NY |
| Hurd | Marcus | Bodega | m | Occidental | s | | 79 | NY |
| Ilse | Frederick & wife | Santa Rosa | m/f | Santa Rosa | m | | 72; 50+ | GER |
| Ilse | Mary | Santa Rosa | f | 103 Tenth St. | w | | 64 | IRL |
| Ilse | Mary, Mrs. | Santa Rosa | f | 104 Tenth St. | w | | 64 | IRL |
| Imfeld | Mary | Sonoma | f | Broadway, Green's Sanitorium | w | 2 | | |
| Ingerson | Capt. James | Bodega | m | Dutch Bill Creek aka Brown Ranch | m | 2 | | |
| Inghan | William | Santa Rosa | m | 1022 Second St. | m | 5 | | |
| Isaac(k)s | Jessie | Russian River | m/f | | m | | | |
| Ives | C. O., Mrs. | Santa Rosa | f | 517 Bosley St. | w | 2 | | |
| Ives | Samson | Santa Rosa | m | 517 Bosley St. | s | | | |
| Jack | Humbolt | Salt Point | m | Jarvis Ranch, Stewarts Point | m | | 100+ | |
| Jacobs | C. M. | Santa Rosa | m | Santa Rosa | | | | |
| Jacobs | C. M., Mrs. | Santa Rosa | f | | | 1 | | |

| 1 SURNAME | 2 GIVEN NAME | 3 TOWNSHIP | 4 SEX | 5 RESIDENCE | 6 MAR. | 7 NO. CHILDREN | 8 AGE | 9 NATIVITY |
|---|---|---|---|---|---|---|---|---|
| Jacobs | Ruth A. | Santa Rosa | f | 414 Third St. | w | 1 | 61 | CT |
| Jacobsen | Christ | Petaluma | m | 410 Upham St. | m | 4 | | |
| Jacobsen | Christ, Mr. & Mrs. | Petaluma | m/f | 410 Upham St. | m | 4 | | |
| James | S. F. | Sonoma | m | Agua Caliente | | | | |
| Jarrett | Lola, Mrs. | Petaluma | f | 918 B St. | w | 3 | | |
| Jensen | J. P., Mrs. | Santa Rosa | f | Fulton | m | 2 | 47; 45 | |
| Jewett | Martha, Mrs. | Santa Rosa | f | 218 Fourth St. | w | 5 | | |
| Jewett | Mattie, Mrs. | Santa Rosa | f | Fourth St. | w | 1 | | |
| Johnson | Anne | Analy | f | Bloomfield | w | 5 | | |
| Johnson | Clara | Santa Rosa | f | Earl St. end of A St. | m | | | |
| Johnson | Elna | Santa Rosa | f | 543 Fifth St. | m | | 57 | SWD |
| Johnson | Elna | Santa Rosa | f | 544 Fifth St. | m | | 59 | SWD |
| Johnson | F. J. | Analy | m | | | | | |
| Johnson | H. W., Mrs. | Santa Rosa | f | St.Helena Ave. | m | 4 | | |
| Johnson | Henrietta | Mendocino | f | Healdsburg | s | | 43 | NY |
| Johnson | Magnus | Santa Rosa | m | 543 Fifth St. | m | | 61 | SWD |
| Johnson | Magnus & wife | Russian River | m/f | | m | | | |
| Johnson | Margaret | Petaluma | f | | w | | | |
| Johnson | Marie | Santa Rosa | f | Quackenbush res. on Matanzas Creek | w | 7 | 60 | SCT |
| Johnson | Mary | Santa Rosa | f | 714 Third St. | w | 1 | 66 | IL |
| Johnson | Mary | Analy | f | Sebastopol | m | | 70 | |
| Johnson | Mary E., Mrs. | Santa Rosa | f | | w | 1 | 63 | IL |
| Johnson | William C. | Santa Rosa | m | Hub Lodging house room 17 | m | | | |
| Johnson | Wm. Clifton | Santa Rosa | m | 742 Charles St. | m | | | |
| Johnston | Margaret | Petaluma | f | J St. | w | | 62 | SCT |
| Jones | Nelson | Mendocino | m | nr. Healdsburg | s | | | OH |
| Jose | Sophia | Santa Rosa | f | | w | 5 | | |

| 1 SURNAME | 2 GIVEN NAME | 3 TOWNSHIP | 4 SEX | 5 RESIDENCE | 6 MAR. | 7 NO. CHILDREN | 8 AGE | 9 NATIVITY |
|---|---|---|---|---|---|---|---|---|
| Jose | Sophia, Mrs. | Santa Rosa | f | 285 Wilson St. | w | 5 | | |
| Judt | John F. | Santa Rosa | m | Santa Rosa | s | | | KY |
| Kaller | Patrick | Santa Rosa | m | West Eighth St. | s | | 68 | IRL |
| Karry | M. A., Mrs. | Santa Rosa | f | 713 Second St. | w | 4 | 34 | IL |
| Kase | Louise | Salt Point | f | Salt Point | m | 7 | | |
| Kelley | Michel | Glen Ellen | m | Glen Ellen | s | | | |
| Keniston | Joseph | Bodega | m | Bodega Corners | m | 3 | 51 | ME |
| Kennedy | Emma | Analy | f | Hilton P. O. | m | 2 | | |
| Kennedy | Maud E. | Mendocino | f | 215 Lincoln St., Healdsburg | s | | | |
| Kenney | Mary, Mrs. | Sonoma | f | Napa St. | w | 2 | 70+ | |
| Kennisten | family | Bodega | | | | | | |
| Kenniston | Joseph | Bodega | m | | m | | 50+ | |
| Kern | (children) | Mendocino | m/f | Healdsburg | | 5 | | |
| Ketcham | George | Mendocino | m | West St. Healdsburg | m | 3 | | |
| Ketchum | George | Mendocino | m | Healdsburg | m | 3 | | |
| Ketchum | Julia | Mendocino | f | nr. Healdsburg | m | 3 | | |
| Kidd | F. A., Mrs. | Santa Rosa | f | Santa Rosa | m | 2 | | |
| Kidd | F. A., Mrs. | Santa Rosa | f | Santa Rosa | m | 3 | | |
| Kilcourse | Bridget, Miss | Petaluma | f | 117 Hopper St. | s | | | |
| Kilgore | Catherine | Santa Rosa | f | 523 Santa Rosa Ave. | w | 1 | 87 | IRL |
| Kill | James M. | Santa Rosa | m | 719 Tupper St | m | 1 | 75 | |
| King | J. H. | Santa Rosa | | 420 Third St. | s | 2 | 69 | MO |
| King | Jos. | Analy | m | Graton | m | 3 | | |
| King | Joseph | Analy | m | | m | | 35 | |
| Kirk | Maggie | Petaluma | f | Baker St. | s | | 74 | |
| Kirkpatrick | H. C. | Santa Rosa | f | 415 Mendocino St. | w | 1 | | |
| Kirry | May, Mrs. | Analy | f | Burnett St, Sebastopol | d | 3 | | |
| Kirry | May, Mrs. | Analy | f | Sebastopol | d | 3 | | |
| Kiser | Lena | Petaluma | f | 601 Kent St. | m | 5 | | |

| 1 SURNAME | 2 GIVEN NAME | 3 TOWNSHIP | 4 SEX | 5 RESIDENCE | 6 MAR. | 7 NO. CHILD-REN | 8 AGE | 9 NATIVITY |
|---|---|---|---|---|---|---|---|---|
| Kleemons #1 | Rosa, Mrs. | Redwood | f | Guerneville | | 4 | | |
| Kleemons #2 | Rose, Mrs. | Redwood | f | Guerneville | w | 4 | | |
| Knapp | Lewis C. | Santa Rosa | m | 328 Second | m | | 70 | NY |
| Knighten | Joseph M. | Santa Rosa | m | Santa Rosa | | | | |
| Knox | J. M. | Santa Rosa | m | nr. Fulton | m | 4 | | |
| Koenig | Ernest | Santa Rosa | m | 1050 Orchard St. | s | | 61 | |
| Kostenhoschen | Theodore | Santa Rosa | m | Germania Hotel | w | | 65 | |
| Kriedel | Mrs. | Santa Rosa | f | Santa Rosa | w | 4 | | |
| Lake | Helen M. | Analy | f | Bloomfield | w | 1 | 76 | |
| Lallamouth | Henry | Bodega | m | Occidental | | | 62 | FRN |
| Lamb | Geneva M. | Mendocino | f | Hayden St., Healdsburg | w | 3 | | |
| Lamb | Geneva M. | Santa Rosa | f | nr. Santa Rosa Wingsworth ranch | w | | 81 | |
| Lancaster | William | Santa Rosa | f | 162 Cherry St. | w | 1 | 81 | USA |
| Lander | Margaret E. | Santa Rosa | f | 657 King St. | w | 1 | | |
| Landeway | Anna | Santa Rosa | f | Santa Rosa | w | | 70 | |
| Lane | E. C., Mrs. | Analy | f | Forestville | w | 3 | | |
| Lane | Elizabeth | Santa Rosa | f | 946 Grand Ave. | w | 2 | 65 | |
| Lane | Elizabeth C. | Analy | f | Forestville | w | 2 | 53 | OH |
| Lane | Elizabeth C. | Santa Rosa | f | 946 Grand Ave. | w | 2 | | |
| Lane | Mrs. | Analy | m | Forestville | w | 4 | | |
| Langren | Louisa | Petaluma | f | | w | | 69 | NY |
| LaPoint | William | | m | | | | | |
| Larrison | Seymour | Cloverdale | m | camps out | s | | | |
| Larsen | Anton | Santa Rosa | m | Oakland House, Roberts Ave. | w | 3 | | |
| Lavin | Timothy | Petaluma | m | Petaluma | s | | 74 | |
| Law | M., Mrs. | Petaluma | f | 219 Bremen St. | m | 3 | | |
| Lawrence | Alva Perry | Analy | m | Forestville | s | | 13 | |
| Lawrence | Katie Amanda | Analy | f | Forestville | s | | 10 | |

| 1 | 2 | 3 | 4 | 5 | 6 | 7 | 8 | 9 |
|---|---|---|---|---|---|---|---|---|
| SURNAME | GIVEN NAME | TOWNSHIP | SEX | RESIDENCE | MAR. | NO. CHILDREN | AGE | NATIVITY |
| Lawrence | Mary J. | Petaluma | f | East Petaluma | m | 5 | | |
| Lawson | M. H. | Santa Rosa | m | west of Santa Rosa | m | 3 | | |
| Leander | Charles | Santa Rosa | m | formerly County Farm | | | 75 | |
| Lebeouff | Fred | Bodega | m | Occidental | s | | 60+ | FR CND |
| Lee | Dora | Mendocino | f | Hayden St., Healdsburg | w | 4 | 40 | |
| Lee | Dora, Mrs. | Mendocino | f | Healdsburg | m | 5 | 45 | PA |
| Lee | Lottie | Mendocino | f | Healdsburg | m | 1 | 23 | MO |
| Lelonarn | Celestine | Mendocino | f | Healdsburg | w | 3 | | |
| Leluarn | Celestine, Mrs. | Mendocino | f | Healdsburg | w | 2 | | |
| Leluarn | John | Mendocino | m | | | 3 | | |
| LeMoine | John | Bodega | m | Occidental | s | | 71 | |
| Lennox | James W. | Sonoma | m | El Verano | s | | 74 | |
| Lennox | Jas. W. | Sonoma | m | El Verano | s | | 74 | |
| Leonard | Mary, Mrs. | Petaluma | f | 117 Hopper St. | w | | | |
| Leonard | S. F., Mr. & Mrs. | Santa Rosa | m/f | 1020 Fifth St. | m | | 76; 75 | ME; MA |
| Letcher | Giles, Mr. & Mrs. | Petaluma | m/f | Prospect St. | m | | | |
| Letcher | Kate, Mrs. | Petaluma | f | 411 Prospect St. | w | | | |
| Lewis | Cora | Russian River | f | Windsor | w | | | |
| Lewis | Ellen A. | Santa Rosa | f | Todd Dist. | w | 5 | | |
| Lewis | Elvira | Santa Rosa | f | 126 Scott St. | a | 5 | | |
| Lewis | Florence, Mrs. | Santa Rosa | f | 314 Brown St. | d | 4 | | |
| Lewis | G. W. & family | Santa Rosa | m | Harris Place no. of Poor House | m | 3 | | |
| Lewis | Harriet | Petaluma | f | Hopper St. | w | 1 | 76 | IN |
| Lewis | James H. | Petaluma | m | Petaluma | m | | 57 | IN |
| Lewis | Martha J. | Bodega | f | Occidental | d | 2 | | |
| Lewis | Martha, Mrs. | Bodega | f | Occidental | m | 1 | | |
| Lewis | Mary | Mendocino | f | Healdsburg | | | | |
| Lewis | R. M. | Mendocino | m | Healdsburg | m | | 83 | |

| 1 SURNAME | 2 GIVEN NAME | 3 TOWNSHIP | 4 SEX | 5 RESIDENCE | 6 MAR. | 7 NO. CHILDREN | 8 AGE | 9 NATIVITY |
|---|---|---|---|---|---|---|---|---|
| Lewis | R. M. | Mendocino | m | Dry Creek | m | | | |
| Lewis | Ralph | Russian River | m | Windsor | m | | | |
| Lewis | Robert | Mendocino | m | Healdsburg | m | | | |
| Lightfoot | Eliza | Cloverdale | f | Washington St. | w | 1 | 76 | |
| Lingron | Alfred | Santa Rosa | m | 707 Henley St. | m | 6 | 50 | |
| Livingston | Cornelia E. | Redwood | f | Guerneville | m | 2 | | |
| Livingston | Ella | Mendocino | f | Healdsburg | m | | | |
| Lockerby | Robert | Vallejo | m | Penngrove | s | | | |
| Long | Tilly | Santa Rosa | f | nr. Tupper St. | s | 4 | 37 | CA |
| Lottritz | John & Mary | Calistoga | m/f | Porter Creek School Dist. | m | | both 60 + | |
| Lottritz | Mary E., Mrs. | Santa Rosa | f | Porter Creek | w | | 74 | GER |
| Louk | Cora L..., Mrs. | Redwood | f | Guerneville | m | 1 | 34 | OR |
| Louk | Olive | Mendocino | f | 321 Sherman St., Healdsburg | w | | | |
| Lounibos | Emile P. | Glen Ellen | m | Kenwood | m | 5 | | |
| Lueders | Henry & wife | Petaluma | m/f | Petaluma | m | | 73 | DNK |
| Maclean | Kate & Margaret, Misses | Mendocino | f | Healdsburg | | | old | |
| Maclean #1 | Katherine & Margaret | Mendocino | f | Healdsburg | s | | | |
| Maclean #2 | Katherine & Margaret | Mendocino | f | Healdsburg | | | | |
| Maclean #3 | Misses | Mendocino | f | Healdsburg | | | | |
| Magetti | Bartolomeo | Sonoma | m | Germany St. | m | 1 | 65 | SWT |
| Maginnis | Thos. | Santa Rosa | m | 155 W. Third St. | m | | | |
| Mahan | Charles | Mendocino | m | Healdsburg | | | 82+ | |
| Maloney | Michael | Santa Rosa | m | Santa Rosa | | | 52 | NY |
| Maloof | Charlie | Santa Rosa | m | 332 Corrilla St. | m | 1 | | |
| Manning | Mary | Redwood | f | Guerneville | m | 6 | | |
| Maren | James | Analy | m | Cunningham Ranch, Sebastopol | s | | | |
| Maren | James | Analy | m | Sebastopol | s | | 72 | |

-24-

| 1 | 2 | 3 | 4 | 5 | 6 | 7 | 8 | 9 |
|---|---|---|---|---|---|---|---|---|
| SURNAME | GIVEN NAME | TOWNSHIP | SEX | RESIDENCE | MAR. | NO. CHILDREN | AGE | NATIVITY |
| Marion | A., Mrs. | Analy | f | 212 Pitt Ave., Sebastopol | m | 1 | | |
| Markham | Susan | Santa Rosa | f | 608 Charles St. | w | 2 | 69 | |
| Marsh | Alida L., Mrs. | Vallejo | f | Cotati | w | 2 | | |
| Marsh | J. S. | Washington | m | Geyserville | w | 4 | | |
| Marsh | J. S. | Santa Rosa | m | Willow St. | w | 3 | | |
| Marsh | John Shelby | Cloverdale | m | 3 miles S. W. of Cloverdale | w | 4 | 83 | |
| Marshall | Izoro K., Mrs. | Ocean | f | Cazadero | w | | | |
| Marshall | Martha J. | Santa Rosa | f | 322 Boyce St. | m | 3 | | |
| Martell | David | Analy | m | Molino | m | 6 | 77 | |
| Marten | Alex | Washington | m | Geyserville | m | | | |
| Martin | Alex | Mendocino | m | Alexander Valley | m | | | |
| Martin | E. J., Mrs. | Santa Rosa | f | Mark West | w | | 58 | TN |
| Martin | Elizabeth J. | Mendocino | f | Healdsburg | w | | 69 | TN |
| Martin | Elizabeth J. | Mendocino | f | North St., Healdsburg | w | | 82 | |
| Martin | Elizabeth Jane | Russian River | f | | w | | 61 | TN |
| Martin | G. W., Mr. & Mrs. | Mendocino | m/f | Alexander Valley | m | | 84; 54 | TN |
| Martin | George W., Mrs. | Mendocino | f | Healdsburg | | | | |
| Martz | Samuel | Santa Rosa | m | 117 Carrillo St. | m | 1 | 81+ | |
| Martz | Samuel | Santa Rosa | m | 117 Carillo St. | m | 1 | 83 | |
| Masa | Susanah | Santa Rosa | f | Santa Rosa | w | | | |
| Masa | Susanah, Mrs. | Santa Rosa | f | Santa Rosa | w | | | |
| Mason | Myrtle, Mrs. | Mendocino | f | Healdsburg | m | 5 | | |
| Mastrup | Mary | Petaluma | f | 759 G St. | | 5 | 43 | DNK |
| Mastrup | Mary | Petaluma | f | 759 G St. | m | | 41 | DNK |
| Mastrup | Mary, Mrs. | Petaluma | f | cor. Sixth & G Sts. | w | 5 | 42 | DNK |
| Mathews | Elizabeth | Cloverdale | f | Commercial St. | w | | | |
| Matsen | Marie P. | Petaluma | f | 718 H St. | w | | | |
| Matsen | Mary P. | Petaluma | f | 718 Fourth St. | w | | | |

-25-

| 1 | 2 | 3 | 4 | 5 | 6 | 7 | 8 | 9 |
|---|---|---|---|---|---|---|---|---|
| SURNAME | GIVEN NAME | TOWNSHIP | SEX | RESIDENCE | MAR. | NO. CHILDREN | AGE | NATIVITY |
| Matthews | Eliza | Cloverdale | f | Cloverdale | w | | | |
| Mausera | Antonio Garcia | Santa Rosa | m | 129 Seventh St. | s | 3 | | |
| Mausera | Antonio Garcia | Santa Rosa | m | 614 Seventh St. | w | 3 | | |
| Maxwell | Alvina | Petaluma | f | 312 Fourth St. | d | 2 | | |
| McBee | Samentha | Redwood | f | | s | 1 | 80 | TN |
| McCaleb | Dona, Mrs. | Santa Rosa | f | 341 W. Eighth St. | d | 3 | | |
| McCarty | L. E., Mrs. | Santa Rosa | f | 130 E St. | w | 2 | | |
| McCarty | L. W., Mrs. | Petaluma | f | 18 Laurell Ave. | w | 2 | | |
| McCombs | Aaron C. | Santa Rosa | m | 224 Wallace St. | m | 5 | | |
| McCoy | Alma, Mrs. | Petaluma | f | Petaluma | d | 3 | | |
| McCriston | Silvester C. | Analy | m | Graton | m | | | |
| McDaniel | Pearl, Mrs. | Santa Rosa | f | 629 Mill St. | w | 3 | 25 | IL |
| McDaniels | Pearl, Mrs. | Santa Rosa | f | Mill St. | w | 3 | 24 | |
| McDonald | Isabella, Mrs. | Santa Rosa | f | 418 Third St. | m | 2 | 80 | SCT |
| McElnay | S. C., Mrs. | Santa Rosa | f | 417 Humboldt St. | m | 2 | | |
| McElnay | S. C., Mrs. | Santa Rosa | f | Joe Davis St. nr. Tenth St. | w | 2 | | |
| McFarland | Vina | Petaluma | f | Fifth St.; bet. F & G Sts. | w | | 70-80 | |
| McFarland | Vina, Mrs. | Petaluma | f | | | | aged | |
| McGreavy | Ellen F. | Santa Rosa | f | 740 Charles St. | w | | | |
| McGuire | Elizabeth | | f | | | 6 | | |
| McGuire | Neil | Cazadero | m | Cazadero | | | 74 | KY |
| McLaughlin | Robert | Bodega | m | | | | 73 | |
| McLean | Margaret | | f | Fisks Mill | m | 4 | | |
| McMillion | Vada | Analy | f | Sebastopol | m | 1 | | |
| McNally | Ella | Petaluma | f | 528 Broadway St. | w | 4 | 38 | WA |
| McNally | Ella, Mrs. | Petaluma | f | 528 Bassett St. | m | 4 | 38 | WA |
| McPeak | Belle, Miss | Analy | f | Forestville | s | | 30 | CO |
| McPeak | Peter F. | Redwood | m | Hilton | s | | | |

| 1 SURNAME | 2 GIVEN NAME | 3 TOWNSHIP | 4 SEX | 5 RESIDENCE | 6 MAR. | 7 NO. CHILDREN | 8 AGE | 9 NATIVITY |
|---|---|---|---|---|---|---|---|---|
| Meador | Bell, Mrs. | Santa Rosa | f | 453 Ellis St. | m | 5 | | |
| Meador | Belle, Mrs. | Santa Rosa | f | 922 Benton St. | m | 2 | | |
| Means | Lycurgus | Russian River | m | | s | 1 | | |
| Means | Lycurgus | Russian River | m | Windsor | d | 2 | | |
| Mecke | Caroline | Petaluma | f | 210 First St. | w | | 66 | |
| Mehan | Patrick | Petaluma | m | | m | 5 | | |
| Mell | Mary | Santa Rosa | f | 300 Santa Rosa Ave. | w | | 71 | |
| Mell | Mary | Santa Rosa | f | Charles & Santa Rosa Ave. | w | | 72 | |
| Mello | Amelia | Analy | f | Sebastopol | w | 3 | | |
| Mello | Emilia C. (Mrs. Geo.) | Analy | f | Sebastopol | w | | | |
| Mello | Geo. | Analy | m | | | | | |
| Merrell | Ellen A. | Santa Rosa | f | 323 Hendley St. | w | | 76 | |
| Merrit | Edward | Analy | m | Bloomfield | s | | 71 | |
| Merrithen | M. G., Mrs. | Petaluma | f | Kent St. | m | 7 | 38 | NE |
| Merritt | S. J., Mrs. | Cloverdale | f | North St. | w | 2 | 79 | |
| Merritt | Sarah J. | Cloverdale | f | School St. | w | 2 | 82 | |
| Merritt | Sarah J. | Cloverdale | f | First St. | w | | 81 | |
| Metcalf | Loretta | Santa Rosa | f | 446 Orchard St. | m | 2 | | |
| Metcalf | Loretta | Santa Rosa | f | 308 Brown St. | w | 2 | | |
| Meyer | Lulu | Santa Rosa | f | 413 First St. | m/s | 4 | 26 | CA |
| Meyer | M. | Santa Rosa | m | 9 Main St. | s | | | |
| Meyers | Lula | Santa Rosa | f | 413 First St. | m | 4 | 26 | CA |
| Miller | Carl, Mrs. | Santa Rosa | f | 608A Charles St. | ds | | | |
| Miller | Carl, Mrs. | Redwood | f | Guerneville | m | | | |
| Miller | Louisa | Santa Rosa | f | 111 Second St. | w | 2 | | |
| Miller | Louisa | Santa Rosa | f | 331 Camilla St. | w | | | |
| Miller | Lucy, Mrs. | Redwood | f | Guerneville | | | | |
| Minear | Mrs. | Santa Rosa | f | 62 Tenth St. | | several | | |
| Mize | Aditha | Santa Rosa | f | Westside Ave. | w | 1 | 50 | KY |

| 1 SURNAME | 2 GIVEN NAME | 3 TOWNSHIP | 4 SEX | 5 RESIDENCE | 6 MAR. | 7 NO. CHILDREN | 8 AGE | 9 NATIVITY |
|---|---|---|---|---|---|---|---|---|
| Monaco | Paulena | Santa Rosa | f | 901 Wright St. | w | | | |
| Monotti | Luigi | Santa Rosa | m | where he gets charity | m | 4 | 75 | SWT |
| Moore | E. J., Mrs. | Santa Rosa | f | 450 Beaver St. | w | 4 | | |
| Moore | Ellen | Petaluma | f | 338 Keokuk St. | w | 3 | 75+ | |
| Moore | Margaret | Santa Rosa | f | 501 Sebastopol Ave. | w | 2 | | |
| Moraga | Jospha, Mrs. | Mendocino | f | Healdsburg | | | 70 | |
| Moraga | Mrs. | Santa Rosa | f | | w | 1 | 70 | |
| Morrill | Dorinda Rilla | Analy | f | Bloomfield | w | 1 | 78 | |
| Morrisey | Kate, Mrs. | Petaluma | f | Petaluma | w | 3 | | |
| Morrison | Mrs. | Santa Rosa | f | Santa Rosa | m | 4 | 39 | |
| Morrow | James H. | Redwood | m | Guerneville | | | 89 | |
| Morrow | James H. | Redwood | m | Fourth St., Guerneville | m | 3 | 93 | |
| Moulton | S. C. | Analy | m | Forestville | | | 78 | |
| Muerth | Alice, Mrs. | Cloverdale | f | Railroad Ave. | m | 1 | | |
| Mulford | Mr. & Mrs. J. | Cloverdale | m/f | Commercial St. | m | 3 | 75; 76 | |
| Muller | Mary | Petaluma | f | Petaluma | w | 1 | 40 | GER |
| Mullin | Delia, Miss | Petaluma | f | Petaluma | | | | |
| Mulvany | R. M., Mrs. | Santa Rosa | f | Santa Rosa | m | 4 | 30 | OR |
| Murphy | Mabel | Santa Rosa | f | 414 Eighth St. | s | | 9 | CA |
| Murphy | Mabel, Miss | Santa Rosa | f | 415 Eighth St. | s | | 8 | CA |
| Murphy | R. W. | Washington | m | Geyserville | w | 8 | 80 | |
| Murphy | Richard W. | Washington | m | | w | | | |
| Myers | Henry | Knights Valley | m | Alexander Valley | s | | 11 | IL |
| Navoni | Batista | Cloverdale | m | Cloverdale | w | | | |
| Navoni | Battista | Santa Rosa | m | Cloverdale | m | 2 | | |
| Neidringhouse | Henry | Mendocino | m | University St., Healdsburg | w | | | |
| Neidringhouse | Mr. | Mendocino | m | University St., Healdsburg | w | 1 | | |
| Nelan | Marcella, Mrs. | Ocean | f | Tyrone Mills | w | | | |

-28-

| 1 SURNAME | 2 GIVEN NAME | 3 TOWNSHIP | 4 SEX | 5 RESIDENCE | 6 MAR. | 7 NO. CHILDREN | 8 AGE | 9 NATIVITY |
|---|---|---|---|---|---|---|---|---|
| Nelson | A. S. | Washington | | Geyserville | s | | 75 | KY |
| Nelson | Cornelia | Santa Rosa | f | 878 Second St. | | 3 | | |
| Nelson | Margaret | Salt Point | f | Annapolis | w | | | |
| Nelson | Margaret | Salt Point | f | Annapolis | w | | 70+ | |
| Nelson | Margaret, Mrs. | Salt Point | f | | | | | |
| Neuman | Marie | Santa Rosa | f | 417 King St. | w | | 75 | |
| Newman | Elizabeth | Santa Rosa | f | 1007 Fourth St. | w | 4 | 75 | IRE |
| Newman | John Allen | Analy | m | nr. Sebastopol | m | | 82 | |
| Newman | John Allen | Analy | m | 3 ½ miles south of Sebastopol | s | | 81 | |
| Newman | Marie, Mrs. | Santa Rosa | f | Humboldt St. | w | | 70 | |
| Newman | W. N. | Mendocino | m | | | | 72 | OH |
| Newton | Hulda | Santa Rosa | f | 1112 Humboldt St. | m | 1 | | |
| Newton | Hulda S. | Santa Rosa | f | 113 Leland St. | m | 1 | | |
| Noriel | J. C. | Santa Rosa | m | 424 First St. | m | 5 | 57 | CHL |
| Noriel | Jesse | Santa Rosa | m | Charles St. | | 1 | | |
| Norris | Anna, Mrs. | Santa Rosa | f | Healdsburg | m | 1 | | |
| Norris | Anna, Mrs. | Mendocino | f | Healdsburg | w | 1 | | |
| Norris | E., Mrs. | Petaluma | f | 418 Howard St. | w | 2 | | |
| Norris | Elizabeth, Mrs. | Petaluma | f | 23 Howard St. | w | | | |
| Northway | I. B., Mrs. | Petaluma | f | 325 Bassett St. | m | 1 | | |
| Norton | John, Mrs. | Bodega | f | Valley Ford | w | 4 | | |
| Norton | John, Mrs. | Bodega | f | Valley Ford | w | 4 | | |
| Norton | Philinda | Mendocino | f | Healdsburg | s | | 72 | OH |
| Nottingham | Mrs. | | f | | | | | |
| O'Bryan | A. L. | Santa Rosa | m | 1010 Mendocino St. | s | | | |
| O'Halleran | Tymothy | Sonoma | m | El Verano | s | | 67 | |
| O'Halloran | Bella Bransteller | Santa Rosa | f | 1119 Orchard St. | w | 2 | | |
| O'Halloran | J. D., Mrs. | Santa Rosa | f | 1119 Orchard St. | m | 4 | | |
| O'Halloran | Timothy | Sonoma | m | El Verano | s | | 68 | |

| 1 SURNAME | 2 GIVEN NAME | 3 TOWNSHIP | 4 SEX | 5 RESIDENCE | 6 MAR. | 7 NO. CHILDREN | 8 AGE | 9 NATIVITY |
|---|---|---|---|---|---|---|---|---|
| Ohlsen | Henry | Santa Rosa | m | 315 Santa Rosa Ave. | s | | | |
| Olmstead | L. W. | Ocean | m | mouth of Russian River | s | | 65 | PA |
| Olmstead | L. W. | Ocean | m | mouth of Russian River | s | | 66 | PA |
| Olmstead | Levy Willis | Ocean | m | Jenner | s | | 79 | |
| Ologue | Mary | Santa Rosa | f | 618 Joe Davis St. | m | 5 | 42 | CA |
| Olway | Abby | Sonoma | f | Napa St. East | w | | 73 | |
| O'Neil | Minnie | Santa Rosa | f | 222 Second St. | m | 2 | | |
| O'Rourke | Mary, Mrs. | Petaluma | f | Petaluma | w | 9 | | |
| Orth | Helene | Petaluma | f | Fourth St. | w | 4 | 42 | GER |
| Orth | Helene, Mrs. | Petaluma | f | Fourth St. bet. G & H Sts. | w | 4 | 40 | GER |
| Ouellet | J. C. | Mendocino | m | Healdsburg | s | | 75 | |
| Pahud | Henriette, Mrs. | Santa Rosa | f | 11 Summer Ave. | | 4 | 67 | RUS |
| Palmer | Thomas B. | | m | | | | 67 | NY |
| Papera | Arseda | Analy | m | Forestville | m | 4 | | |
| Park | Elizabeth, Mrs. | Analy | f | Sebastopol | m | 4 | | |
| Parker | Frederick | Glen Ellen | m | Glen Ellen | s | 3 | 76 | |
| Parker | Joseph P. | Washington | m | Gates Ranch, Geyserville | m | | | |
| Patrick | Jesse | Petaluma | m | Petaluma | m | 2 | 23 | IN |
| Patterson | J. T. | Redwood | m | Guerneville | w | 6 | 61 | TN |
| Patterson | Mary, Mrs. | Santa Rosa | f | 514 Davis St. | d | 2 | | |
| Patterson | Pearl & Rosa | Redwood | f | Guerneville | | | 11 & 9 | CA |
| Paula | George, Mrs. | Petaluma | f | 461 Dana St. | w | 1 | | |
| Pearse | Mary, Mrs. | Santa Rosa | f | 895 Second St. | w | | 76 | |
| Pedro | John | Santa Rosa | m | 653 Mill St. | m | 1 | 63; 72 | SWT |
| Pelizzari | Carlo | Santa Rosa | m | 225 Second St. | m | 5 | 44 | ITL |
| Pelizzari | Carlo | Santa Rosa | m | 225 Second St. | m | 5 | | |
| Pellow | Angelina | Santa Rosa | f | 453 Ellis St. | m | 3 | | |

| 1 SURNAME | 2 GIVEN NAME | 3 TOWNSHIP | 4 SEX | 5 RESIDENCE | 6 MAR. | 7 NO. CHILDREN | 8 AGE | 9 NATIVITY |
|---|---|---|---|---|---|---|---|---|
| Pellow | Angelina | Santa Rosa | f | 205 Second St. | m | 3 | | |
| Perey | Joe | Petaluma | m | 561 I St. | w | | 62 | CHL |
| Perkins | Blanche | Russian River | f | East Windsor | s | | 15 | |
| Perkins | Blanche | Russian River | f | Windsor | s | | | |
| Perrot | E. | Santa Rosa | m | Fifth & North St. | w | | 89 | |
| Perry | Agnes | Mendocino | f | Healdsburg | w | 1 | | |
| Perry | Elizabeth | Santa Rosa | f | 111 Theresa St. | w | | | |
| Perry | Margaret Agnes, Mrs. | Mendocino | f | Healdsburg | | 1 | | |
| Perry | Mary | Santa Rosa | f | 5 Tenth St. | w | 3 | | |
| Peterson | C. D. | Santa Rosa | | 128 Morgan St. | w | 6 | | |
| Peterson | John | Washington | m | Geyserville | s | | | |
| Peterson | John | Washington | m | Geyserville | s | | 79 | |
| Pettis | Lula A. | Analy | f | | m | 6 | | |
| Petty | James | Redwood | m | Monte Rio | s | | | |
| Petty | James Ervin | Redwood | m | Monte Rio | s | | | |
| Phelan | Jennie, Miss | Santa Rosa | f | 117 Eighth St. | w | 3 | | |
| Phelan | Lucinda, Mrs. | Santa Rosa | f | Santa Rosa | w | | 75 | |
| Phillips | Mariah, Mrs. | Santa Rosa | f | | w | | | |
| Philpott | Sarah M. | Mendocino | f | First St., Healdsburg | w | | 52 | CA |
| Phinney | Grace M. | Santa Rosa | f | | | 2 | | |
| Pickrell | Nellie, L. | Petaluma | f | 822 Main St. | m | 4 | | |
| Piezzi | Leonard | Santa Rosa | m | Santa Rosa | s | | | |
| Piezzi(e) | Leonardo | Bodega | m | | | | | |
| Poggi | G. B. | Analy | m | Sebastopol | m | 3 | | |
| Poggi | G. B. | Analy | m | Sebastopol | m | 4 | 70 | ITL |
| Poggi | G. B., Mr. | Analy | m | Sebastopol | m | 4 | | |
| Pollard | Thomas & Elizabeth | Analy | m/f | | m | | 74; 75 | |
| Pollard | Thomas & wife | Analy | m/f | Sebastopol | m | | 70; | |

| 1 SURNAME | 2 GIVEN NAME | 3 TOWNSHIP | 4 SEX | 5 RESIDENCE | 6 MAR. | 7 NO. CHILDREN | 8 AGE | 9 NATIVITY |
|---|---|---|---|---|---|---|---|---|
| Pomroy | Mr. | Analy | m | Sebastopol | | | 71 | |
| Pool | Lydia | Redwood | f | Guerneville | w | 5 | 60 | OH |
| Pope | Jacob | Glen Ellen | m | Glen Ellen | d | 3 | 82 | |
| Porter | Julia | Analy | f | Bodega Ave., Sebastopol | m | 5 | 40 | WI |
| Porter | Lucy | Petaluma | f | Petaluma | | | 76 | |
| Porter | William | Santa Rosa | m | nr. South Park School | | | | |
| Porter | William | Santa Rosa | m | 829 Ripley St. | w | | | |
| Porter | Wm. P. | Santa Rosa | m | Petaluma Rd. | m | 4 | | |
| Post | Frances, Mrs. | Petaluma | f | 136 Liberty St. | m | | | |
| Post | J. B. | | m | | | | | |
| Potter | Edmond | Santa Rosa | m | 528 First St. | s | 1 | 64 | MD |
| Powell | Frank | Santa Rosa | m | Bellevue | m | | 80 | |
| Powers | L., Mrs. | Santa Rosa | f | Santa Rosa | m | | 73 | |
| Pressl[e]y | William H. | Redwood | m | Guerneville | s | | | GA |
| Price | William H. | Santa Rosa | m | Alpine Valley | w | 1 | 87 | |
| Prince | Louis L.; Freddie F. | Redwood | m | Guerneville | | | | |
| Proctor | Sadie | Mendocino | f | Healdsburg | w | 2 | | |
| Pucinelli | Ben | Cloverdale | m | Asti | m | 6 | | |
| Purdy | George Washington | Petaluma | m | Petaluma | s | | 71 | OH |
| Quackenbush | Lettie | Santa Rosa | f | Santa Rosa | | 4 | | |
| Querola | John | Sonoma | m | Napa St. | s | | 70 | ITL |
| Quirk | Margaret | Petaluma | f | Keller St. | s | | 55 | IRL |
| Raddel | Mrs. | Santa Rosa | f | Santa Rosa | | | | |
| Raddle | Ed, Mrs. | Redwood | f | Guerneville | | | | |
| Radel | Edward, Mrs. | Redwood | f | Guerneville | m | 2 | | |
| Raefael | Pedro | Cazadero | m | Cazadero | m | 9 | | |
| Raineri | Lucia | Sonoma | f | | m | 7 | | |
| Ramis | Elliott M. & wife | Santa Rosa | m/f | 115 6th St. | m | | | |

| 1 SURNAME | 2 GIVEN NAME | 3 TOWNSHIP | 4 SEX | 5 RESIDENCE | 6 MAR. | 7 NO. CHILDREN | 8 AGE | 9 NATIVITY |
|---|---|---|---|---|---|---|---|---|
| Read | William B. | Sonoma | m | Agua Caliente | m | | 75 | OH |
| Read | William Bowers | Sonoma | m | Agua Caliente | s | | 76 | OH |
| Redmond | Harriet M. | Mendocino | f | 427 North St., Healdsburg | s | | 72 | |
| Redmond | Harriett M. | Mendocino | f | 312 University St., Healdsburg | s | | 75 | |
| Reed | Laura | Santa Rosa | f | First St. | d | 7 | | |
| Reed | Laura | Santa Rosa | f | 413 First St. | w | 4 | | |
| Reed | Sarah Jane | Santa Rosa | f | 210 Olive St. | w | 1 | 77 | |
| Reeder | Alice H. | Santa Rosa | f | 723 Wright St. | w | 3 | 41 | MO |
| Reeder | Alice H. | Santa Rosa | f | 723 Wright St. | w | 3 | | |
| Reeder | Daisy | Santa Rosa | f | Ware St. | m | 1 | | |
| Reeder | S. W., Mrs. | Santa Rosa | f | | | 4 | | |
| Reedy | Mary | Petaluma | f | 10 Bassett St. | w | 2 | | |
| Reedy | Mary, Mrs. | Petaluma | f | 11 Bassett St. | d | 3 | | |
| Reedy | Mary, Mrs. | Petaluma | f | Bassett St. | d | 3 | | |
| Renfroe | James | Redwood | m | Pocket Canyon | s | | 69 | MO |
| Renfroe | James F. | Redwood | m | Pocket Canyon | | | | |
| Renfroe | James F. | Redwood | m | | | | | |
| Renfroe | James F. | Redwood | m | Guerneville | | | 68 | MO |
| Renfroe | James F. | Redwood | m | Guerneville | s | | 66 | KY |
| Reyburn | W. B. | Santa Rosa | m | | s | | 55 | OH |
| Reynolds | Daniel B. | Santa Rosa | m | 518 Sebastopol Ave. | m | 1 | 55 | OH |
| Reynolds | Daniel B. | Santa Rosa | m | 513 Sebastopol Ave | m | 3 died | | |
| Reynolds | S. K. | Bodega | m | Camp Meeker | | | 83 | |
| Reynolds | S. K. | Bodega | m | Camp Meeker | w | | 83 | |
| Reynolds | Smith K. | Bodega | m | Occidental | w | | | |
| Ribardiere | Susanne | Mendocino | f | Fitch St., Healdsburg | m | 4 | | |
| Rice | D. P. | Analy | m | Occidental | s | | 74 | |
| Rice | Ernest | Mendocino | m | Westside Dry Creek | s | | 65 | |
| Rice | Thomas & wife | Ocean | m/f | Cazadero | m | | | |

-33-

| 1 SURNAME | 2 GIVEN NAME | 3 TOWNSHIP | 4 SEX | 5 RESIDENCE | 6 MAR. | 7 NO. CHILDREN | 8 AGE | 9 NATIVITY |
|---|---|---|---|---|---|---|---|---|
| Richards | Eliza, Mrs. | Santa Rosa | f | | m | | 46; 33 | |
| Richardson | Eliza C., Mrs. | Santa Rosa | f | 125 W. Eighth St. | m | 4 | | |
| Rickett | (children) | Analy | m/f | Forestville | | 3 | | |
| Riley | Clara & Harry | Santa Rosa | f/m | camp nr. Second St. & creek | | 2 | | |
| Ring | R. G. | Petaluma | m | 567 First St. | s | | 77 | ME |
| Ring | R. G. | Petaluma | m | Petaluma | s | | 76 | ME |
| Rippetoe | Dora | Mendocino | f | West St., Healdsburg | m | 4 | 29 | MO |
| Ritter | J. W. | Ocean | m | Cazadero | w | 5 | | |
| Roat | Wm. L., Mr. & Mrs. | Russian River | m/f | Windsor | m | | 81; 76 | |
| Roberson | Malvina J. | Petaluma | f | Petaluma | | 5 | | |
| Roberts | Rose, Mrs. | Petaluma | f | Petaluma | m | 4 | 28 | CA |
| Robertson | F. | Bodega | m | | | | 78 | |
| Robertson | Robert | Petaluma | m | Box 80, Mountain Ave. | s | | 83 | |
| Robertson | Sydney Henry | Analy | m | | m | | | |
| Robinson | F. | Analy | m | | s | | 85 | NC |
| Robinson | Mary, Mrs. | Petaluma | f | Petaluma | m | 2 | | |
| Robison | Fletchey | Analy | | Sebastopol | s | 3 | 86 | NC |
| Rodd | John | Santa Rosa | m | Berry Ln. & Morgan St. | s | | abt. 48 | ENG |
| Rogers | Niles V. | | m | | | | 71 | NY |
| Rogers | Rita Francisca | Petaluma | f | Petaluma | w | 3 | | |
| Rose | D. E., Mrs. | Mendocino | f | Healdsburg | | 7 | | |
| Rose | Jane | Knights Valley | f | nr. Mayacama schoolhouse | m | | 68 | |
| Rose | Mr. & Mrs. | Analy | m/f | | m | | | |
| Rossi | Serafina | Sonoma | f | 411 South Davis | w | 6 | | |
| Roth | A. R. | Bodega | | Occidental | s | | 71 | HLD |
| Roy | Ann, Mrs. | Petaluma | f | | | 1 | | |

-34-

| 1 SURNAME | 2 GIVEN NAME | 3 TOWNSHIP | 4 SEX | 5 RESIDENCE | 6 MAR. | 7 NO. CHILDREN | 8 AGE | 9 NATIVITY |
|---|---|---|---|---|---|---|---|---|
| Roy | Fannie | Petaluma | f | Petaluma | | 1 | | |
| Rudolfi | Attilio | Sonoma | m | East First St. | s | | 51 | ITL |
| Rudolfi | Attilio | Sonoma | m | First St. East | s | | 52 | ITL |
| Rudolfi | Attilio | Sonoma | m | Wiskersham Ranch, Sonoma | s | | | |
| Rudolfi | Attilio | Sonoma | m | Milani Place 1 mile N. from Sonoma | s | | 51 | ITL |
| Ruesch | Christof | Cloverdale | m | | | | | |
| Runyan | Hattie | Santa Rosa | f | 223 Second St. | m | 3 | | |
| Russ | Matilda | Santa Rosa | f | | w | | | |
| Russell | William H. | Santa Rosa | m | N. Fulton Rd. | m | 2 | 88 | MA |
| Ryerson | William | Knights Valley | m | nr. Great Western Mine | s | | 71 | |
| Sabieni | Mary | Santa Rosa | f | 209 Second St. | m | 5 | | |
| Sales | Henery | Knights Valley | m | Rt #3, Healdsburg | s | | | |
| Sales | Luke & family | Santa Rosa | m | | m | 3 | 43; 39 | |
| Salvador | Mr. | Sonoma | m | Stewarts Point | w | | | |
| Samuels | Anna | Santa Rosa | f | First & A Sts. | m | | | |
| Samuels | James, Mrs. | Santa Rosa | f | | w | 5 | | |
| Samuels | Jessie M. | Santa Rosa | f | 16 Pearson St. | m | 2 | | |
| Sandusky | Mattie | Mendocino | f | Healdsburg | w | 4 | 34 | MO |
| Sansbury | Benjamin Franklin | Glen Ellen | m | Kenwood | s | | | |
| Santos | Mary, Mrs. | Ocean | f | Kidd Creek School Dist. | w | 5 | | |
| Santos | Mary, Mrs. | Ocean | f | Kidd Creek School Dist. | w | 4 | | |
| Sawyer | Alice, Mrs. | Petaluma | f | | | small children | | |
| Sawyer | Marsden Albert | Bodega | m | Camp Meeker | s | | | |
| Schefer | Ernest | Santa Rosa | m | Santa Rosa | m | 7 | | |
| Schell | Frank | Petaluma | m | 41 Main St. | s | | 72 | |
| Schlobohm | Albert | Santa Rosa | m | Magnolia Hotel, Fourth St. | w | 1 | 79 | |

| 1 SURNAME | 2 GIVEN NAME | 3 TOWNSHIP | 4 SEX | 5 RESIDENCE | 6 MAR. | 7 NO. CHILDREN | 8 AGE | 9 NATIVITY |
|---|---|---|---|---|---|---|---|---|
| Schrogen | Mary J. | Santa Rosa | f | 8 College Ave. | w | 5 | 73 | |
| Schuster | James Elgin | Bodega | m | Freestone | s | | | |
| Sciacca | G. S. | Santa Rosa | m | 307 Second St. | m | 4 | 63 | |
| Scott | Albert | Santa Rosa | m | 117 West Eighth St. | w | 3 | | |
| Scott | J. H. | | | | | | | |
| Seigel | Frank | Analy | m | McFarlane Ave. & High St., Sebastopol | m | 4 | | |
| Shaeffer | Cynthia | Mendocino | f | Shonnan | m | 1 | | |
| Shaeffer | Cynthia | Mendocino | f | Healdsburg | m | 1 | | |
| Shaw | O. F., Dr. | Petaluma | m | 472 I St. | w | | 65 | NY |
| Sheldon | R. W. | Petaluma | m | Petaluma | s | | 77 | NY |
| Sheldon | R. W. | Petaluma | m | 31 Main St. | s | | 89 | |
| Shepard | Martin | Petaluma | m | Main St. | s | | 70 | NY |
| Shepherd | Morris | Petaluma | m | Eight St. | s | | 69 | OH |
| Sherwood | J. C. | Cloverdale | m | Cloverdale | s | | 92 | |
| Sholes | Martha J. | Cloverdale | f | Mulberry St. | w | 4 | | |
| Sholes | Martha J., Mrs. | Cloverdale | f | Cloverdale | | 3 | | |
| Sibley | Rebecca, Mrs. | Petaluma | f | | w | | 60 | |
| Silva | D., Mrs. | Petaluma | f | Nalago St. | s | | 35 | PRT |
| Silva | Mabel | Cloverdale | f | | w | 4 | | |
| Silva | Manuel D. | Petaluma | m | 623 Galland St. | m | 3 | | |
| Silva | Mary M. | Petaluma | f | Petaluma | w | 8 | | |
| Silvia | Leonor | Petaluma | f | | | | 31 | AZR |
| Silzle | (children) | Mendocino | m/f | Healdsburg | | 6 | | |
| Simoni | Natalina | Santa Rosa | f | 604 Olive St. | w | 3 | | |
| Simpson | Zeptha, Mrs. | | | | | | | |
| Small | Mrs. | Bodega | f | Freestone | | | | |
| Smith | D. W. | Bodega | m | cabin on Fermini Cadelot property, Bay | s | | | |

-36-

| 1 | 2 | 3 | 4 | 5 | 6 | 7 | 8 | 9 |
|---|---|---|---|---|---|---|---|---|
| SURNAME | GIVEN NAME | TOWNSHIP | SEX | RESIDENCE | MAR. | NO. CHILDREN | AGE | NATIVITY |
| Smith | J. Y., Mrs. | Petaluma | f | Petaluma | w | 2 | | |
| Smith | Joseph M. | | m | | | | 63 | IA |
| Smith | Nova N. | Analy | f | 219 Bodega Ave., Sebastopol | w | 4 | | |
| Smith | S. H. | Cloverdale | m | | s | | 77 | MA |
| Smith | S. L., Mrs. | Santa Rosa | f | 103 W. Sixth St. | m | 3 | 45 | IL |
| Smith | Samuel H. | Cloverdale | m | | s | | 76 | MA |
| Smith | Samuel H. | Cloverdale | m | | s | | 75 | |
| Smither | W., Mrs. | Russian River | f | Windsor | m | 9 | | |
| Smithers | W. L. | Santa Rosa | m | Fulton | m | 12 | | |
| Smyth | Mary R., Mrs. | Petaluma | f | Petaluma | | | 46 | |
| Snow | Rubin A. | Petaluma | m | no permanent home | | | | |
| Solorzano | Antonio | Petaluma | m | Main St. | s | | 78 | Santa Barbara |
| Sousa | Marion, Mrs. | Analy | f | RR #1 Box 139 | m | 2 | | |
| Souza | Frank | Analy | m | Green Valley | m | | | |
| Spaich | Emilia, Mrs. | Petaluma | f | San Antonio Dist, Nicasio Road | d | 5 | | |
| Spaich | Emilia, Mrs. | Petaluma | f | 323 Walnut St. | d | 5 | | |
| Spaulding | Ambrose N. | Petaluma | m | 210 West St. | w | | 83 | |
| Speller | George | Analy | m | | | | | |
| Sprunck | Henry P. | Russian River | m | Windsor | w | | 79 | |
| Stafford | B., Mrs. | Santa Rosa | f | South Park | m | 3 | | |
| Stark | H. E., Mrs. | Santa Rosa | f | Petaluma Rd | s | | 59 | IL |
| Stark | Harriot E. | Santa Rosa | f | 331 W. Eighth St. | w | 5 | 77 | |
| Stark | Willie | Mendocino | m | Healdsburg | | | | |
| Starr | Nancy, Mrs. | Santa Rosa | f | Mendocino St. | w | | 72+ | |
| Steinpis | Rosa | Santa Rosa | f | 306 Mendocino St. | m | 2 | 27 | IA |
| Sterling | James A. | Sonoma | m | First St. West | s | | | |
| Stewart | Lovilla | Petaluma | f | 330 Main St | w | 3 | 77 | |

| 1 | 2 | 3 | 4 | 5 | 6 | 7 | 8 | 9 |
|---|---|---|---|---|---|---|---|---|
| SURNAME | GIVEN NAME | TOWNSHIP | SEX | RESIDENCE | MAR. | NO. CHILDREN | AGE | NATIVITY |
| Stewart | Lovilla, Mrs. | Mendocino | f | 139 North St., Healdsburg | w | 3 | 79 | |
| Stochini | Agostino | Santa Rosa | m | Hearn District | m | 2 | 77 | SWT |
| Stodard | Bud | Bodega | m | nr. Freestone | w | 5 | | |
| Storks | Hariet E., Mrs. | Santa Rosa | f | Cannery Camp Ground | w | 3 | 78 | |
| Strock | Emma, Mrs. | Analy | f | 216 Healdsburg Ave., Sebastopol | w | 1 | 60 | |
| Stump | Daniel A. | Santa Rosa | m | 929 Sonoma Ave. | m | 4 | | |
| Sutherland | Ella | Santa Rosa | f | Pressley & Temple Sts. | w | 1 | 75 | |
| Sutherland | Ellen | Santa Rosa | f | First & Main | w | 1 | | |
| Sutherland | Ellen, Mrs. | Santa Rosa | f | Ninth St. | w | 1 | | |
| Suthland | Ellen | Santa Rosa | f | West Eighth St. | w | | | |
| Sweet | James | Bodega | m | O'Farrell Ranch, Freestone | w | | | |
| Sweet | James | Redwood | m | Guerneville | w | 1 | | |
| Talbot | Louis F. | Santa Rosa | m | 323 Carrillo St. | s | | | |
| Talbot | Louis F. | Santa Rosa | m | 323 Carrillo St. | s | | | |
| Talbot | Louis Franklin | Santa Rosa | m | 412 South E St. | s | | 33 | CA |
| Tate | George Sidney | Sonoma | m | Spain St. | w | | 73 | |
| Tate | George Sidney | Sonoma | m | Spain St. | s | | 73 | |
| Taylor | Ina F. | Santa Rosa | f | tent on Palm nr. Orange | w | 1 | | |
| Tew | Clara | Santa Rosa | f | 626 Charles St. | w | 1 | | |
| Thatford | Sarah A., Mrs. | Petaluma | f | 403 Washington St. | w | 1 | 72 | NY |
| Thiesen | C. E. C. S. | Santa Rosa | m | 738 Davis St. | w | | 63 | GER |
| Thomas | D. W. | Analy | m | Sebastopol | m | | 70 | KY |
| Thomas | H. R., Mr. & Mrs. | Petaluma | m/f | cor. Oak & Keokuk Sts. | m | 4 | | |
| Thompson | Julia E. | Santa Rosa | f | 582 Mendocino Ave. | w | 2 | 58 | IA |
| Thompson | Julia E. | Santa Rosa | f | 653 Mill St. | w | 4 | 71 | |
| Thompson | Nellie B. | Santa Rosa | f | 517 Washington St. | w | 4 | | |
| Thompson | William, Mrs. | Santa Rosa | f | Santa Rosa | m | 4 | 42 | AR |
| Thorp | Carlena Anna Marie | Santa Rosa | f | Healdsburg | w | | | |

| 1 | 2 | 3 | 4 | 5 | 6 | 7 | 8 | 9 |
|---|---|---|---|---|---|---|---|---|
| SURNAME | GIVEN NAME | TOWNSHIP | SEX | RESIDENCE | MAR. | NO. CHILDREN | AGE | NATIVITY |
| Thummillen | Elizabeth, Mrs. | Cloverdale | f | | | 4 | | |
| Timmons | H. M. | Santa Rosa | m | cor. First & Main St. | w | 4 | | |
| Tod | Juliet M. & Isabella | Santa Rosa | f | College Ave. | | | | |
| Tojo | Madalena | Sonoma | f | Second St. East | w | 2 | 73 | |
| Tojo | Madalena | Sonoma | f | Napa St. | s | 3 | | |
| Toltschin | J., Mrs. | Santa Rosa | f | 316 Chestnut St. | deserted | 1 | 54 | |
| Tombs | Henry C. & Mrs. | Washington | m/f | Geyserville | m | | 80; 84 | |
| Toombs | G. A. | Santa Rosa | | 714 Third St. | m | 10 | | |
| Toroni | Margherita | Sonoma | f | Spain St. | w | 3 | 69 | |
| Toroni | Margherita | Sonoma | f | Second St. | w | 3 | 71 | |
| Toschi | Tranquilla | Santa Rosa | f | 125 Sixth St. | m | 5 | | |
| Towle | Ida M. | Santa Rosa | f | 105 Theresa St. | w | 1 | | |
| Treat | John J., Mrs. | Mendocino | f | Mason St., Healdsburg | m | 8 | | |
| Trimble | Patrick J. | Petaluma | m | Main St. | s | | 59 | IRL |
| Tritchler | Dora | Cloverdale | f | Cloverdale | w | 4 | 43 | OR |
| Truett | William | Mendocino | m | Healdsburg | m | | | |
| Tuitchlen? | Dora, Mrs. | Cloverdale | f | | | | | |
| Tuney | J. | Santa Rosa | m | Santa Rosa | m | | | |
| Tuney | J. | Santa Rosa | m | Santa Rosa | m | | | |
| Tunnell | Eliza A., Mrs. | Santa Rosa | f | 22 Rutledge St. | w | | 70 | |
| Turner | Annie Maria, Mrs. | Cazadero | f | Cazadero | w | 1 | | |
| Turner | J. H. | Bodega | m | nr. Occidental | m | 1 | 45 | CA |
| Turner | J. H. | Bodega | m | Bodega Bay | m | 1 | 54 | |
| Turner | M., Mrs. | Ocean | f | Duncans Mills | w | 2 | 80 | |
| Turner | Martha | Ocean | f | Duncans Mills | w | 2 | 80 | |
| Turner | Mary, Mrs. | Mendocino | f | Healdsburg | | 2 | | |
| Turner | Peter W. | Santa Rosa | m | Davis & Seventh Sts. | s | | 73 | NY |

-39-

| 1 SURNAME | 2 GIVEN NAME | 3 TOWNSHIP | 4 SEX | 5 RESIDENCE | 6 MAR. | 7 NO. CHILDREN | 8 AGE | 9 NATIVITY |
|---|---|---|---|---|---|---|---|---|
| Turner | Peter W. | Analy | m | Green Valley | | 2 | 74 | NY |
| Turner | S. E., Mrs. | Santa Rosa | f | 217 Fifth St. | w | | 59 | NY |
| Turner | Semantha E., Mrs. | Santa Rosa | f | 328 Second St. | m | 2 | 64 | NY |
| Tyler | Clifton | Redwood | m | Mill St., Guerneville | | | 6 | CA |
| Unger | Julia | Santa Rosa | f | 423 Carillo St. | ds | 2 | | |
| Ursin | Ada | Analy | f | nr. Hessel Station | m | 1 | | |
| Ursin | Ada L. | Analy | f | nr. Hessel Station | m | 1 | | |
| Ursin | Ada, Mrs. | Analy | f | Hessel Station, Sebastopol | m | 1 | | |
| Valentine | Mary | Glen Ellen | f | Kenwood | w | | 80 | MD |
| Van | Mr. & Mrs. | Mendocino | m/f | Healdsburg | m | 1 | | |
| Vance | | Santa Rosa | m/f | Fifth St. | | 2 | | |
| Vance | Robin & Stuart | Santa Rosa | m/f | | | | 7; 3 | |
| VanGeldern | Mathilde | | f | Santa Rosa | | | 64 | Hanover, GER |
| VanGeldern | Matilda | Sonoma | f | Sonoma | | | 61 | |
| VanGeldern | Matilda, Miss | Sonoma | f | | | | | |
| Vann | E. S. | Mendocino | m | Healdsburg | m | | 80 | |
| Vann | E. S. | Mendocino | m | Healdsburg | m | | | |
| Vann | E. S. | Mendocino | m | Center St., Healdsburg | m | | 91 | TN |
| Vann | E. S. & wife | Mendocino | m/f | Healdsburg | m | | 79; 55 | TN |
| Vaughan | E. N., Mrs. | Santa Rosa | f | Seventh & Davis Sts. | m | | | |
| Vaughn | Casan E., Mrs. | Mendocino | f | Santa Rosa | | 1 | 89+ | |
| Veatch | Ellen | Analy | f | 314 Petaluma Ave., Sebastopol | w | | 80 | |
| Vellulïini | Ermida & Annie | Redwood | f | Guerneville | | | 10; 5 | Sonoma Co. |
| Vest | Eli | Santa Rosa | m | Santa Rosa | m | | 33 | MO |
| Vestal | Jacob | Analy | m | Forestville | s | | 78 | IN |
| Vier(s) | Mrs. | Petaluma | f | Petaluma | w | 7 | | |

-40-

| 1 | 2 | 3 | 4 | 5 | 6 | 7 | 8 | 9 |
|---|---|---|---|---|---|---|---|---|
| SURNAME | GIVEN NAME | TOWNSHIP | SEX | RESIDENCE | MAR. | NO. CHILDREN | AGE | NATIVITY |
| Vierra | Anna, Mrs. | Petaluma | f | | | | | |
| Vineyard | Leone | Washington | m | Geyserville | s | 6 | 12 | |
| Vinsent | John | Santa Rosa | m | 303 W. Eighth St. | w | | | |
| Vinyard | Leon | Washington | m | Geyserville | | | 11 | AR |
| vonGeldern | Matilda | Sonoma | f | | | | 64+ | |
| Wagner | Katherine | Analy | f | Graton | m | 7 | | |
| Waldvogel | Marie | Santa Rosa | f | 140 South E St. | w | | | |
| Walk | Lillie Ellen | Santa Rosa | f | 234 Henley St. | m | 5 | | |
| Walker | Ada L., Mrs. | Santa Rosa | f | 527 Second St. | d | 6 | | |
| Walker | B. K. | Santa Rosa | m | Route 5 Box 99 | w | | | |
| Walker | Benjamin K. | Santa Rosa | m | Santa Rosa | w | | 85 | |
| Walker | Lizzie | Mendocino | f | Healdsburg | | 5 | | |
| Walker | Lizzie | Russian River | f | Windsor | | 5 | | |
| Walker | Nancy, Mrs. | Santa Rosa | f | 8 College Ave. | s | 2 | 35 | PA |
| Wall | Ada | Analy | f | Sebastopol | m | 3 | | |
| Wall | Ada, Mrs. | Analy | f | Eleanor Ave., Sebastopol | d | 3 | | |
| Wallace | James | Santa Rosa | m | | | | | |
| Ward | Laura | Petaluma | f | 702 East D St. | m | 5 | | |
| Ward | Laura | Petaluma | f | Forestville Rd. District | m | 6 | | |
| Ward | Laura, Mrs. | Petaluma | f | 533 Vallejo St. | m | 5 | | |
| Ward | Lizzie, Mrs. | Santa Rosa | f | 846 Second St. | w | 3 | 41 | IA |
| Ward | Thomas | Petaluma | m | Third St. | m | 3 | 73 | ENG |
| Ward | William | Analy | m | Spring Hill School Dist. | s | | | |
| Ward | William | Analy | m | Green Valley | s | | | |
| Warne | N. E., Mrs. | Analy | f | Sebastopol | m | | 53 | IA |
| Warne | N. E., Mrs. | Analy | f | Sebastopol | m | | 53 | USA |
| Wassom | Jacob & wife | Mendocino | m/f | Healdsburg | m | | 84; 70 | |
| Webb | William B. | Petaluma | m | 12 Main St. | s | | 79 | |

| 1 SURNAME | 2 GIVEN NAME | 3 TOWNSHIP | 4 SEX | 5 RESIDENCE | 6 MAR. | 7 NO. CHILDREN | 8 AGE | 9 NATIVITY |
|---|---|---|---|---|---|---|---|---|
| Webster | Anthony | Analy | m | Sebastopol | m | | | |
| Welch | Martha | Santa Rosa | f | 711 Madison St. | w | 1 | 80 | |
| Welch | Martha, Mrs. | Santa Rosa | f | 212 Barnett St. | s | | 75 | |
| Welch | Mary, Mrs. | Analy | f | Bloomfield | w | 5 | 76 | |
| Welch | Mrs. | Analy | f | Bloomfield | m | 5 | | |
| Welhe | Irene | Santa Rosa | f | Wilson St. | s | | | |
| Weller | Ada, Mrs. | Santa Rosa | f | 903 Morgan | d | 3 | | |
| Weller | George | Santa Rosa | m | W. Third St. | m | 1 | 64 | IL |
| Wells | J. M. | Mendocino | m | Center St., Healdsburg | m | | | |
| Wells | Oscar J. | Glen Ellen | m | Kenwood | s | | 78 | |
| Wellschott | Theodore & wife | Sonoma | m/f | Sonoma | m | | 70+ | |
| Welschott | Theodore | Sonoma | m | Sonoma | | | 75 | |
| Welsholt | Theodore | Sonoma | m | Sonoma | m | | 72 | |
| Westgate | Charles, Mrs. | Analy | f | Berry Ln., Sebastopol | w | 1 | | |
| Wheeler | A. | Mendocino | m | Healdsburg | m | | old | KY |
| Wheeler | A. | Mendocino | m | Healdsburg | m | 3 | 65 | |
| Wheeler | Mary | Santa Rosa | f | 636 Charles St. | w | 6 | | |
| Whitcomb | O., Mr. & Mrs. | Analy | m/f | Halleberg Ranch, Graton | m | 6 | 69; 66 | |
| White | Catherine R. | Santa Rosa | f | 409 Mendocino Ave. | s | | | |
| White | John | Bodega | m | Occidental | | | | |
| White | John | Bodega | m | Occidental | s | | | ENG |
| Whitney | Cora, Mrs. | Santa Rosa | f | Carrington & Davis Sts. | m | 1 | | |
| Whitson | Charlotte | Petaluma | f | 326 Kentucky St. | w | | 45 | |
| Wiatt | Martha A. | Petaluma | f | Petaluma | | | 70 | Boston, MA |
| Wiatt | Martha A. | Petaluma | f | Petaluma | | | 80 | |
| Wieberts | Richard | Mendocino | m | Healdsburg | m | 1 | | |
| Wilhite | George A. | Bodega | m | in a tent, Bodega Bay | m | 1 | | |
| Wilke | Irene | Santa Rosa | f | 757 Wilson St. | w | | | |

| 1 | 2 | 3 | 4 | 5 | 6 | 7 | 8 | 9 |
|---|---|---|---|---|---|---|---|---|
| SURNAME | GIVEN NAME | TOWNSHIP | SEX | RESIDENCE | MAR. | NO. CHILDREN | AGE | NATIVITY |
| Wilkerson | John F. | Santa Rosa | m | foot hills north of St. Helena Ave. | w | | 71 | |
| Willcox | Eliza | Mendocino | f | Healdsburg | s | 1 | 73 | NY |
| Williams | Cynthia, Mrs. | Cloverdale | f | Mulberry St. | m | 4 | | |
| Williams | George W. & Sarah A. | Santa Rosa | m/f | Santa Rosa | m | | 67; 70 | OH & IN |
| Williams | Ira T., Mrs. | Santa Rosa | f | 714 Henley St. | w | 1 | 73 | |
| Williams | J. W., Mr. & Mrs. | Santa Rosa | m/f | Santa Rosa | m | | | |
| Williams | Mary | Mendocino | f | Healdsburg | s | | 77 | VA |
| Williams | Wm | Sonoma | m | Sonoma | | | | |
| Williams | Mary Ann | Sonoma | f | Healdsburg | s | | 75 | VA |
| Willis | Ada, Mrs. (children) | Santa Rosa | f | 3 Goodman Ave. | d | 8 | 34 | |
| Wilson | Anthony | Santa Rosa | m | 720 First St. | s | | 81 | |
| Wilson | Anton | Santa Rosa | m | 931 Washington St. | w | | | |
| Wilson | Charles K., Mrs. | Salt Point | f | crossroads nr. Sea View | w | | | |
| Wilson | Charles Sovrin | Sonoma | m | Agua Caliente | s | | 81 | |
| Wilson | Florence, Mrs. | Petaluma | f | | | 2 | | |
| Wilson | Florence, Mrs. | Petaluma | f | 614 Main St. | m | 3 | | |
| Wilson | Lillie, Mrs. | Santa Rosa | f | 523 1/2 Fourth St. | d | 5 | | |
| Wilson | Lilly | Santa Rosa | f | 408 College Ave. | d | 5 | | |
| Wilson | Lilly | Santa Rosa | f | Fourth St. | m | 5 | | |
| Wilson | Lilly, Mrs. | Santa Rosa | f | 920 Santa Rosa Ave. | d | 5 | | |
| Wilson | P. L. | Santa Rosa | m | Petaluma Rd. nr. bone factory | m | 3 | | |
| Wilson | Sarah, Mrs. | Redwood | f | Guerneville | | 3 | | |
| Winslow | John | Petaluma | m | race track | s | | 65 | |
| Winter | Bernhardt | Russian River | m | Windsor | w | 1 stepson | | |
| Winter | Bernhardt | Russian River | m | R.F.D. 1, Windsor | m | 1 | | |

| 1 SURNAME | 2 GIVEN NAME | 3 TOWNSHIP | 4 SEX | 5 RESIDENCE | 6 MAR. | 7 NO. CHILDREN | 8 AGE | 9 NATIVITY |
|---|---|---|---|---|---|---|---|---|
| Winton | Robert F. | Santa Rosa | m | 210 F. St. | m | | | |
| Winton | Robert F. | Santa Rosa | m | 210 F St. | m | | | |
| Woldvogel | Mary | Santa Rosa | f | 120 Ninth St. | w | 1 | 51 | SWT |
| Wolfe | N. T. | Mendocino | m | Healdsburg | m | | 66 | |
| Wolfe | N. T. | Mendocino | m | 425 Piper St., Healdsburg | m | | 73 | |
| Wolfe | N. T. & Catherine | Mendocino | m/f | Piper St., Healdsburg | m | | 76; 69 | TN & OH |
| Wood | Jane | Petaluma | f | 684 Keller St. | w | | 87 | ENG |
| Wood | Jane, Mrs. | Petaluma | f | Petaluma | | | 79 | |
| Wood | John | Petaluma | m | Petaluma | m | | | |
| Wood | John | Petaluma | m | Petaluma | m | | 80+ | |
| Wood | John & Mary Jane | Petaluma | m/f | Petaluma | m | | 75; 70 | |
| Wood | W. E., Mrs. | Mendocino | f | Healdsburg | o | | | |
| Woodley | Josie | Santa Rosa | f | 314 Brown St. | m | 3 | | |
| Woods | Katie | Santa Rosa | f | Rutledge St. | w | 3 | | |
| Woods | Katie, Mrs. | Santa Rosa | f | 915 Clark St. | d | 3 | | |
| Woodward | Martha Jane | Santa Rosa | f | 902 Orchard St. | w | | 83 | |
| Wooley | Susan | Analy | f | Humboldt St. | w | | 70 | IN |
| Woolf | Buck, Mrs. | Mendocino | f | Healdsburg | | | | |
| Woolley | Susan | Santa Rosa | f | 29 Sixth St. | w | | 71 | IN |
| Worden | William D. | Analy | m | | | | | |
| Wordin | Annie | Santa Rosa | f | 143 Scott St. | w | | 64 | |
| Workman | Nettie | Redwood | f | Mill St., Guerneville | m | 1 | 24 | CA |
| Wright | Isaac | Petaluma | m | 305 Broadway & Bassett Sts. | m | | 92 | |
| Wyatt | Mrs. & Aunt Peggy | Petaluma | f | beyond Revere House | m/s | 5 | | |
| Yeager | A., Mrs. | Santa Rosa | f | Creek St. | m | 6 | 43 | CA |
| Young | John | Redwood | m | Guerneville | | | 70+ | KY |
| Young | Minnie A. | Santa Rosa | f | 925 Fifth St. | w | | | |

| 1 | 2 | 3 | 4 | 5 | 6 | 7 | 8 | 9 |
|---|---|---|---|---|---|---|---|---|
| SURNAME | GIVEN NAME | TOWNSHIP | SEX | RESIDENCE | MAR. | NO. CHILDREN | AGE | NATIVITY |
| Young | Ada, Mrs. | Santa Rosa | f | 718 Wright St. | w |  | 63 |  |
| Zanolini | M., Mrs. | Analy | f | Bloomfield | m | 7 | 37 | SWT |
| Zanolini | Michael | Analy | m | Bloomfield | m | 6 |  | SWT |
| Zappa | Martin | Santa Rosa | m | South Park | m | 3 |  |  |

Part II

surname, given name, children's names, children's ages, children's birthplaces, lives with whom, relationship

| 1 SURNAME | 2 GIVEN NAME | 10 CHILDREN'S NAMES | 11 CHILDREN'S AGES | 12 CHILDREN'S BIRTHPLACES | 13 LIVES WITH WHOM | 14 RELATIONSHIP |
|---|---|---|---|---|---|---|
| Abino | Rosania | Mary; Maud; Frank; Louisa; Rosa | 14; 13; 13; 12; 10 | | alone | |
| Adams | J. W. | small children | | | wife & children | |
| Adams | Melissa, Mrs. | | | | | |
| Adams | W. J. | | | | | |
| Adams | W. J. | | | | | |
| Albertson | Iver | Malvin; Selma | 3; 18 mos. | Santa Rosa | Mollie Albertson | wife |
| Alexander | Ada Lue, Mrs. | Charles R.; Alexander L.; Malissie Mary Ida; Samuel W. | 12; 10; 6; 20 mos. | | Mrs. Humphreys | mother |
| Alexander | Lou Humphreys, Mrs. | C. R.; Lou; Mary Ida; Sam'l W. | 26; 20; 21; 14 | Petaluma | | |
| Allan | Maude, Mrs. | Alice; Adele | 6; 4 | Rio Vista, CA | Martha Drennon | mother |
| Allen | Bessie May | | | | C. Sawtelle | |
| Allen | W. H. | | | | E. E. Spragues | |
| Alsved | Louisa, Mrs. | | 4; 2 | | John Alsved & children | husband & children |
| Alway | Abby, Mrs. | | | | M. J. Pierce | |
| Amwell(e) | Letta | Tony; Feam; Grace | 14; 13; 10 | CO; NE; IA | children | |
| Andersen | Thomas & wife | | | | together | |
| Anderson | John P. | | | | wife | |
| Anderson | Louisa | | | | | |
| Anderson | Mary | | | | husband | |
| Andrews | Carrie | Annetta Lillian; Walter Joseph | 8; 5 | Petaluma | children | |
| Andrews | Elizabeth, Mrs. | | 1 ½ to 7 | IRL | | |
| Anker | Erik | | | | Mrs. M. Grindle | |
| Anker | Peter & wife | | | | together | |
| Anker | Peter & wife | Jacob | 38 | DNK | | |
| Antone | Peter | Tommy; Annie | 5; 3 | Sonoma Co., CA | | |

| 1 SURNAME | 2 GIVEN NAME | 10 CHILDREN'S NAMES | 11 CHILDREN'S AGES | 12 CHILDREN'S BIRTHPLACES | 13 LIVES WITH WHOM | 14 RELATIONSHIP |
|---|---|---|---|---|---|---|
| Archer | N. A., Mrs. | Maud Etta Kennedy; Paul S. | 32; 10 | Sonoma Co., CA | Maud (feebleminded), dau; Paul, grandson | |
| Archer | N. A., Mrs. | Maude Kennedy (dau.); Paul S. (grandson) | 33; 11 | CA | alone with children | mother & grandmother |
| Arnett | Alice | Floyd; Vivian; Lenard; Naomi | 16; 14; 12; 10 | Bodega | children | |
| Arnett | John H. | | | | | |
| Arnold | Joe, Mrs. | | | | | |
| Arnold | T. J., Mrs. | | | | Mrs. Annie A. Malory | |
| Arnold | Temassah | Louise; Francis; Truimi?; Willie; Margarete | 16; 12; 10; 8; 2 | CA | alone with children | |
| Ash | Arethusa, Mrs. | | 6; 8 | | Mr. Ash & child | grandmother |
| Asman | Louis, Mrs. | Louisa; Carl; Louis | 15; 13; 6 | Eureka, CA | | |
| Asman | Louise | Helene; Karl; Louis | 16; 14; 7 | CO; CA; CA | Belle Vossos | |
| Asmussen | Alfred, Mrs. | Anna; Alfred; Felton; Willie; Ellwood; Norville | 15; 13; 11; 9; 6; 4 | all SF | | |
| Azevedo | Manuel | | | | J. M. Souza | |
| Badgley | Edgar Jasper | Ira; Jessie; Edgar; Linus; Edna; Eldon | 14; 12; 10; 8; 7; 4 | KS; KS; IL; IL; CA; CA | | |
| Bailey | James | | | | Mrs. Bailey | wife |
| Bailey | Samuel H. | | | | alone | |
| Bailey | William | | | | | |
| Bain | Mrs. | | | | | |
| Bainbridge | Benj. | all of age | | | | |
| Baker | Elvira J. | William M.; Albert; Oliver E. | 50; 40; 30 | MO; CA | William M. Baker | |
| Balzari | Rosa | James | 19 | Santa Barbara | son | |
| Burnes | J. R., Mrs. | Mrs. Garrett Kidd | | | brother | |
| Barker | John | | | | | |
| Barnes | Peggy | | | | | |

| 1 SURNAME | 2 GIVEN NAME | 10 CHILDREN'S NAMES | 11 CHILDREN'S AGES | 12 CHILDREN'S BIRTHPLACES | 13 LIVES WITH WHOM | 14 RELATIONSHIP |
|---|---|---|---|---|---|---|
| Barnes | Peggy | | | | | |
| Barnes | Wm. | | | | | |
| Barry | Anna | | | | children | |
| Bartlow | Emma, Mrs. | Norval; Bud | 12; 10 | Red Bluff; Chico, CA | | |
| Bartow | Helen, Mrs. | Gladys E. Vallier; Myron H. Vallier; Caroline | 13; 11; 5 | Petaluma; Petaluma; Willits, CA | | |
| Battaglia | Mary | Victoria | 21 mos. | Santa Rosa | Mrs. Groli | |
| Batten | Christina | | 60; 55; 44 | | alone | |
| Batten | Cora | George; Gerald | 8; 7 | WA; CA | Mrs. J. H. Lockard | mother |
| Batten | Cora | George; Gerald | 11; 10 | WA; CA | Blitz Paxton | |
| Baxman | Lewis | small | | | wife and children | |
| Beansford | Ida B. | | | | Mary A. Bransford | mother |
| Beckett | Mrs. | | small | | | |
| Bee | Alice, Mrs. | | | | | |
| Bee | Alice, Mrs. | large family | | | | |
| Bee | Mary A. | Martin; Myrtle Walker; Maud Seecot; Chester; Henrietta | 31; 29; 27; 25; 17 | 1st 2 Santa Rosa; last 3 Guerneville | 17 year old dau. | |
| Bee | Mary A. | | 33; 31; 29; 27; 19 | Santa Rosa; Guerneville | Henrietta Bee | |
| Bee | Mary, Mrs. | little children | 5; 3; 1 | | | |
| Beebe | T. J. | | | | alone | |
| Beebe | Thomas J. | | | | Thomas Hickley | |
| Bell | Mary | | all under 7 | | | |
| Bell | Peter & Clara E. | | | | wife, Clara E. Bell | |
| Bemiss | Sam | | | | | |
| Bemiss | Samuel | | | | | |
| Bemiss | Samuel | | | | alone | |

| 1 SURNAME | 2 GIVEN NAME | 10 CHILDREN'S NAMES | 11 CHILDREN'S AGES | 12 CHILDREN'S BIRTHPLACES | 13 LIVES WITH WHOM | 14 RELATIONSHIP |
|---|---|---|---|---|---|---|
| Bemiss | Samuel | | | | alone | |
| Bemiss | Samuel | | | | alone | |
| Benson | Mathis Charles | Russel; Martha | 10; 8 | Rio Vista, CA | wife & children | |
| Bentel | Bertha | Elfred Scot; Elsie Beutel | 32; 21 | Santa Cruz, CA; Sonoma Co | | |
| Berlin | David & Agnes (children) | | | | | |
| Berry | Emma, Mrs. | Lelia; Josie; Birddie; Nelly | 16; 12; 10; 8 | | | |
| Berry | | | oldest 15 | | | |
| Berryessa | Jacinto | boy | 25 | CA | John W. Lhauren | none |
| Berryessa | Jacinto | | | | George McCutchan | |
| Berwert | Frank | | | | Mrs. J. Sutter | sister |
| Betrix | Emile | | | | | |
| Bilow | Anna, Mrs. | Charlie | 10 | GER | Mr. Carter | none |
| Binder | Charles | | | | | |
| Binegar | W. L. | | | | Siemer Bros. | |
| Biret | Grace | Sutherland; Edith | 13 | Guerneville | Ed Beebe | sister |
| Birkhoff | C. | Hattie; Rosie; Robert; Herman; Jesse | 11; 9; 7; 3; 1 ½ | ?; ?; ?; Santa Rosa, Santa Rosa | | |
| Bish | Abraham | all married four living in county | | | dau. | dau. |
| Bishop | George W. | both of age | | | W. Liter | son-in-law |
| Bishop | Mattie | | | | Mr. Ring | |
| Black | Sarah | | | | alone | |
| Blair | John | | | | | |
| Blake | E. M., Mrs. | | 30 | Napa Valley, CA | alone | |
| Blank | Cord, Mrs. | | all minors; youngest 9 mos. | | | |
| Blank | Cord, Mrs. | | | | | |
| Bledsoe | Thomas | | | | alone | |
| Blele | Christian O. | | | | William Knott | |

| 1 | 2 | 10 | 11 | 12 | 13 | 14 |
|---|---|---|---|---|---|---|
| SURNAME | GIVEN NAME | CHILDREN'S NAMES | CHILDREN'S AGES | CHILDREN'S BIRTHPLACES | LIVES WITH WHOM | RELATIONSHIP |
| Boids | Erminia | | | | | |
| Borgwardt | A. | | | | | |
| Bowman | Francis J. | Henry Alford; Joseph Roy; Jesse | 21; 15; 13 | Santa Cruz; Santa Clara; Santa Clara, CA | children | |
| Boyd | Ben, Mrs. | | | | | |
| Boyd | W. M., Mrs. | Moris Vernon; Gilbert Hope; Alice May; Beatrice Aileen; Herold Wilson; Raymond Lincoln; Dorothy Eveline ; Evert Wendel | 12; 10; 8; 7; 6; 5; 4; 6 mos. | CA; MA; CA; CA; CA; CA; CA | | |
| Bradford | Herbert | | | | | wife & 2 children |
| Bransford | Ida | | | | Z. W. Bransford | parents |
| Bray | E. C. | | | | | |
| Bray | Elisha G. | | | | | |
| Breaks | Charles H. | ages 7 to 14 | | | alone | |
| Bremer | Caroline | | | | Belle Parkinson | |
| Breshear | Clara | Elvin; Julius | 3; 1 | CA | alone | |
| Brimigian | Samuel | | | | | |
| Broomhall | John | Carlos; Gertie; Albert; Horace; Mrs. Harley J. Vincent; one unknown | 17; 15; 7 | | Mrs. Harley J. Vincent | dau. |
| Brown | Amanda, Mrs. | | | | | |
| Brown | Charlotte | | | | rents room | |
| Brown | Charlotte, Mrs. | | | | | |
| Brown | F. L., Mrs. | Ernest | 11 | Humboldt Co.; Sonoma Co., CA | | |
| Brown | Fanny, Mrs. | | | | | |
| Brown | M., Mrs. | Eugene; Viola; Norman; Frank | 11; 10; 9; 5 | SF; SF; SF; Graton | | |
| Brown | Nancy | | | | Mrs. C. H. Gardner | |
| Browning | Tandy | | | | alone | |

| 1 | 2 | 10 | 11 | 12 | 13 | 14 |
|---|---|---|---|---|---|---|
| SURNAME | GIVEN NAME | CHILDREN'S NAMES | CHILDREN'S AGES | CHILDREN'S BIRTHPLACES | LIVES WITH WHOM | RELATIONSHIP |
| Bruce | Florence I. | Glaydys; Delbert; John; Marion | 7; 7; 6; 5 | 1st 3 St. Helena, CA; NV | | |
| Brunk | Margaret, Miss | | | | L. Shank | |
| Bryant | Rachael | | | | alone with small child | |
| Bryant | Rachel J., Mrs. | Francis Cecil Stocton | 2 | Healdsburg | | |
| Buckland | Mary J., Mrs. | George Piper | 56 | | | |
| Buckner | Mary J. | | | | alone | |
| Buckner | Mary J., Mrs. | | | | Mrs. Poggie (niece) | niece |
| Buckner | Mary Jane | | | | Davis known as Shiver | |
| Buell | Lillian | Park Allen; Orrin Rafael; Friend Leo | 13; 11; 9 | | son-in-law | |
| Bulotti | James | | | | Hotel d'Italia Unita | |
| Burke | (children) | | 16; 14; 12; 10; 8; 6; 4 | | | |
| Burkhardt | Joseph & Margaret | | | | | |
| Bums | John J. | | | | | |
| Burns | Sarah | | oldest 10 youngest 2 | | children | |
| Burns | Thomas | | | | | |
| Bush | J. J., Mrs. | Mrs. D. Conley; Mrs. H. Carter; Mrs. E. Cox; Mrs. M. Rahn | 50; 39; 27; 25 | CA | Mrs. Adams | |
| Butler | A. M. | | | | alone | |
| Butler | Bettie | | | | Mrs. S. L. Ashley | |
| Butler | Mr. & Mrs. | | | | Mrs. Butts | |
| Butts | John W. | | | | wife and children | |
| Byrnes | Jennie | | | | Lizzie Kidd | |
| Cadd | Edwin | | | | F. J. Wheaton | stepson |
| Cadden | Thomas | | | | alone | |

| 1 | 2 | 10 | 11 | 12 | 13 | 14 |
|---|---|---|---|---|---|---|
| SURNAME | GIVEN NAME | CHILDREN'S NAMES | CHILDREN'S AGES | CHILDREN'S BIRTHPLACES | LIVES WITH WHOM | RELATIONSHIP |
| Cain | Robert M. | | | | | |
| Camario | Fernando | | | | J. J. Alves Ranch | |
| Cambra | M. J. & family | | oldest 9; youngest 8 mos. | | | |
| Camenzina | Joseph | Hermina; Carl; Ida; John; Matilda; Anna | 10; 8; 6; 5; 1; 1 wk. | | alone | |
| Cameron | Douglas | | 9; 7; 4; 2 | Sioux City, IA; Petaluma; Healdsburg; Ukiah, CA | | |
| Cameron | Mary | Lawrence; Bruce; Douglas; Mary; baby | 10; 8; 6; 4; 9 mos. | IA; last 4 CA | | |
| Campbell | Mary E. | | dau. | | | |
| Campbell | T. T., Mrs. | | | | | |
| Capell | Susan Francis | Charles M.; Minnie W. Brimfield | 39; 33 | | alone | |
| Capell | Susan Francis | | | | alone | |
| Capponi | Elena | | | | Mark ; Egido Capponi | nephews |
| Capponi | Elena | | | | Marco Capponi | nephew |
| Capponi | Enrico & wife | | | | | |
| Capri | Rosa | Mario Rossi | 17 | SF | alone with son | |
| Capri | Rosa | John Mario | 18 | SF | son | |
| Capucci | Marie Gianpietri | Paoline | 12 | Marsiglia, FRN | mother | |
| Capucci | Mary | Paolina | 7 | Marseille, FRN | F. Lombarde | |
| Capucci | Mary, Mrs. | Frank; Pauline | 23; 15 | ITL | | |
| Caretto | Peter | Delia | 7 mos. | Healdsburg | B. McKendry | none |
| Carillo | Vincento | Susie; Nick (both adults) | both adults | | Susie | dau. |
| Carlson | John | | | | alone | |
| Carlson | John | | | | Mrs. M. Ludolff | none |
| Carr | James | | | | Mrs. A. F. Hibbitts | niece |

| 1 | 2 | 10 | 11 | 12 | 13 | 14 |
|---|---|---|---|---|---|---|
| SURNAME | GIVEN NAME | CHILDREN'S NAMES | CHILDREN'S AGES | CHILDREN'S BIRTHPLACES | LIVES WITH WHOM | RELATIONSHIP |
| Carrell | Ethel, Mrs. | James; Myrtle; Irene; Birdie; Charlie; Dorothy; Grace | 17; 15; 11; 9; 7; 5; 17 mos. | | | |
| Carriger | Elizabeth, Mrs. | | 18; 14; 11; 9 | | | |
| Carrillo | Joaquin | | oldest 12 | | wife and children | |
| Carrillo | Joaquin | | young | | family | |
| Carstensen | Henry | Helen; Gladys; Raymond | 6; 7; 8 | Petaluma | family | |
| Carstensen | Henry & wife | Raymond; Gladys; Helen | 9; 8; 7 | Petaluma | | |
| Casares | Laura, Mrs. | | minor | | | |
| Caton | Anna | Ramos; Louisa | | | Charles Silva | none |
| Cavalli | Irene, Mrs. | Dora; Ellen; Virginia; Alice | 11; 9; 6; 3 | CA | children | |
| Chaffee | Homer H. | | 28 | CA | Mrs. L. Conners | son |
| Chaffee | Jarvis | | 7; 10; 12 | | wife & children | |
| Charity | John | | | | | |
| Charles | M. L. | | | | | |
| Charles | M. L. | | | | | |
| Charles | Martin Luther | | | | alone | |
| Chase | N. G., Mrs. | Margie; Marie | 15; 10 | Santa Cruz Co., CA | | |
| Chicca | Americo | Frank; Emma | 2yrs. 6mos.; 11mos. | Santa Rosa; Santa Rosa | | |
| Childres | Ruann, Mrs. | Martha Angeline; Phebe Emily; Nellie; Myrtle; Easley (gr-gr-grandchild) | 43; 38; 33; 28; 7 | 3 in IL; CA | gr-gr-granddau. | |
| Christensen | Anna M. | Helen, Alice; Gladys; Francis; 2 others over 15 years | 11; 9; 2; 1 | Sonoma Co. | in rented home | |
| Christensen | C. P. | Christian; James M. | | | | |
| Clanton | Rose Velmer | | | | B. Franklin | |
| Clapp | Florence | Elmer | 10 | LaJolla, San Diego Co., CA | rents from R. J. Butts | |

-54-

| 1 | 2 | 10 | 11 | 12 | 13 | 14 |
|---|---|---|---|---|---|---|
| SURNAME | GIVEN NAME | CHILDREN'S NAMES | CHILDREN'S AGES | CHILDREN'S BIRTHPLACES | LIVES WITH WHOM | RELATIONSHIP |
| Clark | Ellena, Mrs. | | small child | | | |
| Clark | J. H., Mr. & Mrs. | | | | wife | |
| Clay | Ann, Mrs. | | | | | |
| Clay | Annie, Mrs. | | | | | |
| Clements | Maria | Mathew | 43 | | | |
| Clements | Mary | Mathew | 50 | AUS | alone | |
| Clinesmith | Mary | | | | F. J. Bowman | dau. |
| Cloer | Sarah | Grace; Vada McMillen | 24; 29 | | | |
| Cloer | Sarah C. | Bell Cunningham; Vada McMullin; Anna Wood; Grace Mier; Harrison; Albert; William | 42; 39; 35; 33; 30; 27; 21 | AR | Vada McMillin | dau. |
| Coburn | Lulu, Mrs. | George; Walter | 14; 16 | | along | |
| Cody | Thomas Michle | | | | Jos. Cain | |
| Coffer | E. M., Mrs. | Frank; Lillian Wardell | 30; 21 | NY; ID | alone | |
| Coffey | Clara Bell - see H. C. Kirpatrick | | | | | |
| Collins | Charles T. | George; Charlie; Raymond; Oliver; Marion | 12; 10; 9; 7; 2 | Sonoma Co. | children | sons & dau. |
| Combs | Robert R. | | | | Mary Combs | wife |
| Comstock | B. F. | | | | | |
| Conklin | I., Mrs. | | under 8 years | | | |
| Conkling | Fannie | Jay; Charlie; Marion; Ruth | 15; 12; 9; 7 | all CA | | |
| Conners | Thomas | | | | Mrs. A. P. Ganyard | |
| Connor | Thomas | | | | Mrs. Polk | |
| Cook | Ella | Carl; Ethel | 11; 8 | | Dr. Ruddock | |
| Cook | Ella, Mrs. | | | | alone | |
| Cook | Jesse | | | | Mrs. Daisy Reeder | dau. |
| Cook | Madelia | | from 2 mos. to 7 yrs. | Santa Rosa | | |

| 1 SURNAME | 2 GIVEN NAME | 10 CHILDREN'S NAMES | 11 CHILDREN'S AGES | 12 CHILDREN'S BIRTHPLACES | 13 LIVES WITH WHOM | 14 RELATIONSHIP |
|---|---|---|---|---|---|---|
| Cook | Solome, Mrs. | | oldest 11 | | | |
| Cooper | Robert F. | Earl; Frank; Elsie; Minnie; Fred; Mary; Hazel; Edna | 16; 14; 12; 10; 8; 6; 4; 3 mos. | | | |
| Cornett | Agnes, Mrs. | | | | 3 small children | |
| Cornwall | Henrietta | | | | | |
| Corri | Joquin | | 2; 15 mos. | | wife and children | |
| Cotrell | (family) | | oldest 10 | | family | husband |
| Cottey | Annie L. | Vivian; Everett; Dorothy | 10; 7; 6 mos. | all in Oakland, CA | mother & children | |
| Cotty | A., Mrs. | Vyvyan; Everett; Dorothy | 14; 11; 4 | Oakland; Oakland; Santa Rosa | Mrs. S. Critchlow | |
| Coulson | Lucinda | Author; Golden; Erle | 1; 3; 11 mos. | Petaluma | | |
| Cox | Ann E. | | | Santa Rosa | | |
| Cox | J. J. | | | | | |
| Cox | William | Henry; W. D. | about 40; about 43 | | wife | |
| Coyle | Michael, Mrs. | | 1 infant & 4 little children | | | |
| Crampton | Eugene R. | Erna J.; Lucille Louise | 10; 2 | Reno, NV & Petaluma | wife & children | |
| Crealy | George | | | | | |
| Cromwell | Rebeca, Mrs. | | | | | |
| Cromwell | William T. | | | | wife | |
| Crozier | P. B., Mrs. | | | | | |
| Culbertson | Alex | | | | Behmer Tenement House | |
| Culbertson | Alexander | | | | alone | |
| Culbertson | Alexander | | | | | |
| Culken | C. | | 12 | SF | himself, wife and 1 child | |
| Cunningham | Mrs. | | | | | |

-56-

| 1 SURNAME | 2 GIVEN NAME | 10 CHILDREN'S NAMES | 11 CHILDREN'S AGES | 12 CHILDREN'S BIRTHPLACES | 13 LIVES WITH WHOM | 14 RELATIONSHIP |
|---|---|---|---|---|---|---|
| Cunningham | Nettie | | | | | |
| Cunningham | Nettie | | | | Mr. & Mrs. John Hurd | sister & brother-in-law |
| Cunningham | W. A. & J. | | | | | |
| Curry | Patrick | | | | | |
| Curry | Patrick | | | | | |
| Curry | Patrick | one unnamed; John | 30 | | wife | |
| Curry | Patrick | Ellen; John | dau. 13; son 9 | | | |
| Curry | Patrick & family | | 14; 10 | | family | |
| Damerell | Rebecca, Mrs. | Beulah Lee; Owen Clinton; Ben. Lorin; Wesley Earl; Brattan Logan; Charles Bernice | 14; 13; 9; 7; 5; 5 | | | |
| Damrell | R., Mrs. | Beulah; Owen; Lorin; Earl; Bernice; Bratton | 16; 14; 10; 8; 6; 6 | | | children |
| Darden | George | Mrs. T. P. Jones | | | | |
| Dart | L., Mrs. | | | | G. H. Rugg | |
| Dart | L., Mrs. | | | | Virginia Rugg | |
| Darwell | J. M. | | | | | |
| Davidson | Augustus W. | grown up and away | | | wife | yes |
| Davis | C. H., Mrs. | Willis Howard | 6 ½ | Lawton, OK | | |
| Davis | Grace | | 8; 6; 4 | WA; CA | children | |
| Davis | J., Mrs. | | | | | |
| Davis | Manuel | Manuel; Mary; Clara; John | 27; 25; 20; 17 | PRT; PRT; Petaluma; Vine Hill Dist. | alone | |
| Davis | Mary | Roy; Herbert; Frederick | 11; 9; 4 | | Mrs. D. B. Bolton | none |
| Davis | Minnie | Ella May; George; Emerald | 6; 4; 3 | WA; Yuba Co,; Yuba Co, CA | children | |
| Davison | H. W. | | | | M. J. Buckley | |
| Davison | Henry W. | | | | | |

| 1 SURNAME | 2 GIVEN NAME | 10 CHILDREN'S NAMES | 11 CHILDREN'S AGES | 12 CHILDREN'S BIRTHPLACES | 13 LIVES WITH WHOM | 14 RELATIONSHIP |
|---|---|---|---|---|---|---|
| Davison | Henry W. | | | | | |
| Davison | Henry W. | | | | | |
| Davison | John William | Theo Earl; William Edwin; Ida May; Russel Emmet; Hellen Janette | 13; 10; 6; 3; 9 mos. | 1 Sacramento, 2 Healdsburg, 1 Santa Rosa | children | |
| Deal | George | | | | | |
| Dean | Edwin B. | | | | Chas. Spincer | |
| de Bendeleben | Oufried | | | | alone | |
| DeCeveness | Nicholas | | | | Mrs. A. M. Bantar | |
| deMooy | Ella Palmer, Mrs. | | 16 | Napa, CA | alone | |
| Denny | C., Mrs. | | 13; 7 | | | |
| Derrickson | J. W. | Willard | 10 | MO | wife & child | |
| Deskin | E. | Sadie; Geneva; Elsie; Eddie; Preston; Pleasant | 14; 12; 9; 7; 5; 2 | CA; CA; CA; IA; CA; CA | | |
| Devereaux | R. E. | Edward; George; Walter | 9; 13; 11 | San Rafael, CA | George B. Douglas | |
| Devine | Mary E. | | | | Delia Ann Hawley | |
| Dicks | Margaret, Mrs. | | | | H. C. David | son-in-law |
| Dinucci | Isabella | Louie (crippled); Fred | 16; 14 | SF | children | |
| Divers | Caroline | | | | | |
| Divers | Edward, Mrs. | | | | | |
| Dixon | William | | | | | |
| Dodson | M. J., Mrs. | Henry; James; Ruby | 12; 10; 7 | | | |
| Doggett | Vida Mc L. | Averil; Muriel; Vida; Margaret | 15; 14; 11; 9 | Napa Co.; Napa Co.; Napa Co.; Sonoma Co. | | |
| Dohrman | Mrs. | small children | | | | |
| Doidge | Mary L. | Annie | 12 | | husband & child | |
| Doidge | Richard | Annie | 13 | | wife & dau. | wife & dau. |
| Doidge | Richard | Annie | 13 | | wife Mary S.; Annie | wife; child |

-58-

| 1 SURNAME | 2 GIVEN NAME | 10 CHILDREN'S NAMES | 11 CHILDREN'S AGES | 12 CHILDREN'S BIRTHPLACES | 13 LIVES WITH WHOM | 14 RELATIONSHIP |
|---|---|---|---|---|---|---|
| Doidge | Richard | Annie | 13 | | wife & child | |
| Doidge | Richard | | | | wife, Mary | |
| Doidge | Richard | | | | wife & dau. | |
| Dolan | Andrew | | | | alone | |
| Dolan | Andrew | | | | alone | |
| Dolan | Andrew | | | | alone | |
| Donnolly | Bridget | | | | Owen Donnolly | |
| Donnolly | M., Mrs. | small children | oldest 9 | | | |
| Dorman | Louise, Mrs. | large family of children | | | | |
| Doss | Seth B. | all married except Lewis who is feeble minded | 30 | | wife & son | |
| Dotterer | Minnie | daus. | | | two daus. & two grandchildren | |
| Dowd | Z. Z., Mr. | | young | | family | |
| Dower | James | | | | Geo. H. Ziller | |
| Doyle | M., Mrs. | David; Alsui | 13; 8 | CA | | |
| Drake | Mabel Flora | Elva; Florence; Mildred | 9; 7; 5 | Petaluma | children | |
| Drake | S. G. | | | | | |
| Drake | S. G. | | | | | |
| Duarte | Sarah | helpless children | | | | |
| Duarte | Sarah | dau. | 5 | | family | |
| Dudley | Mrs. | | | | | |
| Dudley | Nellie, Mrs. | little girl | | | | |
| Dudley | Nellie, Mrs. | young dau. | | | | |
| Dudley | Nellie, Mrs. | | 13 | | child | |
| Dudly | Mrs. | little girl | | | | |
| Duke | Catherine | | | | alone | |
| Duke | Catherine | | | | alone | |
| Dunbar | Haln Killigrew | | | | Gilbert C. Jenkins | none |
| Dunbar | Haln, K. | | | | alone | |

| 1 SURNAME | 2 GIVEN NAME | 10 CHILDREN'S NAMES | 11 CHILDREN'S AGES | 12 CHILDREN'S BIRTHPLACES | 13 LIVES WITH WHOM | 14 RELATIONSHIP |
|---|---|---|---|---|---|---|
| Duncan | Charlotte, Mrs. | | youngest 15 mos. | | children | |
| Dunham | Cora | Agnes; Earl; Lorin | 16; 12; 9 | Mendocino Co., CA | alone | |
| Dyer | Louie | | | | M. J. Mullaly | step-dau. |
| Eby | Sophia Elgin | | 14 | | alone | |
| Edwards | L., Mrs. | Robert Parker | 39 | | alone | |
| Edwards | Leavina | Robert Parker | 33 | | alone | |
| Elkerton | E. D. | Frankie; Milo; Maudie; Bulah; George; Marian; Bessie | 16; 14; 11; 8; 6; 3; 1 | all Sonoma Co. | | |
| Elliott | Charles, Mrs. | Edwinnie; Chas; Ralph; Billie; Charlott | 5½; 4½; 3; 2; 8 mos. | all CA | alone | |
| Elliott | Chas., Mrs. | Winnie; Charlie; Ralph; Billie; Charlott | 5, 4; 3; 2; ½ | Sonoma Co. | | |
| Elliott | W. N. | | | | | |
| Elliott | William N. | | | | alone | |
| Ellis | William J. | | | | | |
| Ellison | Minnie, Mrs. | | | | children | |
| Ellison | Minnie, Mrs. | Ina; Geraldine | 18; 16 | Cazadero | Ina Gourley | mother |
| Elshio | Antonio F. | | | | wife & 8 children | |
| Emerson | Henry | | | | Mrs. Callie Emerson | dau.-in-law |
| Entrena | Filomena | Joseph; Antonio | 29; 34 | SPN | 2 sons | |
| Eprosen | Felix | | | | | |
| Evans | James A. | Willie; Alonzo; Clarence; Tolbert; Alta; Lily | 15; 17; 12; 10; 8; 6 | CA | | |
| Fadigan | Edward | | | | | |
| Fancher | John A. | Melville Acorn; Horrel Acorn; Elmer Acorn; James; Carl; Lida | 14; 9; 12; 2; 4; 3 mos. | Humboldt Co.; Lida in Willits, CA | | |
| Fawcett | Mary | | | | alone | |

| 1 | 2 | 10 | 11 | 12 | 13 | 14 |
|---|---|---|---|---|---|---|
| SURNAME | GIVEN NAME | CHILDREN'S NAMES | CHILDREN'S AGES | CHILDREN'S BIRTHPLACES | LIVES WITH WHOM | RELATIONSHIP |
| Faylor | Mary, Mrs. | Josiah; Orson; Mary Walker; John; Nellie Fisher | 52; 50; 48; 47; 45 | UT;UT; UT; last two Sonoma Co. | alone | |
| Felitz | Mary | | | | | |
| Fergeson | Levi | | | | alone | |
| Ferguson | Levi | | | | on ranch of Mr. Tomlin | |
| Fergusson | Levi | | | | alone | |
| Finley | Carrie Ann | Winnie Alberta; Henry Harrison; Hattie Lucil; Lillian Eva; Jefferson Davis | 12; 11; 9; 3; 2 | CA | children | |
| Finley | N., Mrs. | Emma; Ada | 40; 38 | Sonoma Co. | | |
| Finley | Nancy, Mrs. | Emma J. Boddy; Ada Hotton | 41; 39 | Sonoma Co. | alone | |
| Fish | Mary, Mrs. | 7 dependent on her | | | | |
| Fisher | L. F., Mrs. | Freddie; Arther; Larance; Frorance; Jonnie; Rube | 13; 11; 9; 6; 3; 1 ½ | 5 in Sonoma Co., 1 in NV | children | |
| Fisher | T. L. | Earl; Pearl; Mildred; Carrie; Murrel; Salome | 11; 9; 7; 6; 4; 2 | CA | family | |
| Fitch | R. J. | R. A.; Rosy; Victor; Victoria; Alfred; Minnie; August | 20; 16; 14; 10; 8; 6; 3 | August & Rosy CA; the rest in MEX | children | |
| Fitzpatrick | Mrs. | | | | | |
| Flanigan | Richard | | | | | |
| Fletcher | Charles H. | | | | alone | |
| Fletcher | Charles H. | | | | alone | |
| Fletcher | Chas. H. | | | | alone | |
| Flood | Lena, Mrs. | girl | 18 | SF | alone | |
| Fochetti | Bernardo | | | | alone | |
| Ford | Benjamin F. | Vella | 11 | Sonoma Co. | Mrs. Thierkoff | |
| Forpeilha | Rosa T. | Manuel; John; Ijelica; Calos | 7; ?; ?; 10 mos. | | | |
| Foster | Augusta C., Mrs. | | | | | |

| 1 SURNAME | 2 GIVEN NAME | 10 CHILDREN'S NAMES | 11 CHILDREN'S AGES | 12 CHILDREN'S BIRTHPLACES | 13 LIVES WITH WHOM | 14 RELATIONSHIP |
|---|---|---|---|---|---|---|
| Foster | G. H., Mrs. | | | | alone | |
| Fouder | Elizabeth | | | | | |
| Fouts | Elizabeth | Lena; Martha | 24; 21 | | Maria Knecht | |
| Fowler | Cinfoliana | | | | alone | |
| Fowzer | William J. | | | | | |
| Francisco | A. | Amelia; Mary; Clarence; Tony | 16; 13; 10; 8 | Mendocino Co; Sonoma Co.; Sonoma Co.; Sonoma Co. | | |
| Francisco | Antone | small children | | | | |
| Franklin | Ann, Mrs. | | | | | |
| Franklin | Ann, Mrs. | | | | dau. & grandchildren | |
| Fraser | A. F. | | | | H. B. Cook | |
| Frederickson | Annie | | | | children | |
| Frediani | Caterina | Elsie; Charlie | 12; 6 | ITL; Napa Co., CA | | |
| Friend | Robert & Carline | | | | | |
| Frugoli | Francisco | Annie; Ida; Joe | 15; 12; 8 | 2 in Reno, NV; 1 in Santa Clara Co., CA | family | |
| Frugoli | Francisco | Annie; Ida; Joe | 17; 15; 10 | Reno, NV | wife and children | |
| Funk | L., Mrs. | Fritz | 25 | SF | | |
| Funk | Louise, Mrs. | Fritz | 18 | | | |
| Furia | Lazzaro | Angelina; Rosea | 3; 11 mos. | SF & Santa Rosa | family | |
| Furia | Lazzaro | Angiolina; Rosi; Adolfo | 6; 4; 1 ½ | SF; Santa Rosa; Santa Rosa | | |
| Furlong | Thos. | | | | | |
| Futterer | Conrad | | | | | |
| Futterer | Conrad | | | | wife | |
| Futterer | Conrad & Louisa | | | | | |
| Gager | George G. | | | | alone | |

| 1 | 2 | 10 | 11 | 12 | 13 | 14 |
|---|---|---|---|---|---|---|
| SURNAME | GIVEN NAME | CHILDREN'S NAMES | CHILDREN'S AGES | CHILDREN'S BIRTHPLACES | LIVES WITH WHOM | RELATIONSHIP |
| Gallaudett | E. J., Mrs. | | | | alone | |
| Gamboggi | Rosa | | | | | |
| Ganyard | G. L., Mrs. | | | | | |
| Garnero | Mary | Clara | 4 | Santa Rosa | F. Lombardi | none |
| German | Kate | | | | | |
| German | Katie, Mrs. | girls | 1; ?; 6 | | | |
| Gerrick | Ella | Emma; Etta; George; Arthur | 13; 8 ;7; 4 | | children | |
| Giauque | Elizabeth | Nellie Holmes; Garland Berry (adopted) | 10; 8 | | alone | |
| Giauque | Elizabeth | Amos; Lou | 40; 35 | Napa Co. | alone | |
| Gibson | G. W. | George; Lillie; Lottie; Edward; Robert | 17; 14; 11; 6; 2 | Sacramento; Placerville, CA | family | |
| Gibson | G. W. | George; Lillie; Lottie; Edward; Robert | 18; 15; 12; 7; 3; 2 mos. | CA; VA | | |
| Gilcrist | Mrs. | son | adult | CA | | |
| Glidden | Charles & Esther | | | | themselves | |
| Gober | Elizabeth | James Henry; Charles Van Buren; Tennessee Elizabeth; Eliza Ellen; Lillie May | 16; 14; 12; 10; 6 | | children | |
| Goetjen | C. & wife | Emma; Annie; Fred; Ida; Adolph | 43; 39; 41; 36; 34 | SF | John Gutermute | |
| Goetjen | C., Mr. & Mrs. | all married | 30 to 43 | SF | | |
| Golett | Jane | | | | alone | |
| Gould | Mollie B. | Minnie; Flossie | 15; 10 | | Mrs. McCrosky | |
| Gounsky | Fannie, Mrs. | | all small | | | |
| Gounsky | J., Mrs. | | 9 to 1 | | | |
| Gounsky | Mrs. | | 11 to not quite 2 yrs. | | | |
| Grace | Anne | | | | | |

| 1 SURNAME | 2 GIVEN NAME | 10 CHILDREN'S NAMES | 11 CHILDREN'S AGES | 12 CHILDREN'S BIRTHPLACES | 13 LIVES WITH WHOM | 14 RELATIONSHIP |
|---|---|---|---|---|---|---|
| Grace | Annie, Mrs. | | | | | |
| Gray | Olive | | young | | | |
| Green | Charles | | | | | |
| Green | Hannah, Mrs. | John; Charles; Sadie | 40; 37; 35 | | alone | |
| Green | Nellie M. | Mary; Zelma | 10; 8 | MO; CA | children | |
| Green | Richard | | | | | |
| Greening | S. J., Mrs. | single daus.; 2 confined to bed from sickness | 15; 18; 21 | | daus. | |
| Greenleaf | T., Mrs. | Walter; Delbert; John; Genevieve; Mildred; Hiram | 14; 10; 9; 5; 4; 1 | | husband & children | |
| Greenleaf | T., Mrs. | | | | husband & 6 children | |
| Gregory | Charles M. | | | | Mr. & Mrs. Marcus Snook | |
| Griffin | J. M. | | | | | |
| Griggs | Arthur Odell | Lena Anderson; Ruth Anderson; Ralph Anderson; Vivian Anderson; LeRoy Odell Griggs | 17; 15; 12; 7; 6 mos. | Ukiah, Covelo, Ukiah, El Dorado, CA | R. Sherwood | |
| Grube | Joseph | | | | alone | |
| Guerin | Frank Merritt | | | | D. D. Morton | none |
| Guilfoyle | Mary | William; John; Richard; Luisa; Frank; Joseph; Mary | 40; 39; 38; 36; 34; 33; 31 | | alone | |
| Gussman | Santo | Frank; Casey; Josie | 47; 45; 35 | CHL; Marin Co., CA; Sonoma Co. | | |
| Gustavsen | Gus | | | | Mr. & Mrs. W. T. Liggett | |
| Hale | Ada | | | | dau. | |
| Hale | Ada E. | children all grown | | | | |
| Hall | Roxania | | | | Warren Hall | |
| Hall | William | Roxy; Warren | 53; 38 | | Roxy Hall | dau. |
| Hall | William | | | | dau. | |

| 1 SURNAME | 2 GIVEN NAME | 10 CHILDREN'S NAMES | 11 CHILDREN'S AGES | 12 CHILDREN'S BIRTHPLACES | 13 LIVES WITH WHOM | 14 RELATIONSHIP |
|---|---|---|---|---|---|---|
| Hamele | Anna | | | | alone | |
| Hamlin | Chas. J. | | | | alone | |
| Hammele | Anne | | | | alone | |
| Handfest | George | | | | H. O. Ludolff | none |
| Hanford | John | | | | alone | |
| Hansen | A., Mrs. | | | | alone | |
| Hansen | Euchtho | | | | alone | |
| Hansen | Peter | Harry; Mabel | 6; 3 | SF; Sebastopol | | |
| Hansen | Peter | Harry; Mabel | 8; 4 | SF; Sebastopol | | |
| Happy | J. H., Mrs. | | | | his family | |
| Harbine | Charles | Sarah G. | 34 | MO | wife | |
| Harbine | Chas. | | | | | |
| Harbine | Chas. E. | Sarah Gertrude | 35 | MO | wife, Susan | husband |
| Hardin | Amelia, Mrs. | | | | Geo. | |
| Hardin | Mr. & Mrs. | | | | | |
| Harding | Anna M., Mrs. | | | | E. M. Cutter | |
| Hardt | Augusta, Mrs. | Chas; George; William; Mary; Louise; Minnie | 45; 30; 29; 35; 33; 27 | Sonoma Co. | | |
| Hardy | Rebecca | | | | alone | |
| Harman | Albert M. | | | | alone | |
| Harmon | Charles | | | | Mrs. Mabel Kinzie | |
| Harmon | Lizzie, Mrs. | | | | alone | |
| Harrison | N., Mrs. | | | | | |
| Harrison | Nannie, Mrs. | | | | | |
| Hart | Joseph | | | | | |
| Hasting | F. D. | Mary Kennedy; Joseph; Emma Owens; Nelson; Clara Holchester; Milton | 46; 44; 42; 40; 38; 27 | Sonoma Co. | own home | |
| Hasting(s) | F. D. | Joseph; Mrs. Kennedy; Mrs. Owens; Nelson; Milton | doesn't know | doesn't know | wife | |

| 1 SURNAME | 2 GIVEN NAME | 10 CHILDREN'S NAMES | 11 CHILDREN'S AGES | 12 CHILDREN'S BIRTHPLACES | 13 LIVES WITH WHOM | 14 RELATIONSHIP |
|---|---|---|---|---|---|---|
| Hastings | Edward & Mary | | | | | |
| Hastings | Emily | | | | Dr. Brower & daus. | |
| Hauser | A., Mrs. | Edmond; Alfred | 63; 60 | Stubbekgobing, DNK | | |
| Hauskneckt | Henry | Lena; Henrrietta; Sallie; Elise; Charles; George; Fred | 17; 14; 12; 9; 16; 5; 4 | | family | |
| Hawley | Delia Ann | | | | | |
| Hawley | Delia, Mrs. | | | | Mary Devine | |
| Hayhurst | William | | | | | |
| Haynes | W. R. | | (infants) | | wife | |
| Heinsen | Maggie | | all under 8 | | wife | |
| Heiss | Edwin, Mrs. | Eddie | 9 | Santa Rosa | four children | |
| Hekeler | Philip H. | | | | at home | |
| Hekeler | Philip Henry | | | | | |
| Henderson | J. H. | | | | | |
| Henley | Daniel | | | | | |
| Herford | Thomas | Gertrude M. Heithim; Flora A. Ambeynson; John A.; Harriet E. Cole | 38; 35; 32; 24 | 1st in Occidental; others in Freestone | Harriet E. Cole | dau. |
| Heryford | Nick | | | | | |
| Hesse | Louisa, Mrs. | | | | wife; 3 small children | |
| Hesse | Louisa, Mrs. | | bet. 7 and 12 | | | |
| Hester | Clara | Mary; Robert; James; Beulah | 12; 10; 6; 3 | CO; CA; CA; CA | children | |
| Hester | Clara, Mrs. | Mary A.; Robert G.; James W.; Beulah L. | 11; 9; 5; 2 | CO; CA; CA; CA | | |
| Hester | Clara, Mrs. | Mary; Robert; James; Beulah | 12; 10; 6; 3 | CO; CA; CA; CA | | |
| Hetzel | C. F. | Irene Rowe; Ruth; Olga; Louise; Zelma; Lydia; | 21; 20; 19; 17; 15; 13; 11; 6; 3 | Guerneville | | |

-66-

| 1 SURNAME | 2 GIVEN NAME | 10 CHILDREN'S NAMES | 11 CHILDREN'S AGES | 12 CHILDREN'S BIRTHPLACES | 13 LIVES WITH WHOM | 14 RELATIONSHIP |
|---|---|---|---|---|---|---|
| Hetzel | C. F. | Hattie; Clarence; C. F. | | | children | |
| Hetzel | C. F. | Irene; Ruthe; Olga; Mia Louise; Zelma; Sydia; Hattie; Clarence; C. F. | 21; 20; 19; 17; 15; 13; 11; 6; 3 | CA | | |
| Hetzel | Carl | Irne Rowe; Ruthe; Louise; Olga; Elma; Synda; Hattie; Clarance; Charles | 21; 20; 18; 16; 14; 12; 10; 5; 2 | Guerneville | wife & children | |
| Hevel | E. L. | | | | wife | |
| Hillbrant | Ethel | May; Amy; Nellie; Laura | 18; 16; 14; 7 | 1st two Yuba Co.; last two Sonoma Co. | | |
| Hinkley | Eleanor | | | | Mrs. Nellie B. Thompson | |
| Hinkley | Eleanor, Miss | | | | Nellie B. Thompson | aunt |
| Hinrichsen | John W. | | | | | |
| Hinrichsen | Therese | Clara; Annie; Josie; Harry; Lelda | 13; 7; 5; 3 10 mos. | | husband, John W. | Husband |
| Hofer | George | all dead | | Cincinnati, OH | | |
| Hoffman | E. E., Mrs. | Clifford; Marian | 13; 6 | Petaluma | Capt. Montgomery of Salvation Army | |
| Hofmann | Carl C. | | | | alone | |
| Holbrock | William | | | | J. H. Weise | |
| Holmes | Clara L. | | | | | |
| Hopper | Harlow | | | | G. R. Hopper, brother | brother |
| Horgan | Kate, Mrs. | Michae; Lizzie; Thomas; Julia; Mary; Maggie; Eugene; John | 21; 19; 17; 15½; 14; 12; 10; 8 | Ocean Township | | |
| Horgan | Mrs. | Michael; Lizzie; Gula; Thomas; Mary; Eugene; John; Margaret | 23; 21; 17; 19; 16; 11; 10; 13 | Willow Creek. | children | |
| Houx | John W. & wife | | | | | |

| 1 | 2 | 10 | 11 | 12 | 13 | 14 |
|---|---|---|---|---|---|---|
| SURNAME | GIVEN NAME | CHILDREN'S NAMES | CHILDREN'S AGES | CHILDREN'S BIRTHPLACES | LIVES WITH WHOM | RELATIONSHIP |
| Howard | Amy M. | | 24; 26; 32 | Placer County, CA | alone | |
| Howard | Amy, Mrs. | Carl; Henry; Phillip; Benny; Maggie Stutsman; Dell Martin | 21; 26; 30; 40; 35; 33 | | | none |
| Howard | J. G. | | | | Manuel Constance | |
| Howard | J. G. | C.E.; Frank; Herbert | 38; 40; 42 | Napa Co., CA | alone | |
| Howard | Jas. G. | Charles Eugene; Franklin; Herbert | 42; 40; 38 | St Helena, CA | | |
| Howard | John C. | | | | wife & 3 children | |
| Howard | John C. | Henry; Carl | 15; 12; 8 | | wife & children | |
| Howard | John C. | | 12; 9 | | J. A. Philabaum | |
| Howe | H. | Gracie; Robert | 17; 15 | Napa, CA | Mrs. Lyttaker | |
| Howe | Julia | Phillip Green; Willard Howe | 29; 17 | Alameda; SF, CA | | |
| Howeth | Mary | | eldest is 13 | | with 6 children | |
| Hoyt | Charles | | | | sister | |
| Hughes | David W. | | | | | |
| Humphreys | W. F. | | | | wife & 2 children | |
| Humphries | Charles | | | | Catherine Humphres | |
| Humphries | Emma, Mrs. | minor children | | | | |
| Hurd | Marcus | | | | Andrew J. Blaney | none |
| Hurd | Marcus | | | | A. J. Blaney | |
| Ilse | Frederick & wife | | | | | |
| Ilse | Mary | | | | alone | |
| Ilse | Mary, Mrs. | | | | alone | |
| Imfeld | Mary | Josephine Kiser; Joseph | adults | | Mrs. L. H. Green | |
| Ingerson | Capt. James | Rosie; Jimmie | 10; 9 | | | |
| Inghan | William | Clara; Blache; Lillian; Milford; Florence | 9; 7; 6; 4; 3 | MI; MI; 3 Santa Rosa | | |
| Isaac(k)s | Jessie | | | | | |

| 1 SURNAME | 2 GIVEN NAME | 10 CHILDREN'S NAMES | 11 CHILDREN'S AGES | 12 CHILDREN'S BIRTHPLACES | 13 LIVES WITH WHOM | 14 RELATIONSHIP |
|---|---|---|---|---|---|---|
| Ives | C. O., Mrs. | Alice McCombs; Daisy McCombs (grandchildren) | 13; 10 | CA | grandchildren | |
| Ives | Samson | | | | | |
| Jack | Humbolt | | | | | |
| Jacobs | C. M. | | | | | |
| Jacobs | C. M., Mrs. | girl | | | wife & invalid dau. | |
| Jacobs | Ruth A. | Stella M. | over 18 | | dau. | |
| Jacobsen | Christ | Edith; Alma; Hans; Frank | 5; 3; 2; 1 | SF, SF; Sunny Slope; Petaluma | | |
| Jacobsen | Christ, Mr. & Mrs. | Edith; Alma; Hans; Frank | 24 Dec. 1907; 16 Dec.1909; 19 July 1911; 26 June 1912 | SF, SF, Petaluma, Petaluma | | |
| James | S. F. | | | | wife; C. F. Faber | |
| Jarrett | Lola, Mrs. | George; Helen; August | 20; 23; 30 | Bolinas, Marin Co., CA | E. Blackburn | |
| Jensen | J. P., Mrs. | Mary; Esther | 12; 9 | Sonoma Co. | | |
| Jewett | Martha, Mrs. | Augustus L; Grace; Earl; Leona Lois; Ivan | 29; 26; 24; 22; 14 | Sonoma Co. | dau. | |
| Jewett | Mattie, Mrs. | Leora | 14 | Guerneville | | |
| Johnson | Anne | Nora Colburn; Nellie Williams; Mary Dunbar; Martin; Louis | | Bloomfield | Mary Dunbar | |
| Johnson | Clara | | | | Mrs. Samatha Johnson, 60 yr. old widow; her mother-in-law | mother; dau. |
| Johnson | Elna | | | | | |
| Johnson | Elna | | | | alone | |
| Johnson | F. J. | | | | | |
| Johnson | H. W., Mrs. | Gertrude; Cecilia; Margaret; | 14; 12; 10; 8 | Sacramento; Ft. | husband & children | |

| 1 SURNAME | 2 GIVEN NAME | 10 CHILDREN'S NAMES | 11 CHILDREN'S AGES | 12 CHILDREN'S BIRTHPLACES | 13 LIVES WITH WHOM | 14 RELATIONSHIP |
|---|---|---|---|---|---|---|
| Johnson | Henrietta | Dolores | | Bragg, CA | Charles Johnson | child |
| Johnson | Magnus | | | | wife | |
| Johnson | Magnus & wife | | | | | |
| Johnson | Margaret | | | | | |
| Johnson | Marie | Carl; John; Harold; Martin; Laurie; Mrs. Josie Schaffer; Lula | 27; 26; 24; 22; 18; 20; 17 | | R. M. Quackenbush | none |
| Johnson | Mary | William E. | 28 | | L. B. Gardner | none |
| Johnson | Mary | | | | alone | |
| Johnson | Mary E., Mrs. | | | | | |
| Johnson | William C. | | | | | |
| Johnson | Wm. Clifton | | | | | |
| Johnston | Margaret | | | | alone | |
| Jones | Nelson | | | | alone | |
| Jose | Sophia | | oldest 10; youngest 3 | | | |
| Jose | Sophia, Mrs. | | 1 to 10 | | | |
| Judt | John F. | | | | | |
| Kaller | Patrick | | | | | |
| Karry | M. A., Mrs. | Hila; Myrtle; Alice; Walter; Karry | all under 13 years | | children | |
| Kase | Louise | | | | 7 small children | |
| Kelley | Michel | | | | alone | |
| Keniston | Joseph | girls | | | | |
| Kennedy | Emma | Margorie; Frieda | 18; 14 | | | |
| Kennedy | Maud E. | | | | Alice C. Meyer | sister |
| Kenney | Mary, Mrs. | | | | 2 daus. | |
| Kennisten | (family) | | | | | |
| Kenniston | Joseph | | | | wife and children | |

| 1 | 2 | 10 | 11 | 12 | 13 | 14 |
|---|---|---|---|---|---|---|
| SURNAME | GIVEN NAME | CHILDREN'S NAMES | CHILDREN'S AGES | CHILDREN'S BIRTHPLACES | LIVES WITH WHOM | RELATIONSHIP |
| Kern | (children) | Hester Ellen; Walter J.; Myrtle; George; Earnest | 14; 12; 10; 8; 6 | CA | Elizabeth Pitts | grandmother |
| Ketcham | George | | | | wife & dau. | |
| Ketchum | George | Mrs. Minnei Heoque; Herbert; Fannie | 45; 39; 35 | MO; Monterey Co.; Monterey Co., CA | Wife Julia | wife |
| Ketchum | Julia | Minnie Heogue; Herbert Ketchum; Fannie Ketchum | 45; 39; 33 | Monterey Co., CA | George & Fannie Ketchum | husband & dau. |
| Kidd | F. A., Mrs. | | young | | with 2 children | |
| Kidd | F. A., Mrs. | | 15; 12; 11 | | | |
| Kilcourse | Bridget, Miss | | | | Mrs. Mary Leonard | sister |
| Kilgore | Catherine | Catherine Hottinger | | | Catherine Hottinger | dau. |
| Kill | James M. | Carrie | 38 | Santa Rosa | wife | wife |
| King | J. H. | both married | | | Joe Richardson | none |
| King | Jos. | Elsie; Dorthy; Mable | 5; 3; ½ | Graton | | |
| King | Joseph | | | | | |
| Kirk | Maggie | | | | Mrs. Madalina | |
| Kirkpatrick | H. C. | Clara Bell Coffey | | | | |
| Kirry | May, Mrs. | Dora; Melvin (sickly); Elmer | 21 ½; 20; 18 | | | |
| Kirry | May, Mrs. | Dora; Melvin; Elmer | 21 ½; 20; 18 | Humboldt Co., CA | | |
| Kiser | Lena | Mabel; Lillian; Mathilda; Lena; Frederick | 18; 16; 13; 11; 8 | Hollister, CA | children | |
| Kleemons #1 | Rosa, Mrs. | | young | | children | |
| Kleemons #2 | Rose, Mrs. | | | | | |
| Knapp | Lewis C. | | | | alone | |
| Knighten | Joseph M. | | | | | |
| Knox | J. M. | Flora; Emma; Frank; Elizabeth | 42; 52; 55; 42 | IN; IN; IN; CA | wife | wife |
| Koenig | Ernest | | | | Charles Thorn | |

| 1 SURNAME | 2 GIVEN NAME | 10 CHILDREN'S NAMES | 11 CHILDREN'S AGES | 12 CHILDREN'S BIRTHPLACES | 13 LIVES WITH WHOM | 14 RELATIONSHIP |
|---|---|---|---|---|---|---|
| Kostenhoschen | Theodore | | | | | |
| Kriedel | Mrs. | | minor children | | | |
| Lake | Helen M. | Mrs. W. A. Lloyd | 43 | Bloomfield | Mr. & Mrs. W. A. Lloyd | dau. |
| Lallamouth | Henry | | | | | |
| Lamb | Geneva M. | | 61; 64; 57 | CA | Mrs. L. C. French | |
| Lamb | Genevra M. | Mrs. Thomas Wheaton; George Spittler | | | alone | |
| Lancaster | William | George William | 21 | Placerville, CA | alone | |
| Lander | Margaret E. | Ruth | 22 | Santa Rosa | dau. | |
| Landeway | Anna | | | | | |
| Lane | E. C., Mrs. | baby; boy; dau. | 3 mos.; 5; 12 | | | |
| Lane | Elizabeth | | | | | |
| Lane | Elizabeth C. | Arnie A. Conklin; Egan Lane | 16; 11 | | alone | |
| Lane | Elizabeth C. | Annie Conkling; Joe | 30; 26 | CA | sons | |
| Lane | Mrs. | | | | | |
| Langren | Louisa | small children | | | | |
| LaPoint | William | | | | | |
| Larrison | Seymour | | | | | |
| Larsen | Anton | Leila Mary; Norman Anton; Blanche Parmelia | 10; 5 yrs. 3 mos.; 1 yr. 3 mos. | Santa Rosa | children live with Mrs. E. Anker | no relation |
| Lavin | Timothy | | | | | |
| Law | M., Mrs. | Lotta; Leola; Eldwynn | 9; 7; 3 | Seattle, WA | Susan Trimble | sister |
| Lawrence | Alva Perry | | | | father | |
| Lawrence | Katie Amanda | | | | father | |
| Lawrence | Mary J. | | | | | |
| Lawson | M. H. | Leroy; Birdie; Beatrice | 26; 20; 18 | Yolo Co., CA | E. L. Lawson | son |

| 1 SURNAME | 2 GIVEN NAME | 10 CHILDREN'S NAMES | 11 CHILDREN'S AGES | 12 CHILDREN'S BIRTHPLACES | 13 LIVES WITH WHOM | 14 RELATIONSHIP |
|---|---|---|---|---|---|---|
| Leander | Charles | | | | alone | |
| Lebeouff | Fred | all half orphans | | | children | |
| Lee | Dora | minors | | | children | |
| Lee | Dora, Mrs. | | | | children | |
| Lee | Lottie | | | | | |
| Lelonarn | Celestine | | | | | |
| Leluarn | Celestine, Mrs. | | 5; 8 | | | |
| Leluarn | John | | small children | | | |
| LeMoine | John | | | | | |
| Lennox | James W. | | | | alone | |
| Lennox | Jas. W. | | | | alone | |
| Leonard | Mary, Mrs. | | | | Miss Kelcousse | sister |
| Leonard | S. F., Mr. & Mrs. | only child 24 years ago | | | | |
| Letcher | Giles, Mr. & Mrs. | | | | | |
| Letcher | Kate, Mrs. | | | | Raymonds House | |
| Lewis | Cora | | | | | |
| Lewis | Ellen A. | David T.; Robert L.; Gorden E.; Orval E.; Nellie V. | 15; 11; 9; 6; 3 | CA | children | |
| Lewis | Elvira | Thelma; Sarah; Paul; John; George | 10; 8; 5; 3; 1 | S.F.; SF; Petaluma; Santa Rosa; Hayward, CA | | |
| Lewis | Florence, Mrs. | Maretta; Freda; Melvin; Marquetta | 10; 8; 4; 14 months | CA | | |
| Lewis | G. W. & family | | small | | family | |
| Lewis | Harriet | James | 55 | | James Lewis | son |
| Lewis | James H. | | | | Harriett Lewis | |
| Lewis | Martha J. | | | | Amanda Bale | |
| Lewis | Martha, Mrs. | Mildred | 17 | | Amanda Bole | sister |
| Lewis | Mary | | 3 grandchildren | | | |

| 1 SURNAME | 2 GIVEN NAME | 10 CHILDREN'S NAMES | 11 CHILDREN'S AGES | 12 CHILDREN'S BIRTHPLACES | 13 LIVES WITH WHOM | 14 RELATIONSHIP |
|---|---|---|---|---|---|---|
| Lewis | R. M. | | | | wife | |
| Lewis | R. M. | | | | wife | |
| Lewis | Ralph | | | | wife | |
| Lewis | Robert | | | | Mary | wife |
| Lightfoot | Eliza | grown son with large family | | | alone | |
| Lingron | Alfred | Anna; Alfred; Maria; Walter; Carl; Paul | 12; 10; 9; 7; 5; 3 | Santa Rosa; rest in Berkeley, CA | | |
| Livingston | Cornelia E. | | 8; 5 | | Mrs. Hannah Murray | mother |
| Livingston | Ella | | | | | |
| Lockerby | Robert | | | | | |
| Long | Tilly | Dolly Lavina; Gracie Mary; Edmunt; Decader | 8; 6; 4; 1 | | alone | |
| Lottritz | John & Mary | | | | | |
| Lottritz | Mary E., Mrs. | | | | alone | |
| Louk | Cora L., Mrs. | Ernest | 4 | | on farm of Thomas R. Inslen | |
| Louk | Olive | | 35; 29; 27; 24; 20 | | 78 year old mother | |
| Lounibos | Emile P. | Adeline; Emile; Dorothy; Elizabeth; Eugene | 14; 12; 9; 5; 2 | Kenwood & Santa Rosa | family | |
| Lueders | Henry & wife | | | | wife | |
| Maclean | Kate & Margaret, Misses | | | | with brother, Alexander, who is old and infirm | |
| Maclean #1 | Katherine & Margaret | | | | sisters; Alexander | brother |
| Maclean #2 | Katherine & Margaret | | | | | |
| Maclean #3 | Misses | | | | | |
| Magetti | Bartolomeo | son | adult | | | |
| Maginnis | Thos. | | | | Manuel Constant | |

| 1 SURNAME | 2 GIVEN NAME | 10 CHILDREN'S NAMES | 11 CHILDREN'S AGES | 12 CHILDREN'S BIRTHPLACES | 13 LIVES WITH WHOM | 14 RELATIONSHIP |
|---|---|---|---|---|---|---|
| Mahan | Charles | | | | | |
| Maloney | Michael | | | | | |
| Maloof | Charlie | | 8 | Santa Rosa | wife & child | |
| Manning | Mary | | oldest 13 | | husband & children | |
| Maren | James | | | | Rob Cunningham | |
| Maren | James | | | | Cunningham Ranch | |
| Marion | A., Mrs. | Louis | 10 | CA | husband, Alexander, & son | stepson |
| Markham | Susan | Ralph Green; Earl Green | 34; 31 | | | |
| Marsh | Alida L., Mrs. | Dora E.; Elmer J. | 16; 12 | Mtn. City, KS | Mrs. J. Lopus | none |
| Marsh | J. S. | Edith Gibson; Isabell McAllister; Rosa Qinliven; Mollie Hiatt | 45; 40; 42; 38 | | William Bruner | |
| Marsh | J. S. | Mrs. W. E. Hiatt; Mrs. A D. McAllaster; Mrs. Jesie Bruner | 42; 46; 55 | Sonoma Co. | | sisters-in-law |
| Marsh | John Shelby | children grown & married | | | W. E. Hiatt | |
| Marshall | Izoro K., Mrs. | | | | | |
| Marshall | Martha J. | Charles; May Anderson; Cleveland | 39; 41; 30 | TX; AR; MO | alone | |
| Martell | David | | | | | |
| Marten | Alex | John; Edward; Thomas; Glenn; Harry; Anna | 15; 13; 11; 5; 4; 11 mos. | Sonoma Co. | Geo. T. McCutchan | |
| Martin | Alex | | | | wife | |
| Martin | E. J., Mrs. | | | | John & Mary Anderson | nephew |
| Martin | Elizabeth J. | | | | | |
| Martin | Elizabeth J. | | | | Mrs. Owens | |
| Martin | Elizabeth Jane | | | | alone | |
| Martin | G. W., Mr. & Mrs. | | | | | |
| Martin | George W., Mrs. | | | | | |

| 1 | 2 | 10 | 11 | 12 | 13 | 14 |
|---|---|---|---|---|---|---|
| SURNAME | GIVEN NAME | CHILDREN'S NAMES | CHILDREN'S AGES | CHILDREN'S BIRTHPLACES | LIVES WITH WHOM | RELATIONSHIP |
| Martz | Samuel | George | 40? | | Cornelia A. Martz | wife |
| Martz | Samuel | George | 42 | Oakland, CA | wife, Cornelia | |
| Masa | Susanah | | | | | |
| Masa | Susanah, Mrs. | | | | | |
| Mason | Myrtle, Mrs. | Byrl; John; Robert; Mary; Louise | 15; 12; 10; 8; 5 | IA; IL; CA | children | sons & daus. |
| Mastrup | Mary | | | | | |
| Mastrup | Mary | | all under 11 | | | |
| Mastrup | Mary, Mrs. | Anna; Andrew; Ivan; James; Louis | 13; 11; 9; 7; 7 | | | |
| Mathews | Elizabeth | | | | | |
| Matsen | Marie P. | | | | | |
| Matsen | Mary P. | | | | alone | |
| Matthews | Eliza | | | | | |
| Mausera | Antonio Garcia | Salvador; Josepha; Maria | 9; 7; 2 | SPN; CA | Manuel Lopez | |
| Mausera | Antonio Garcia | Salvador; Josepha; Maria | 10; 7; 3 | SPN; SPN; Santa Rosa | Francisco Gonzales | |
| Maxwell | Alvina | Elaine; Maurice | 7; 6 | CA | Isabelle Rogers | grandmother |
| McBee | Samentha | dau. married; other adult children | | | Mrs. M. A. McPeak | |
| McCaleb | Dona, Mrs. | Arlie; Linus; Desbia | 9; 8; 4 | Wash. Co., AR; Wash. Co., AK; Adair Co., OK | children | mother |
| McCarty | L. E., Mrs. | W. W. Austin; Gula B. Austin | 17; 15 | TX | son & dau. | |
| McCarty | L. W., Mrs. | Austin, William W.; Milk, G. B., Mrs. | 19; 18 | TX | alone | |
| McCombs | Aaron C. | Wallace J. Moore; Donald E. Moore; Rena Estelle Moore; Amis Dudlley Moore; Malcom W. | 11; 9; 7; 4 | AZ; NM; MEX | | |

| 1 | 2 | 10 | 11 | 12 | 13 | 14 |
|---|---|---|---|---|---|---|
| SURNAME | GIVEN NAME | CHILDREN'S NAMES | CHILDREN'S AGES | CHILDREN'S BIRTHPLACES | LIVES WITH WHOM | RELATIONSHIP |
| McCoy | Alma, Mrs. | ?; Mervin; Fay | 15; 10; 5 | ?; Petaluma; Sebastopol | children | |
| McCriston | Silvester C. | | | | wife | |
| McDaniel | Pearl, Mrs. | Eula; Gracie; Ada | 7; 5; 3 | | | |
| McDaniels | Pearl, Mrs. | Ada Eunice; Grace Elizabeth; Eula May | 2; 4; 6 | | alone | |
| McDonald | Isabella, Mrs. | Mrs. Bouteri; Mrs.Hodgson | 39; 37 | | Angus McDonald | |
| McElnay | S. C., Mrs. | Lizzie Weldon; Kate Field | | | | |
| McElnay | S. C., Mrs. | Mrs. Kate Weldon; Mrs. Lizzie | abt 30 both | | | |
| McFarland | Vina | | | | alone | |
| McFarland | Vina, Mrs. | | | | | |
| McGreavy | Ellen F. | | | | | |
| McGuire | Elizabeth | children (two in arms) | | | | |
| McGuire | Neil | | | | | |
| McLaughlin | Robert | | | | | |
| McLean | Margaret | | young | | 4 young children | |
| McMillion | Vada | Pearl | 10 | | with aged mother | |
| McNally | Ella, Mrs. | James; Charles; Robert; Tod | 11; 10; 9; 6 | Santa Rosa | | |
| McPeak | Belle, Miss | | | | William Lawrence | |
| McPeak | Peter F. | | | | alone | |
| Meador | Bell, Mrs. | all grown | | | nurse | |
| Meador | Belle, Mrs. | married daus. | | | rents small house | |
| Means | Lycurgus | dau. | 16 | CA | alone | |
| Means | Lycurgus | Mrs. Myrtle Jones; Violet M. | 20; 17 | Sonoma Co. | alone | |
| Mecke | Caroline | | | | | |
| Mehan | Patrick | 2 boys; 3 girls | to young to work | | M. Levin | |

| 1 SURNAME | 2 GIVEN NAME | 10 CHILDREN'S NAMES | 11 CHILDREN'S AGES | 12 CHILDREN'S BIRTHPLACES | 13 LIVES WITH WHOM | 14 RELATIONSHIP |
|---|---|---|---|---|---|---|
| Mell | Mary | | | | alone | |
| Mell | Mary | | | | | |
| Mello | Amelia | son; dau.; dau. | 31; 36; 25 | Sebastopol | single dau. | dau. |
| Mello | Emilia C. (Mrs. Geo.) | | | | | |
| Mello | Geo. | | | | | |
| Merrell | Ellen A. | | | | | |
| Merrit | Edward | | | | alone | |
| Merrithen | M. G., Mrs. | Robt.; Ray; Bill; Florence | 11; 9; 7; 5 | CA | alone | |
| Merritt | S. J., Mrs. | Mrs. Chas. L. Ingram; Frank | 42; 50 | MI | alone | |
| Merritt | Sarah J. | | | | alone | |
| Merritt | Sarah J. | | | | Mrs. Hale | sister |
| Metcalf | Loretta | Bunah; Cecil | 11; 7 | CA | Mrs. Barry | |
| Metcalf | Loretta | Buena; Cecil | 13; 9 | SF; Petaluma | Mrs. Hushower | |
| Meyer | Lulu | Garland; Vina; George; Hannah | 7; 5 ½; 4; 6 mos. | | Mrs. Giaugue | mother |
| Meyer | M. | | | | Clara D. White | |
| Meyers | Lula | | 7; 5; 4; 3 mos. | | Elizabeth Giaugue | |
| Miller | Carl, Mrs. | | | | | |
| Miller | Carl, Mrs. | | | | | |
| Miller | Louisa | Herbert; Maud | 16; 16 | Santa Cruz, CA | | |
| Miller | Louisa | | | | alone | |
| Miller | Lucy, Mrs. | | | | | |
| Minear | Mrs. | | | | | |
| Mize | Aditha | | | | son | |
| Monaco | Paulena | | | | alone | |
| Monotti | Luigi | Mary Berbiera; Alea Monotti; Geodetti Monico; Catherina Monotti | 51; 43; 40; 37 | | alone | |

| 1 SURNAME | 2 GIVEN NAME | 10 CHILDREN'S NAMES | 11 CHILDREN'S AGES | 12 CHILDREN'S BIRTHPLACES | 13 LIVES WITH WHOM | 14 RELATIONSHIP |
|---|---|---|---|---|---|---|
| Moore | E. J., Mrs. | Wallace J.; Donald E.; Rena E.; Dudley | 9; 7; 5; 2 | AZ; AZ; NM; NM; CA | | |
| Moore | Ellen | James; Cooper; Mary; Ellen Morrow | all about 50 | Petaluma | Ellen Morrow | dau. |
| Moore | Margaret | Mary Kearns; Matilda Kearns (grandchildren) | 8; 6 | Skagway, AK | grandchildren | |
| Moraga | Jospha, Mrs. | | | | | |
| Moraga | Mrs. | Manuel | | | | |
| Morrill | Dorinda Rilla | Samuel J. Pharris | 48 | Petaluma | son | |
| Morrisey | Kate, Mrs. | | small; oldest 6 | | | |
| Morrison | Mrs. | son; dau.; son; dau. | 17; 15; 11; 9 | | 4 children | |
| Morrow | James H. | | | | | |
| Morrow | James H. | Mrs. Belle Graham; Mrs. Emma Steinwirg; Mrs. Myrtle Flor | | | | |
| Moulton | S. C. | | | | | |
| Muerth | Alice, Mrs. | | 14 | SWT | alone | sister; aunt |
| Mulford | Mr. & Mrs. J. | Theodore; Ida S.; Ola W. | 50; 45; 37 | | | |
| Muller | Mary | | 11 | | | |
| Mullin | Delia, Miss | | | | | |
| Mulvany | R. M., Mrs. | | 11; 7; 3; 1; (one cripple) | | | |
| Murphy | Mabel | | | | A. M. Butler | |
| Murphy | Mabel, Miss | | | | A. M. Butler | |
| Murphy | R. W. | Mrs. R. J. Murray; John; Richard Jr.; Frank; Mrs. Kate Wagy; Jennie Cameron; Wallace; Mrs. Ida Gummer | 41; 39; 36; 31; 28; 26; 20; 18 | California | Ida Gummer & husband | dau. & son-in-law |
| Murphy | Richard W. | | | | alone | |
| Myers | Henry | | | | Jos. & Della Kraschel | uncle & aunt |

| 1 SURNAME | 2 GIVEN NAME | 10 CHILDREN'S NAMES | 11 CHILDREN'S AGES | 12 CHILDREN'S BIRTHPLACES | 13 LIVES WITH WHOM | 14 RELATIONSHIP |
|---|---|---|---|---|---|---|
| Navoni | Batista | | | | Frank Pacini & wife | |
| Navoni | Batista | Lessandrina; Vittoria | 45; 52 | SWT | Lessandrina | dau. |
| Neidringhouse | Henry | | | | Mrs. Nosler | |
| Neidringhouse | Mr. | Mrs. Carl Hilderbrand | about 40 | | alone | |
| Nelan | Marcella, Mrs. | | | | | |
| Nelson | A. S. | | | | | |
| Nelson | Cornelia | John H.; Charles W.; Emma Eugley | 40; 50; 62 | | alone | |
| Nelson | Margaret | | | | Hugh Montague | |
| Nelson | Margaret | | | | Hugh Montague | |
| Nelson | Margaret, Mrs. | | | | J. S. McClellan | |
| Neuman | Marie | | | | alone | |
| Newman | Elizabeth | | | | | |
| Newman | John Allen | | | | Lorenzo D. Newman | brother |
| Newman | John Allen | | | | Lorenzo Dow Newman | brother |
| Newman | Marie, Mrs. | | | | | |
| Newman | W. N. | | | | | |
| Newton | Hulda | Horace B. | 33 | Del Norte Co., CA | | |
| Newton | Hulda S. | Horace B. | | | E. C. Newton | |
| Noriel | J. C. | | 15; 10; 9; 6; 4 | | | |
| Noriel | Jesse | Susie | 14 | Santa Rosa | | |
| Norris | Anna, Mrs. | Lewis H. | 6 | CA | Mrs. F. N. Gully | |
| Norris | Anna, Mrs. | | 6 | Santa Rosa | Mr. & Mrs. F. Tully | none |
| Norris | E., Mrs. | Mrs. Francis; Mollie Cabman | 25; 30 | TN | | |
| Norris | Elizabeth, Mrs. | | | | Mrs. Costello | |
| Northway | I. B., Mrs. | Martha | 7 | Petaluma | alone with child | |

| 1 SURNAME | 2 GIVEN NAME | 10 CHILDREN'S NAMES | 11 CHILDREN'S AGES | 12 CHILDREN'S BIRTHPLACES | 13 LIVES WITH WHOM | 14 RELATIONSHIP |
|---|---|---|---|---|---|---|
| Norton | John, Mrs. | | | | | |
| Norton | John, Mrs. | | small children | | | |
| Norton | Philinda | | | | | |
| Nottingham | Mrs. | | | | | |
| O'Bryan | A. L. | | | | Miss Francis E. McGee, trained nurse | |
| O'Halleran | Tymothy | | | | alone | |
| O'Halloran | Bella Bransteller | Iris Stella | 14; 12 | Sonell, MO; Santa Rosa | Mrs. S. D. Moran | sister |
| O'Halloran | J. D., Mrs. | Stella Branstetter; Iris Branstetter; Jimmie; Mary | 14; 11; 4; 21 mos. | Milan, MO; Santa Rosa; Graton; Graton | S. D. Moran | brother-in-law |
| O'Halloran | Timothy | | | | | |
| Ohlsen | Henry | | | | John Olsen | |
| Olmstead | L. W. | | | | alone | |
| Olmstead | L. W. | | | | | |
| Olmstead | Levy Willis | | | | | |
| Ologue | Mary | Fred; Lousiana; Janey; Josey; Kity | 14; 11; 10; 9; 7 | | 5 children | |
| Olway | Abby | | | | M. J. Pierce | |
| O'Neil | Minnie | Annie; Willie | 8; 12 | OR | Mrs. Cota | |
| O'Rourke | Mary, Mrs. | | 1 ½ to 14 | | | |
| Orth | Helene | Walter; Louis; Pauline; William | 15; 13; 11; 10 | | | |
| Orth | Helene, Mrs. | | | | 4 young children | |
| Ouellet | J. C. | | | | alone | |
| Pahud | Henriette, Mrs. | Constand; Matalia; Leon; Alice | 7; 5; 4; 1 yr. 7 mos. | | children | |
| Palmer | Thomas B. | | | | | |
| Papera | Arseda | Giovanni; Marianna; Angelina; Elizabeth | 38; 35; 30; 25 | ITL; ITL; ITL; ITL | | son & dau.-in-law |

| 1 SURNAME | 2 GIVEN NAME | 10 CHILDREN'S NAMES | 11 CHILDREN'S AGES | 12 CHILDREN'S BIRTHPLACES | 13 LIVES WITH WHOM | 14 RELATIONSHIP |
|---|---|---|---|---|---|---|
| Park | Elizabeth, Mrs. | Greta; Ethel; Gilbert; Lois | 8; 5; 3; 10 mos. | CA; CA; CA; CA | | |
| Parker | Frederick | Fred; Edwin; Lily Belle | 47; 43; 41 | | alone | |
| Parker | Joseph P. | | | | wife | |
| Patrick | Jesse | | | | wife & 2 children | |
| Patterson | J. T. | Hester; John; Mary; James; Pearl; Rosa | 24; 22; 18; 15; 10; 8 | | children | |
| Patterson | Mary, Mrs. | James H.; Mrs. Clara Carrington | 49; 43 | Santa Rosa | Mrs. Alice Mervey | |
| Patterson | Pearl & Rosa | | | | | |
| Paula | George, Mrs. | Mrs. John Ronald Paula | 29 | CA | Geo. W. Heason | |
| Pearse | Mary, Mrs. | | | | | wife |
| Pedro | John | Charles, married, lives SF | | | wife | |
| Pelizzari | Carlo | Adelina; Girrolo; Giacinto; Serafina; Carlo | 11; 8; 7; 4; 3 mos. | ITL; CA | wife & family | |
| Pelizzari | Carlo | Adelina; Guido; Giacinta; Serafina; Alberto | 12; 9; 8; 5; 10 mos. | ITL; ITL; ITL; CA; CA | wife & children | |
| Pellow | Angelina | Jimmie; Philip; Mary | 5; 2 ½; 3 mos. | CA | children | |
| Pellow | Angelina | Jimmie; Philip; Mary | 6; 3; 7 mos. | CA; CA; CA | children | |
| Perey | Joe | | | | alone | |
| Perkins | Blanche | | | | Major Philbert | |
| Perkins | Blanche | | | | | |
| Perrot | E. | | | | | |
| Perry | Agnes | infant | | | widowed mother | |
| Perry | Elizabeth | | | | | |
| Perry | Margaret Agnes, Mrs. | boy | 2 | | | |
| Perry | Mary | Frank; Elva; Viola | 15; 13; 15 mos. | 1st two Monterery Co., CA; Viola in Sebastopol | children | |
| Peterson | C. D. | Rosa; Emma; Lone; Anne; Edith; Chris | 40; 38; 36; 32; 28 | Rosa in Java; others in Santa | F. Wancent? | |

| 1 SURNAME | 2 GIVEN NAME | 10 CHILDREN'S NAMES | 11 CHILDREN'S AGES | 12 CHILDREN'S BIRTHPLACES | 13 LIVES WITH WHOM | 14 RELATIONSHIP |
|---|---|---|---|---|---|---|
| Peterson | John | | | Rosa | | |
| Peterson | John | | | | alone | |
| Pettis | Lula A. | Florence; Lelland; Lucille; Hellen; Ina; Edna | 15; 14; 9; 7; 4; 2 | first two Healdsburg; others Sebastopol | | |
| Petty | James | | | | | |
| Petty | James Ervin | | | | | |
| Phelan | Jennie, Miss | | | | Ida Rhoades | sister |
| Phelan | Lucinda, Mrs. | Jennie Phelan; Kate Palmer; Ida Rhoades | 55; 52; 39 | U. S. | Kate Palmer | dau. |
| Phillips | Mariah, Mrs. | | | | | |
| Philpott | Sarah M. | | | | 10 year old child | |
| Phinney | Grace M. | Grace M.; Evelena | 2; 1 | CA | Mrs. J. Harrow | grandmother |
| Pickrell | Nellie, L. | Dayle E.; Glenn F.; Elwyn G.; Verne S. | 9; 8; 6; 21 mos. | Stockton; Cordelia, CA; Healdsburg; Galt, CA | | |
| Piezzi | Leonard | | | | | |
| Piezzi(e) | Leonardo | | | | | |
| Poggi | G. B. | | | | wife; 3 children | |
| Poggi | G. B. | G. B., Jr.; Mary; Jospeh; Gabrial | 18; 16; 14; 12 | | | |
| Poggi | G. B., Mr. | | | | | |
| Pollard | Thomas & Elizabeth | | | | | |
| Pollard | Thomas & wife | | | | | |
| Pomroy | Mr. | | | | wife | |
| Pool | Lydia | Margaret Shoemake; Lee; John; Lizzie McKean; Charley | | | Lizzie Pool McKean | dau. |
| Pope | Jacob | Georg; Francis Gronwald; | | | J. Carrgan | |

-83-

| 1 SURNAME | 2 GIVEN NAME | 10 CHILDREN'S NAMES | 11 CHILDREN'S AGES | 12 CHILDREN'S BIRTHPLACES | 13 LIVES WITH WHOM | 14 RELATIONSHIP |
|---|---|---|---|---|---|---|
| Porter | Julia | Anna Tenitz | | | | |
| Porter | Lucy | May; Ella; Eva; Drusilla; Jimmy | | | mother & children | |
| Porter | William | | | | alone | |
| Porter | William | | | | Charles Lambert | |
| Porter | Wm. P. | Garland Baree; Vina Meyer; Hannah Meyer; Geo. Meyer | 13; 11; 6; 9 | Napa Co., CA | | |
| Post | Frances, Mrs. | | | | alone | |
| Post | J. B. | | | | | |
| Potter | Edmond | step-dau. who is orphan | 24 | | Francis Hilton | step-dau. |
| Powell | Frank | | | | alone | |
| Powers | L., Mrs. | | | | | |
| Pressl[e]y | William H. | | | | | |
| Price | William H. | Alice | 58 | NC | R. J. McKay | |
| Prince | Louis L.; Freddie F. | | children | | Mrs. Livingstone | mother |
| Proctor | Sadie | James Walter; Ira LeRoy (grandchildren) | 6; 8 | Healdsburg | Mr. & Mrs. J. H. Derrick | |
| Pucinelli | Ben | Rafael; Amador; Mary; Lita; Lena; Joseph | 12; 11; 8; 7; 5; 18 mos. | ITL; ITL; rest SF | | |
| Purdy | George Washington | | | | | |
| Quackenbush | Lettie | | | | 4 dependent children | |
| Querola | John | | | | alone | |
| Quirk | Margaret | | | | | |
| Raddel | Mrs. | | | | | |
| Raddle | Ed., Mrs. | | | | | |
| Radel | Edward, Mrs. | | | | | |

| 1 | 2 | 10 | 11 | 12 | 13 | 14 |
|---|---|---|---|---|---|---|
| SURNAME | GIVEN NAME | CHILDREN'S NAMES | CHILDREN'S AGES | CHILDREN'S BIRTHPLACES | LIVES WITH WHOM | RELATIONSHIP |
| Raefael | Pedro | all deceased | | Sonoma Co. | Mrs. Antone | sister |
| Raineri | Lucia | Emma; Linda; Rosie; Mary; George; Guerino; Sophina | 11; 8; 7; 6; 5; 4; 2 | MA; MA; MA; MA; MA; Santa Rosa; Sonoma | | |
| Ramis | Elliott M. & wife | | | | | |
| Read | William B. | | | | alone | |
| Read | William Bowers | | | | | |
| Redmond | Harriet M. | | | | | |
| Redmond | Harriet M. | | | | Mr. & Mrs. Harris | |
| Reed | Laura | Laura; Joseph; Roland; Olive; Thomas; Elsie; Lillian | 14; 12; 11; 9; 7; 5; 3 | CA | children | |
| Reed | Laura | Joseph; Olive; Thomas; Elsie | 14; 11; 9; 7 | 1st 3 Monterey Co; last, Sonoma Co. | | |
| Reed | Sarah Jane | Samuel | 40 | SF | Mrs. Abigal Trijon | |
| Reeder | Alice H. | Ed L.; George; Charles | ?; ?; 11 | | married son, Ed | son |
| Reeder | Alice H. | E. L.; George P.; Charles L. | 34; 31; 25 | Joplin, MO; Carthage, MO; Santa Rosa | | |
| Reeder | Daisy | Lane | 9 | Santa Rosa | child | |
| Reeder | S. W., Mrs. | small children | | | | |
| Reedy | Mary | Edward; Bernardine | 6; 2 ½ | MT | | |
| Reedy | Mary, Mrs. | Edward; Bernard; Bernardine | 5; 2; 2 | Chicago, IL; SD; SD | | |
| Reedy | Mary, Mrs. | Edwin; Bernard; Bernard F. | 5; 26 mos.; 26 mos. | | father | |
| Renfroe | James | | | | alone | |
| Renfroe | James F. | | | | | |
| Renfroe | James F. | | | | | |
| Renfroe | James F. | | | | alone | |
| Renfroe | James F. | | | | | |

| 1 SURNAME | 2 GIVEN NAME | 10 CHILDREN'S NAMES | 11 CHILDREN'S AGES | 12 CHILDREN'S BIRTHPLACES | 13 LIVES WITH WHOM | 14 RELATIONSHIP |
|---|---|---|---|---|---|---|
| Reyburn | W. B. | | | | | |
| Reynolds | Daniel B. | | | | wife; dau. | |
| Reynolds | Daniel B. | Mable died Aug. 1897 age 20; Percy died Jan. 1898; Bessie died Aug. 1899 age 15 | | | wife, Emma E. | |
| Reynolds | S. K. | | | | alone | |
| Reynolds | S. K. | | | | F. W. Newbert | |
| Reynolds | Smith K. | | | | | |
| Ribardiere | Susanne | Susan; Alex; George; Rosa | 9; 7; 3; 18 mos. | AUT; AUT; CA; CA | | |
| Rice | D. P. | | | | | |
| Rice | Ernest | | | | | |
| Rice | Thomas & wife | | | | | |
| Richards | Eliza, Mrs. | | | | | |
| Richardson | Eliza C., Mrs. | Mary; Forest; Burkett; Paul | 10; 9; 6; 4 | 3 in TX; 1 in Santa Rosa | children | |
| Rickett | (children) | Minerva; Margie; Charles | | | | |
| Riley | Clara & Harry | Clara; Harry | 10; 6 | Placer Co; Yuba Co., CA | J. C. Howard & wife | grandparents |
| Ring | R. G. | | | | Mattie Bishop | |
| Ring | R. G. | | | | Mrs. Bishop | |
| Rippetoe | Dora | Lulu; Cora; Agnes; Dora | 7; 6; 3; 9 mos. | | alone | |
| Ritter | J. W. | Alma; Mary; Will; Ida; Dan | 35; 33; 30; 26; 24 | | | |
| Roat | Wm. L., Mr. & Mrs. | | | | | |
| Roberson | Malvina J. | | 14 to 4 mos. | | | |
| Roberts | Rose, Mrs. | | | | | |
| Robertson | F. | | | | | |
| Robertson | Robert | | | | John Scheel | |

| 1 | 2 | 10 | 11 | 12 | 13 | 14 |
|---|---|---|---|---|---|---|
| SURNAME | GIVEN NAME | CHILDREN'S NAMES | CHILDREN'S AGES | CHILDREN'S BIRTHPLACES | LIVES WITH WHOM | RELATIONSHIP |
| Robertson | Sydney Henry | | | | wife | |
| Robinson | F. | | | | alone | |
| Robinson | Mary, Mrs. | | small | | | |
| Robison | Fletchey | Laura; Alice; Nelson | 35; 20; 33 | | alone | |
| Rodd | John | | | | J. Vincent | |
| Rogers | Niles V. | | | | | |
| Rogers | Rita Francisca | | | | | |
| Rose | D. E., Mrs. | small children | 11 and under | | | |
| Rose | Jane | | | | alone | |
| Rose | Mr. & Mrs. | | | | | |
| Rossi | Serafina | Mary; Emil; Louis; Angel; Rose; Antonietta | 20; 19; 17; 12; 10; 9 | Mary in Sonoma; others Bennett Valley | | |
| Roth | A. R. | | | | alone | |
| Roy | Ann, Mrs. | | child | | | |
| Roy | Fannie | dau. | 8 | | | |
| Rudolfi | Attilio | | | | A. Pinelli, A. | |
| Rudolfi | Attilio | | | | A. Pinelli | |
| Rudolfi | Attilio | | | | Leveroni brothers, on Grace ranch | |
| Rudolfi | Attilio | | | | alone | |
| Ruesch | Christof | | | | | |
| Runyan | Hattie | Henry; Eva; Mabel | 16; 6; 3 | all Santa Rosa | | |
| Russ | Matilda | | | | | |
| Russell | William H. | Emma Churchill; Judith Chauncey | | | wife | |
| Ryerson | William | | | | | |
| Sabieni | Mary | James; Daisy; Eliza; Angelina; Joseph | 8; 6; 6; 2; 4 | 1st 2 Santa Rosa; last 2 Angels Camp, CA | | |

| 1 | 2 | 10 | 11 | 12 | 13 | 14 |
|---|---|---|---|---|---|---|
| SURNAME | GIVEN NAME | CHILDREN'S NAMES | CHILDREN'S AGES | CHILDREN'S BIRTHPLACES | LIVES WITH WHOM | RELATIONSHIP |
| Sales | Henery | | | | James E. Bidwell | |
| Sales | Luke & family | | 11; 8; 3 | | | |
| Salvador | Mr. | married dau. | | | Minnie Smith | |
| Samuels | Anna | | | | Bob Samuels | |
| Samuels | James, Mrs. | small children | | | | |
| Samuels | Jessie M. | Ella; Eugene | 5; 2 | Santa Rosa; Sacramento | Mrs. Ella Forgett | grandchildren |
| Sandusky | Mattie | Morgan; John; Roy; Alice | 13; 7; 5; 4 | | children | |
| Sansbury | Benjamin Franklin | | | | Charles Howard | brother |
| Santos | Mary, Mrs. | Stephen Smith; Annie; Josie; Ceclia; baby | 11; 7; 5; 3; 6 mos. | Sebastopol; rest at Jenner | John Smith | |
| Santos | Mary, Mrs. | Annie; Josie; Cecilia; Delores | 10; 8; 6; 3 | Sonoma Co. | children | |
| Sawyer | Alice, Mrs. | | | | alone | |
| Sawyer | Marsden Albert | | | | | |
| Schefer | Ernest | Ernest; Elise; Emma; Walter; Bertha; Willie; Richard | 15; 14; 10; 8; 7; 6; 2 | SWT; SWT; SWT; WI; WI; Berkeley, CA; Santa Rosa | | |
| Schell | Frank | | | | alone | |
| Schlobohm | Albert | | 32 | SC | C. G. Christian | |
| Schrogen | Mary J. | Margaret Bailey; Mary DePue; John Wheeler; Anna DeRoco; Alonzo Wheeler | 54; 45; 33; 28; 30 | MO; MO; IL; IL; IL | Mrs. Hawley | |
| Schuster | James Elgin | | | | sister Alice | sister |
| Sciacca | G. S. | Francescios; Elena; Rosalia; Margherita | 3; 5; 7; 10 mos. | St Helena, CA; Santa Rosa | Mrs. Jacob Mack | |
| Scott | Albert | George; Mammie; James | 27; 24; 14 | MI; KS; WA | son | |
| Scott | J. H. | | | | | |
| Seigel | Frank | four married children | | GER | wife | |
| Shaeffer | Cynthia | Marvin | 3 | Healdsburg | | |

| 1 | 2 | 10 | 11 | 12 | 13 | 14 |
|---|---|---|---|---|---|---|
| SURNAME | GIVEN NAME | CHILDREN'S NAMES | CHILDREN'S AGES | CHILDREN'S BIRTHPLACES | LIVES WITH WHOM | RELATIONSHIP |
| Shaeffer | Cynthia | | | CA | child | |
| Shaw | O. F., Dr. | | | | alone | |
| Sheldon | R. W. | | | | Wm. Hill ranch | |
| Sheldon | R. W. | | | | Otto Schinkel | none |
| Shepard | Martin | | | | brother | |
| Shepherd | Morris | | | | Martin Shepherd | brother |
| Sherwood | J. C. | | | | | |
| Sholes | Martha J. | 2 dead; 2 living; youngest 40 | | | alone | |
| Sholes | Martha J., Mrs. | | young | | family | |
| Sibley | Rebecca, Mrs. | | | | | |
| Silva | D., Mrs. | | | | alone with children | |
| Silva | Mabel | Hazel; Wanda; Charlie; Geordia | 8; 5; 2; 7 mos. | all Sonoma Co. | Eugene Gressot | father |
| Silva | Manuel D. | Mrs. J. L. Prader; Mrs. F J. Peter; Maude F. | 36; 35; 33 | Sausalito; Jamestown, CA; Jamestown, CA | | |
| Silva | Mary M. | | 16 and under | | | |
| Silvia | Leonor | | | | Mrs. Mary Perry | |
| Silzle | (children) | Lena; Benjamin; Kate; Wm.; Minnie; Roy | 15; thru 2 yrs. | | Uncle Geo. Silzle, guardian | |
| Simoni | Natalina | Erico; Mary; Julie | 10; 8; 7 | Erico, ITL; Sonoma Co. | alone | |
| Simpson | Zeptha, Mrs. | | | | | |
| Small | Mrs. | | | | | |
| Smith | D. W. | | | | | |
| Smith | J. Y., Mrs. | | | | | |
| Smith | Joseph M. | | | | | |
| Smith | Nova N. | Oliver P.; Reba L.; Robert L.; Gusta N. | 9; 7; 4 ½; 3 | NE | Mrs. Annie R. Phillips | mother |

| 1 SURNAME | 2 GIVEN NAME | 10 CHILDREN'S NAMES | 11 CHILDREN'S AGES | 12 CHILDREN'S BIRTHPLACES | 13 LIVES WITH WHOM | 14 RELATIONSHIP |
|---|---|---|---|---|---|---|
| Smith | S. H. | | | | alone | |
| Smith | S. L., Mrs. | Grace; Melvin; Hope | 15; 8; 5 | | | |
| Smith | Samuel H. | | | | Mrs. Wheelock | |
| Smith | Samuel H. | | | | | |
| Smither | W., Mrs. | Walter; Asa; Ida; Annie; Zora; Willie; Wallace; Emma; Lloyd | 24; 17; 14; 12; 10; 8; 7; 5; 3 | Sonoma Co. (1st 7); Yolo Co., CA (last 2) | husband and children | |
| Smithers | W. L. | Etta Pritchett; Ruby Nisner; Walter; Wanda Morrell; Lucy; Asa; Ida; Annie; Lora; Willie; Wallace; Emma | ?; ?; 22; ?; 16; 13; 12; 10; 6; 5; 3; 2 | Solano Co.; Sonoma Co.; Yolo Co., CA | | |
| Smyth | Mary R., Mrs. | | | | | |
| Snow | Rubin A. | | | | | |
| Solorzano | Antonio | | | | | mother & sisters |
| Sousa | Marion, Mrs. | Grace; Marion Walter | 2; 6 mos. | Green Valley, Sonoma Co. | alone | |
| Souza | Frank | | | | wife, Mary | |
| Spaich | Emilia, Mrs. | Mickey; Julia; Maria; Lena; Emilia | 14; 13; 12; 10; 4 | SF; SF; SF; Petaluma; Petaluma | Frank Bondietti | |
| Spaich | Emilia, Mrs. | Michael; Julia; Marie; Lina; Emily | 17; 16; 15; 13; 7 | SF; SF; SF; Petaluma; Novato, CA | children | |
| Spaulding | Ambrose N. | | | | E. W. Evans | |
| Speller | George | | | | | |
| Sprunck | Henry P. | | | | alone | |
| Stafford | B., Mrs. | Everett; Milton; Nettie | 14; 11; 7 | Colusa Co., CA | children | |
| Stark | H. E., Mrs. | | | | | |
| Stark | Harriot E. | A. J.; Mrs. L. M. Ahrndt; U. S.; H. | 42; 36; 33; 28 | | G. W. S. Wade | none |

| 1 SURNAME | 2 GIVEN NAME | 10 CHILDREN'S NAMES | 11 CHILDREN'S AGES | 12 CHILDREN'S BIRTHPLACES | 13 LIVES WITH WHOM | 14 RELATIONSHIP |
|---|---|---|---|---|---|---|
| Stark | Willie | | | | T. W. Ward | |
| Starr | Nancy, Mrs. | | | | alone | |
| Steinpis | Rosa | | 9; 11 | | C. D. Peterson | father (in county hospital) |
| Sterling | James A. | | | | | |
| Stewart | Lovilla | Ed L.; Ulysses; Mrs. Barton | married with family | | Joseph F. Ryan | |
| Stewart | Lovilla, Mrs. | Edgar; Ulysses; Helen | 53; 48; 42 | IA; MO; CA | Mrs. Barton | dau. |
| Stochini | Agostino | Severina Tognacca; Nina Genazzi | 48; 45 | | Severina Tognacca | dau. |
| Stodard | Bud | Harry; Mable; Fred; Clarrence; Eddy | 13; 11; 10; 8; 6 | ?; WA; CA; CA; CA | | |
| Storks | Hariet E., Mrs. | Andrew Jackson; Yula; Henry | 42; 32; 30 | OR; OR; NV | alone | |
| Strock | Emma, Mrs. | H. M. | 41 | | Mrs. H. M. Strock | |
| Stump | Daniel A. | 2 sons; 2 daus.; married and gone | | | wife, Carrie | |
| Sutherland | Ella | James | 40 | | Thos. Campion | |
| Sutherland | Ellen | James | 48 | | Clara D. White | |
| Sutherland | Ellen, Mrs. | not seen since quake | | | Mrs. Al Barnes | |
| Suthland | Ellen | | | | alone | |
| Sweet | James | | | | | |
| Sweet | James | James | 38 | Sonoma Co. | | |
| Talbot | Louis F. | | | | Mrs. M. W. Talbot, M. W. | mother |
| Talbot | Louis F. | | | | Mary W. Talbot | |
| Talbot | Louis Franklin | | | | Mary W. Talbot | mother |
| Tate | George Sidney | | | | alone | |
| Tate | George Sidney | | | | | |
| Taylor | Ina F. | Ellison R. | 13 | NE | alone | |

| 1 SURNAME | 2 GIVEN NAME | 10 CHILDREN'S NAMES | 11 CHILDREN'S AGES | 12 CHILDREN'S BIRTHPLACES | 13 LIVES WITH WHOM | 14 RELATIONSHIP |
|---|---|---|---|---|---|---|
| Tew | Clara | Willie | 7 | CA | son | |
| Thatford | Sarah A., Mrs. | male | | | alone | |
| Thiesen | C. E. C. S. | | | | Miss G. Thiesen | dau. |
| Thomas | D. W. | | | | | |
| Thomas | H. R., Mr. & Mrs. | | 11; 10; 7; 4 | | | |
| Thompson | Julia E. | Jean; Walter | 18; 23 | | alone | |
| Thompson | Julia E. | all over 21 | over 21 | CA | alone | |
| Thompson | Nellie B. | Jack; Harold; Wallace; Irene | 13; 10; 9; 3 | SF; Alameda; Santa Rosa; Santa Rosa | | |
| Thompson | William, Mrs. | | | | with 4 children | |
| Thorp | Carlena Anna Marie | | | | F. C. Blayer | |
| Thunmillen | Elizabeth, Mrs. | little children | | | | |
| Timmons | H. M. | Bergie; Fred; Ethel; Floy | 33; 31; 28; 24 | 2 in WI; 2 in OR | alone | |
| Tod | Juliet M. & Isabella | application made by Wm. Crawford; parents were William & Minnie Grace Tod; more info on parents | 13; 11 | Santa Rosa | | |
| Tojo | Madalena | Guiseppe; Giovanni | 33; 42 | ITL | | |
| Tojo | Madalena | adult children; residence unknown | | | alone | |
| Toltschin | J., Mrs. | Clara Hall | 22 | Pasadena, CA | | |
| Tombs | Henry C. & Mrs. | | | | | |
| Toombs | G. A. | Pearl; Robert; Alveria; Rowena; Charley; Ruby; James; Woodrow; Clarence; Lena | 19; 17; 16; 14; 10; 8; 6; 3; 18 mos.; 9 mos. | Eureka, CA; Reno, NV | | |
| Toroni | Margherita | Mary Ricci; Katie Scarpellini; Ida Canobbio | 45; 38; 31 | SWT; Sonoma; Sonoma | alone | |
| Toroni | Margherita | Mary Ricci; Katie | 46; 40; 33 | SWT; CA; CA | Ida Canobbio | dau. |

| 1 | 2 | 10 | 11 | 12 | 13 | 14 |
|---|---|---|---|---|---|---|
| SURNAME | GIVEN NAME | CHILDREN'S NAMES | CHILDREN'S AGES | CHILDREN'S BIRTHPLACES | LIVES WITH WHOM | RELATIONSHIP |
| Toschi | Tranquilla | Scarpellini; Ida Canobbio | | | Peter Bonugi | nephew |
| Towle | Ida M. | Joseph; John; Isabella; Virginia; Eugenia | 13; 12; 10; 7; 5 | Lexington, KY | | |
| Treat | John J., Mrs. | Mrs. Gertrude Bergin | 29 | Hampton, IA | Mrs. C. Batten | |
| | | Paul; Elizabeth; Dan; Charlie; Katherine; John; George; Stella | 17; 16; 14; 13; 9; 6; 4; 2 | 1st 2 San Jacinto; next 2 Los Angeles, rest in San Pedro | | |
| Trimble | Patrick J. | | | | | |
| Tritchler | Dora | Jos.; Otie; Chas.; Ollie | 21; 20; 18; 23 | | alone | |
| Truett | William | | | | | |
| Tuitchlen? | Dora, Mrs. | | | | | |
| Tuney | J. | | | | family | |
| Tuney | J. | | | | family | |
| Tunnell | Eliza A., Mrs. | | | | | |
| Turner | Annie Maria, Mrs. | | | ENG | family | dau. |
| Turner | J. H. | Robert Franklin | 2 | Bodga Bay | alone | |
| Turner | J. H. | | 11 | Monroe Co., IN | alone | |
| Turner | M, Mrs. | John A.; James H. | 50; 47 | IN | | |
| Turner | Martha | J. H. Howard; John A. Howard | 51; 48 | | | |
| Turner | Mary, Mrs. | | 15; 2 mos. | | alone | |
| Turner | Peter W. | | | | alone | |
| Turner | Peter W. | Laura Huffman; May Marshall; both married | | | | |
| Turner | S. E., Mrs. | | | | brother | |
| Turner | Semantha E., Mrs. | Mrs. Frank Marshall; Mrs. Wm. Huffman | | | Mrs. Graham | |
| Tyler | Clifton | | | | Mr. & Mrs. B. C. Boyd | none |
| Unger | Julia | Julia; Peter | 2 ½; 5 | St. Louis, MO | | |

| 1 SURNAME | 2 GIVEN NAME | 10 CHILDREN'S NAMES | 11 CHILDREN'S AGES | 12 CHILDREN'S BIRTHPLACES | 13 LIVES WITH WHOM | 14 RELATIONSHIP |
|---|---|---|---|---|---|---|
| Ursin | Ada | Melvin E. | 8 | Penngrove | husband & son | |
| Ursin | Ada L. | Melvin | 11 | Berkeley, CA | John Ursin | husband |
| Ursin | Ada, Mrs. | | 10 | CA | husband & son | |
| Valentine | Mary | | | | J. F. Clowan & wife | dau. |
| Van | Mr. & Mrs. | | son abt. 14 | | | |
| Vance | Robin & Stuart | | 6; 9 | | Mrs. Mary Mountjoy | grandmother |
| Vance | Mathilde | | | | grandmother | |
| VanGeldern | Matilda | | | | | |
| VanGeldern | Matilda, Miss | | | | | |
| VanGeldern | E. S. | | | | | |
| Vann | E. S. | | | | wife, age about 50 | |
| Vann | E. S. | | | | wife & step-son | |
| Vann | E. S. & wife | | | | | |
| Vaughan | E. N., Mrs. | | | | Eugene Heith | |
| Vaughn | Casan E., Mrs. | Elijah K. | | | | |
| Veatch | Ellen | | | | Dadney, May, Mrs. | |
| Vellulini | Ermida & Annie | | | Sonoma Co. | Ermida lives with Mrs. Martinelli (aunt); Annie lives with Napoleone Velluini (uncle) | |
| Vest | Eli | | | | wife | |
| Vestal | Jacob | | | | Jacob Fouts | grandson |
| Vier(s) | Mrs. | small children | | | | |
| Vierra | Anna, Mrs. | 1 invalid dau. & 5 minors | | | with 6 children | |
| Vineyard | Leone | | | | J. L. Benton | uncle |
| Vinsent | John | | | | Mrs. N. Vincent | |
| Vinyard | Leon | | | | J. L. Benton | nephew |
| VonGeldern | Matilda | | | | | |

| 1 | 2 | 10 | 11 | 12 | 13 | 14 |
|---|---|---|---|---|---|---|
| SURNAME | GIVEN NAME | CHILDREN'S NAMES | CHILDREN'S AGES | CHILDREN'S BIRTHPLACES | LIVES WITH WHOM | RELATIONSHIP |
| Wagner | Katherine | Joseph; Bertha; Lottie; Helen; Regina; Edward; Louise | 13; 11; 10; 8; 7; 4; 1 | 1st 5 in Trenton, NJ; others in Los Angeles | husband & children | |
| Waldvogel | Marie | | | | | |
| Walk | Lillie Ellen | Edna; Ernest; Cora Belle; John; Ella L. | 13; 11; 7; 3; 2 | 1st 2 Sebastopol; Oakland, last 2 Santa Rosa | husband & children | |
| Walker | Ada L., Mrs. | all married adults | | | alone | |
| Walker | B. K. | | | | | |
| Walker | Benjamin K. | | | | E. E. Sprague | |
| Walker | Lizzie | | all minors | | | |
| Walker | Lizzie | | 14; 10; 7; 6; 5 | | | |
| Walker | Nancy, Mrs. | | | | children | |
| Wall | Ada | Flora; Nina; Everett | 3; 3; 1 | Sebastopol | mother, Mrs. Florence Garrison | |
| Wall | Ada, Mrs. | Flora Jannett; Nina Natolie; Everett Samuel | 5; 5; 3 | Sebastopol | weak mother; Mrs. William Garrison | mother |
| Wallace | James | | | | | |
| Ward | Laura | Helen; James; Elena; Winnifred; Weston | 9; 8; 5; 4; 2 | Petaluma | Mrs. C. Carter | mother |
| Ward | Laura | Helen; James; Elma; Winifred; Weston; Paul | 12; 11; 9; 7; 5; 2 | Petaluma | | |
| Ward | Laura, Mrs. | Hellen; James; Elma; Winefred; Weston | 10; 9; 6; 5; 3 | 1st 4 Petaluma; Walla Walla, WA | | |
| Ward | Lizzie, Mrs. | Bertha; Hattie May; Jessie Myrtle | 13; 11; 6 | | | |
| Ward | Thomas | Neslon; Charley; Emma | 40; 30; 38 | | alone | |
| Ward | William | | | | John Meagher | |
| Ward | William | | | | | |
| Warne | N. E., Mrs. | | | | sister | |
| Warne | N. E., Mrs. | | | | Mrs. Bruner | |

| 1 SURNAME | 2 GIVEN NAME | 10 CHILDREN'S NAMES | 11 CHILDREN'S AGES | 12 CHILDREN'S BIRTHPLACES | 13 LIVES WITH WHOM | 14 RELATIONSHIP |
|---|---|---|---|---|---|---|
| Wassom | Jacob & wife | | | | | |
| Webb | William B. | | | | alone | |
| Webster | Anthony | | | | Joshua Fix; with wife & child | |
| Welch | Martha | | | | alone | |
| Welch | Martha, Mrs. | | | | | |
| Welch | Mary, Mrs. | Anna McGrew; Maggie; Cole; Kate; Mollie Way; John H.; | 52; 50; 49; 42; 46 | Sarasota Springs, NY | alone | |
| Welch | Mrs. | | | | | |
| Welhe | Irene | | | | | |
| Weller | Ada, Mrs. | Belma; Edna; Milton | 10; 9; 6 | Mendocino Co., CA | Case | |
| Weller | George | James | 18 | Alameda Co., CA | | |
| Wells | J. M. | | | | | |
| Wells | Oscar J. | | | | | |
| Wellschott | Theodore & wife | | | | | |
| Welschott | Theodore | | | | wife, aged 72 or 73 | |
| Welsholt | Theodore | | | | wife, Margaret, 60 | |
| Westgate | Charles, Mrs. | Ruby | 14 | CA | Mrs. Ivy Scott | mother |
| Wheeler | A. | | | | wife | |
| Wheeler | A. | | young | | wife & children | |
| Wheeler | Mary | Henry; Isabel; Emma; George; Nettie; Myrtle | 45; 36; 39; 35; 29; 25 | Mill Creek (Healdsburg area) | Mrs. G. H. Exley, G. H. | none |
| Whitcomb | O., Mr. & Mrs. | | | | Mrs. Whitcomb's mother, Mrs. Schowalter (86), lives with them | |
| White | Catherine R. | | | | alone | |
| White | John | | | | | |
| White | John | | | | | |

| 1 | 2 | 10 | 11 | 12 | 13 | 14 |
|---|---|---|---|---|---|---|
| SURNAME | GIVEN NAME | CHILDREN'S NAMES | CHILDREN'S AGES | CHILDREN'S BIRTHPLACES | LIVES WITH WHOM | RELATIONSHIP |
| Whitney | Cora, Mrs. | Mrs. Florence King | 25 | IN | | |
| Whitson | Charlotte | | | | | |
| Wiatt | Martha A. | | | | alone | |
| Wiatt | Martha A. | | | | | |
| Wieberts | Richard | | | | wife & child | |
| Wilhite | George A. | Marry Carnes | 13 | CA | Trimon Candlot | |
| Wilke | Irene | | | | alone | |
| Wilkerson | John F. | | | | alone | |
| Willcox | Eliza | Mrs. J. J. Groves | | | | |
| Williams | Cynthia, Mrs. | Fred; Ruth; James; Helen | 12; 8; 5; 1 yr. 2 mos. | TN; CA; CA; CA | | |
| Williams | George W. & Sarah A. | | | | wife | |
| Williams | Ira T., Mrs. | | 50 | | John Robinson | |
| Williams | J. W., Mr. & Mrs. | | | | | |
| Williams | Mary | | | | alone | |
| Williams | Wm | | | | | |
| Williams | Mary Ann | | | | alone | |
| Willis | Ada, Mrs. (children) | Adah; Freda; Evelyn; George; Ruth; Homer; Donald; Mervin | 4; 2; 3; 6; 8; 10; 12; 15 | 4 in Santa Rosa; 4 in CO | 6 children | |
| Wilson | Anthony | | | | alone | |
| Wilson | Anton | | | | | |
| Wilson | Charles K., Mrs. | | | | alone | |
| Wilson | Charles Sovrin | | | | alone | |
| Wilson | Florence, Mrs. | | 2; 5 mos. | | | |
| Wilson | Florence, Mrs. | girls | 9; 7; 5 | | | parents |
| Wilson | Lillie, Mrs. | Iva; Roy; Alice; Lester; Freddie | 13; 12; 10; 8; 6 | CND | | |
| Wilson | Lilly | Iva M.; Roy E.; Ione E.; | 12; 10; 8; 6; 4 | British Columbia, | children | |

| 1 | 2 | 10 | 11 | 12 | 13 | 14 |
|---|---|---|---|---|---|---|
| SURNAME | GIVEN NAME | CHILDREN'S NAMES | CHILDREN'S AGES | CHILDREN'S BIRTHPLACES | LIVES WITH WHOM | RELATIONSHIP |
| Wilson | Lilly | Lester E.; Feddie N. | | CND | children | |
| Wilson | Lilly, Mrs. | Iva M; Roy E.; Alice; Lester; Fred E. | 14; 12; 11; 9; 7 | B. C., CND | alone | |
| Wilson | P. L. | Iva May; Roy Edward; Iona Alice; Lester Franklin; Frederick White | 11; 9; 8; 6; 4 | Vancouver, BC | wife | |
| Wilson | Sarah, Mrs. | Frank; Wm.; Orrie Anderson | all grown | CA; CA; CA | | |
| Winslow | John | | | | | |
| Winter | Bernhardt | | 8 | | A. Stockburger | |
| Winter | Bernhardt | adopted | abt. 9 yrs. | GER | Stokburger | |
| Winton | Robert F. | | | | | |
| Winton | Robert F. | | | | | |
| Woldvogel | Mary | Joseph | 22 | | | |
| Wolfe | N. T. | | | | | |
| Wolfe | N. T. | | | | | |
| Wolfe | N. T. & Catherine | | | | | |
| Wood | Jane | | | | alone | |
| Wood | Jane, Mrs. | | | | | |
| Wood | John | | | | | |
| Wood | John | | | | with aged wife | |
| Wood | John & Mary Jane | | | | | |
| Wood | W. E., Mrs. | Edna Walters | 12 yrs. 6 mos.; born 29 July 1896 | Nevada Co., CA | grandchild | |
| Woodley | Josie | George; Donald; Vivian | 5; 2 ½; 18 mos. | Napa, CA | | |
| Woods | Katie | Thomas; Victoria; Walter | 4; 2; 9 mos. | 1 in Stockton, CA; 2 in Santa Rosa | children | |
| Woods | Katie, Mrs. | Thomas; Victoria; Walter | 3; 1 ½; 4 mos. | 2 in Stockton, CA; 2 in Santa Rosa | | |

## Part III

surname, given name, reason for application, property owned, habits of sobriety, source of income, amount of money requested (R$), date of request (day, month, year), amount of award/comments

| 1 | 2 | 15 | 16 | 17 | 18 | 19 | 20 | 21 | 22 | 23 |
|---|---|---|---|---|---|---|---|---|---|---|
| SURNAME | GIVEN NAME | REASON FOR REQUEST | PROPER-TY | SOBRI-ETY | SOURCE OF INCOME | R $ | | DATE OF REQUEST | | AMOUNT AWARDED/ COMMENTS |
| Abino | Rosania | disability of her leg | none | good | none | 5 | 24 | Mar. | 1900 | |
| Adams | J. W. | invalid; unable to work; | | | | | 5 | Aug. | 1889 | |
| Adams | Melissa, Mrs. | blind; unable to work | none | good | none | 8 | 4 | Apr. | 1900 | $6.00 on 4 Apr. 1900 |
| Adams | W. J. | some kind of cancerous disease | | | | | 3 | Feb. | 1890 | |
| Adams | W. J. | sick and unable to work; destitute | | | | | | | 1892 | |
| Albertson | Iver | sick for 10 months and unable to work | none | good | none | 15 | 10 | July | 1911 | $15.00 10 July 1911 |
| Alexander | Ada Lue, Mrs. | no income | none | good | none | 10 | | | 1900 | $6.00 May 1900 |
| Alexander | Lou Humphreys, Mrs. | | small residence | good | none | 8 | 15 | Mar. | 1913 | |
| Allan | Maude, Mrs. | | none | | none | 15 | | | | $15.00 11 Dec. 1916 |
| Allen | Bessie May | orphan; sister 15 or 16, unable to support both of them | | | | | 9 | Oct. | 1890 | |
| Allen | W. H. | sick | none | good | none | 6 | 2 | May | 1915 | $6.00 13 Aug. 1915 |
| Alsved | Louisa, Mrs. | no work & husband sick | 2 ½ acres | good | none | 8 | 18 | Sept. | 1900 | $6.00 3 Oct. 1900 |
| Alway | Abby, Mrs. | old age | none | good | none | 10 | 11 | Mar. | 1913 | |
| Amwell(e) | Letta | sick & unable to work; husband's whereabouts unknown | none | good | what Tony is able to earn | 8 | 4 | Mar. | 1907 | $8.00 7 Mar. 1907 |
| Andersen | Thomas & wife | man confined to bed, no one to help | none | good | none | 8 | 6 | July | 1912 | $8.00 5 Aug. 1912 |
| Anderson | John P. | old age; bodily | none | strict | | 5 | | | | $5.00 8 July 1892; |

| 1 | 2 | 15 | 16 | 17 | 18 | 19 | 20 | 21 | 22 | 23 |
|---|---|---|---|---|---|---|---|---|---|---|
| SURNAME | GIVEN NAME | REASON FOR REQUEST | PROPER-TY | SOBRI-ETY | SOURCE OF INCOME | R $ | | DATE OF REQUEST | | AMOUNT AWARDED/ COMMENTS |
| | | infirmity | | sobriety | | | | | | came to CA in 1871; was postmaster of Mark West |
| Anderson | Louisa | no means of support | | strict sobriety | none | 5 | | | | $5.00 2 Feb. 1892 |
| Anderson | Mary | old and unable to work | some furniture | strict sobriety | none | 5 | | | | $5.00 8 July 1892 |
| Andrews | Carrie | husband does not contribute to support children | none | good | none | 25 | | | | $10.00 8 Sept. 1914 |
| Andrews | Elizabeth, Mrs. | | | | | | | | | $7.00 9 Jan. 1892 |
| Anker | Erik | old age | none | strictly temper-ance | none | 12 | 19 | Feb. | 1917 | $6.00 12 Mar. 1917 |
| Anker | Peter & wife | in county hospital; unable to work; wife almost deaf | home; lot heavily mortgaged | good | none | 12 | 3 | Aug. | 1912 | $12.00 6 Aug. 1912 |
| Anker | Peter & wife | old age | house; barn; 3 lots mortgaged | good | none | 10 | | | | $10.00 8 Mar. 1915 |
| Antone | Peter | sick | none | good | none | 10 | 4 | Feb. | 1908 | filed 5 Feb. 1909 |
| Archer | N. A., Mrs. | old | home mortgaged | good | none | 10 | 18 | Mar. | 1912 | $8.00 6 Apr. 1912 |
| Archer | N. A., Mrs. | children are mentally weak and totally dependent | | good | occasional charity from friends | 15 | 31 | Mar. | 1913 | |
| Arnett | Alice | cannot support children on what little work she is able to get | 3 acres Shasta County | good | none | 15 | 1 | Feb. | 1915 | |
| Arnett | John H. | old and debilitated | none | good | none | 10 | 31 | Dec. | 1912 | $10.00 9 Jan. 1913 |

| 1 SURNAME | 2 GIVEN NAME | 15 REASON FOR REQUEST | 16 PROPERTY | 17 SOBRIETY | 18 SOURCE OF INCOME | 19 R $ | 20 | 21 DATE OF REQUEST | 22 | 23 AMOUNT AWARDED/ COMMENTS |
|---|---|---|---|---|---|---|---|---|---|---|
| Arnold | Joe, Mrs. | destitute and unable to earn living deserted by husband | | | | | 17 | Nov. | 1890 | |
| Arnold | T. J., Mrs. | unable to help herself | none | good | none | 8 | 8 | Dec. | 1913 | |
| Arnold | Temassah | unable to support herself and children | none | good | house work | 10 | 1 | Feb. | 1913 | |
| Ash | Arethusa, Mrs. | no way to support grandsons | none | | none | 10 | 22 | Mar. | 1918 | $10.00 8 Apr. 1918 |
| Asman | Louis, Mrs. | ill | none | good | none | 11 | 2 | Feb. | 1909 | $11.00 3 Mar. 1909 |
| Asman | Louise | poor health; unable to perform sufficient work | some real estate; no income from it | good | none | 11 | 7 | Feb. | 1910 | $10.00 1910 |
| Asmussen | Alfred, Mrs. | husband not able to work | none | good | $20.00/mo. for janitor work | 8 | 9 | Mar. | 1915 | |
| Azevedo | Manuel | partly paralyzed; unable to work | none | good | none | 8 | 31 | Dec. | 1914 | |
| Badgley | Edgar Jasper | prolonged sickness | 8 acres mortgaged | good | none | 10 | 31 | Jan. | 1914 | $10.00 2 Feb. 1914 |
| Bailey | James | unable to work | small house & lot | sober | | 6 | 2 | June | 1900 | $5.00 4 June 1900 |
| Bailey | Samuel H. | physical disability following paralysis | none | sober | none | 8 | 2 | June | 1915 | $8.00 15 June 1915 |
| Bailey | William | feeble and indigent | cabin on the bay | | | 6 | 17 | Nov. | 1891 | $5.00 8 Dec. 1891; resided Bodega Bay 30+ years |
| Bain | Mrs. | invalid with rheumatism; children | | | | | 4 | May | 1886 | |

| 1 | 2 | 15 | 16 | 17 | 18 | 19 | 20 | 21 | 22 | 23 |
|---|---|---|---|---|---|---|---|---|---|---|
| SURNAME | GIVEN NAME | REASON FOR REQUEST | PROPERTY | SOBRIETY | SOURCE OF INCOME | R $ | | DATE OF REQUEST | | AMOUNT AWARDED/ COMMENTS |
| Bainbridge | Benj. | unable to help | | | | | | | | |
| Baker | Elvira J. | unable to work at present | none | good | none | | | Oct. | 1912 | $6.00 9 Oct. 1912 |
| Balzari | Rosa | old age; no means of support | 10 acres with no improvements | good | US pension $12.00 mo. | 10 | 15 | Mar. | 1913 | |
| Barker | John | | none | no habits | | 6 | | | | |
| Barnes | J. R., Mrs. | old and unable to work | none | good | none | 4 | 6 | July | 1910 | |
| Barnes | Peggy | unable to work; needs to take care of sick brother | none | the best | none | 10 | 1 | May | 1916 | $10.00 13 May 1916 |
| Barnes | Peggy | no means of support | | | | | 22 | June | 1888 | |
| Barnes | Wm. | old age | | | | 5 | | | | $5.00 3 Mar. 1890 |
| Barry | Anna | rheumatism | none | good | | 8 | 9 | May | 1884 | |
| Bartlow | Emma, Mrs. | poor health | none | good | none | 30 | 7 | Dec. | 1899 | $5.00 2 Jan. 1900 |
| Bartow | Helen, Mrs. | elderly | none | good | none except her labor | 8 | 6 | Aug. | 1915 | rejected |
| Battaglia | Mary | sick | none | good | none | 12 | 16 | Nov. | 1914 | $8.00 9 Dec. 1914 |
| Batten | Christina | sick | small house | exemplary | none | | 19 | Aug. | 1909 | $7.00 21 Aug. 1909 |
| Batten | Cora | old age | none | good | none | 10 | | | | $10.00 15 Aug. 1910 |
| Batten | Cora | destitute and unable to earn enough | none | | | 10 | | | | $10.00 27 May 1913 |
| Baxman | Lewis | have to board children out | | | | 10 | | Feb. | 1890 | 25 Feb. 1890 |
| | | blind; unable to earn livelihood | | | | | | | | |

| 1 | 2 | 15 | 16 | 17 | 18 | 19 | 20 | 21 | 22 | 23 |
|---|---|---|---|---|---|---|---|---|---|---|
| SURNAME | GIVEN NAME | REASON FOR REQUEST | PROPERTY | SOBRIETY | SOURCE OF INCOME | R $ | | DATE OF REQUEST | | AMOUNT AWARDED/ COMMENTS |
| Beansford | Ida B. | invalid | none | good | none | 8 | | Mar. | 1913 | |
| Beckett | Mrs. | destitute | none | | | | 6 | Oct. | 1885 | |
| Bee | Alice, Mrs. | destitute | none | | none | | 3 | Mar. | 1891 | $7.50 4 Mar. 1891 |
| Bee | Alice, Mrs. | poor health | | | | | | | | $ 7.50 10 Sept. 1892 |
| Bee | Mary A. | heart trouble | none | good | none | 10 | 4 | Jan. | 1911 | $8.00 7 Jan. 1911 |
| Bee | Mary A. | dislocated shoulder and weak right arm | none | good | none | 8 | 8 | Mar. | 1913 | described herself as "Grass Widow" |
| Bee | Mary, Mrs. | deserted by husband, Millard; cannot support herself & children | house rent free | | | | 27 | July | 1884 | |
| Beebe | T. J. | blind and unable to work | none | yes | none | 17 | 5 | Nov. | 1899 | |
| Beebe | Thomas J. | blind since age 7 | none | sober | none | 10 | 3 | Mar. | 1913 | |
| Bell | Mary | sick and unable to work | | | | 10 | | | | $8.00 3 Oct. 1892 |
| Bell | Peter & Clara E. | old age; poor health | none | good | none | 10 | 15 | Feb. | 1916 | $10.00 13 Mar. 1916 |
| Bemiss | Sam | unable to work; rheumatism | none | has drunk some; will abstain in future | none | 6 | 21 | Jan. | 1915 | $6.00 28 Jan. 1915 |
| Bemiss | Samuel | rheumatism in both legs | none | good | none | 6 | | Oct. | 1915 | rejected |
| Bemiss | Samuel | | none | used to drink but sworn off | none | 7 | 26 | July | 1915 | rejected |
| Bemiss | Samuel | rheumatism in legs and hips | none | good | none | 7 | | | | |
| Bemiss | Samuel | rheumatism in knee | none | good | none | 8 | | | | $5.00 6 Feb. 1911 |
| Benson | Mathis Charles | lung trouble | none | good | none | 20 | 8 | Mar. | 1916 | $20.00 13 Mar. |

| 1 | 2 | 15 | 16 | 17 | 18 | 19 | 20 | 21 | 22 | 23 |
|---|---|---|---|---|---|---|---|---|---|---|
| SURNAME | GIVEN NAME | REASON FOR REQUEST | PROPER-TY | SOBRI-ETY | SOURCE OF INCOME | R $ | | DATE OF REQUEST | | AMOUNT AWARDED/ COMMENTS |
| | | | | | | | | | | 1916 |
| Bentel | Bertha | E. Scott, blind, deaf, dumb, 1 leg and arm off; Elsie, muscular rheumatism | | | | 15 | 12 | Feb. | 1917 | $15.00 12 Feb. 1917 |
| Berlin | David & Agnes | man feeble; wife in bad health | | | | | 13 | Jan. | 1892 | $8.00 2 Feb. 1892 |
| Berry | (children) | mother, Emma, died; ask continued support of children | | | | 20 | 1 | Nov. | 1890 | withdrawn 8 Nov. 1890 |
| Berry | Emma, Mrs. | unable to earn enough | | | | 10 | 9 | Feb. | 1890 | $10.00 14 Feb. 1890 |
| Berryessa | Jacinto | physical disability; unable to earn living | none | good | none | 7 | 21 | Mar. | 1913 | |
| Berryessa | Jacinto | | none | good | | 7 | | | | |
| Berwert | Frank | sick | none | good | none | 8 | 25 | Jan. | 1912 | $8.00 6 Feb. 1912 |
| Betrix | Emile | consumption | | | | | 7 | May | 1907 | $10.00 2 Mar. 1907 |
| Bilow | Anna, Mrs. | paralyzed on right side | none | none | none | 8 | 18 | Nov. | 1901 | $5.00 4 Dec. 1901 |
| Binder | Charles | lost eye sight; petition to enter County Hospital | | | | | 30 | Oct. | 1897 | |
| Binegar | W. L. | crippled | none | good | none | 5 | 1 | Mar. | 1911 | $5.00 8 Mar. 1911 |
| Biret | Grace | poor health | none | yes | none | 8 | | | 1911 | $8.00 8 Nov. 1911 |
| Birkhoff | C. | taking care of children; wife ill | | | none | | 23 | Apr. | 1909 | $12.00 26 Apr. 1909 |
| Bish | Abraham | sick | none | good | none | 5 | 15 | Mar. | 1900 | $5.00 19 Mar. 1900 |
| Bishop | George W. | unable to work | none | temperate | none | 5 | 29 | June | 1900 | $5.00 6 July 1900 |
| Bishop | Mattie | unable to work | none | good | non | 5 | 30 | Mar. | 1900 | $5.00 5 Apr. 1900 |
| Black | Sarah | unable to work | none | sober | none | 6 | 20 | Feb. | 1915 | $6.00 8 Mar. 1915 |
| Blair | John | feeble, blind | | | | | 1 | Apr. | 1907 | |

| 1 | 2 | 15 | 16 | 17 | 18 | 19 | 20 | 21 | 22 | 23 |
|---|---|---|---|---|---|---|---|---|---|---|
| SURNAME | GIVEN NAME | REASON FOR REQUEST | PROPER-TY | SOBRI-ETY | SOURCE OF INCOME | R $ | | DATE OF REQUEST | | AMOUNT AWARDED/ COMMENTS |
| Blake | E. M., Mrs. | heart trouble | none | good | none | 10 | 10 | June | 1914 | $6.00 3 Aug. 1914 |
| Blank | Cord, Mrs. | husband recently died | | | | | | | 1891 | filed 3 Mar. 1891; $10.00 |
| Blank | Cord, Mrs. | | | | | 10 | | | | $8.00 5 Jan. 1892 |
| Bledsoe | Thomas | unable to work | none | good | none | 8 | 27 | Apr. | 1914 | $8.00 29 Apr. 1914 |
| Blele | Christian O. | old age; limbs sore; cannot work | none | sober | none | 6 | 3 | Aug. | 1914 | $6.00 15 Sept. 1914 |
| Boids | Erminia | husb. went away; old age | house heavily mortgaged | good | none | | 6 | Jan. | 1909 | $6.00 8 Jan. 1909 |
| Borgwardt | A. | consumption | | | | 8 | 3 | Dec. | 1892 | $8.00 7 Dec. 1892 |
| Bowman | Francis J. | unable to work; cares for invalid son | household furniture | sober | none | 20 | 13 | Apr. | 1910 | $10.00 14 Apr. 1910 |
| Boyd | Ben, Mrs. | husband in county jail | | | | 10 | | | | $6.00 7 June 1892 |
| Boyd | W. M., Mrs. | desertion | none | good | none | 25 | 2 | Oct. | 1913 | $25.00 9 Oct. 1913 |
| Bradford | Herbert | sick | none | | none | 5 | | | 1900 | $5.00 4 Sept. 1900 |
| Bransford | Ida | helpless; cannot walk | none | good | none | | | | | $8.00 27 July 1912 |
| Bray | E. C. | sick, unable to work | none | | $8.00 Mexican War pension | | 1 | Aug. | 1892 | 30 year resident of county |
| Bray | Elisha G. | old age | none | good | Pension | 8 | 31 | Mar. | 1900 | $2.00 2 Apr. 1900 |
| Breaks | Charles H. | sick; 5 children to support | none | good | none | 5 | 17 | Mar. | 1900 | $5.00 20 Mar. 1900 |
| Bremer | Caroline | poor health; unable to work | none | good | none | 5 | 2 | Dec. | 1899 | not allowed 4 Dec. 1899 |
| Breshear | Clara | deserted by husband; feeble health | none | good | small earnings | 15 | | | | $10.00 4 Apr, 1910 |
| Brimigian | Samuel | old age; rheumatism; | none | sober | none | 8 | 3 | Mar. | 1913 | |

| 1 | 2 | 15 | 16 | 17 | 18 | 19 | 20 | 21 | 22 | 23 |
|---|---|---|---|---|---|---|---|---|---|---|
| SURNAME | GIVEN NAME | REASON FOR REQUEST | PROPER-TY | SOBRI-ETY | SOURCE OF INCOME | R $ | | DATE OF REQUEST | | AMOUNT AWARDED/ COMMENTS |
| Broomhall | John | unable to work | | | | | | | | |
| Brown | Amanda, Mrs. | feeble and unable to do heavy work | none | good | $30.00 per quarter | 10 | 12 | Mar. | 1907 | $8.00 2 May 1907 |
| Brown | Charlotte | unable to work | none | good | none | 5 | 31 | May | 1900 | |
| Brown | Charlotte, Mrs. | old age | none | good | Civil War pension $12.00 | 10 | 13 | Mar. | 1913 | |
| Brown | F. L., Mrs. | rheumatism | none | good | pension | 10 | | | 1909 | $8.00 24 May 1909 |
| Brown | Fanny, Mrs. | child is sickly and needs mother at home | none | good | none | 8 | 10 | Mar. | 1910 | $7.00 10 Mar. 1910 |
| Brown | M., Mrs. | destitute | | | | | 7 | Aug. | 1889 | $24.00 2 Feb. 1914 |
| Brown | Nancy | poor health | none | good | none | | | | | |
| Browning | Tandy | can only work part-time | none | sober | none | 5 | 6 | Mar. | 1913 | |
| Bruce | Florence I. | unable to work | cottage and 2 acres | good | none | 5 | | | 1899 | $5.00 5 June 1899 |
| Brunk | Margaret, Miss | unable to support her children | none | good | none | 20 | 22 | June | 1910 | $12.00 7 July 1910 |
| Bryant | Rachael | unable to work | | ok | $10.00 per month from Masonic Lodge | 8 | 5 | Dec. | 1900 | $5.00 15 Dec. 1900 |
| Bryant | Rachel J., Mrs. | raising grandchild | none | good | small gratuity from Masons | 7 | 14 | Mar. | 1913 | |
| Buckland | Mary J., Mrs. | cripple, unable to work | none | good | none | 7 | 1 | Aug. | 1909 | $7.00 4 Aug. 1909 |
| | | | | | | 8 | | Mar. | 1900 | $5.00 23 Mar. 1900 |

| 1 | 2 | 15 | 16 | 17 | 18 | 19 | 20 | 21 | 22 | 23 |
|---|---|---|---|---|---|---|---|---|---|---|
| SURNAME | GIVEN NAME | REASON FOR REQUEST | PROPER-TY | SOBRI-ETY | SOURCE OF INCOME | R $ | | DATE OF REQUEST | | AMOUNT AWARDED/ COMMENTS |
| Buckner | Mary J. | poor health; friend unable to support her | | | | 10 | 2 | Dec. | 1889 | |
| Buckner | Mary J., Mrs. | rheumatism for 6 yrs. | | | | 8 | | | | $6.00 filed 1 Mar. 1890 |
| Buckner | Mary Jane | sick & old | none in this state (Illinois) | sober | small gifts occasionally | 6 | | | | $5.00 6 Apr. 1891 |
| Buell | Lillian | lame | none | | none | 75/yr | 28 | May | 1914 | filed 13 June 1914 widowed 4 years |
| Bulotti | James | sick & destitute | | | non | | 4 | Apr. | 1911 | $6.00 4 Apr. 1911 |
| Burke | (children) | both parents sick | | | | | | | | $10.00 9 Dec. 1891 |
| Burkhardt | Joseph & Margaret | infirm and unable to support themselves | | | | | 29 | Jan. | 1886 | |
| Bums | John J. | lost leg & hand; partially blind | none | sober | none | 10 | | | | $10.00 11May 1916 |
| Burns | Sarah | sick & unable to work | none | very good | none | 10 | | | | $8.00 |
| Burns | Thomas | old age | none | temperate | none | 8 | 12 | June | 1900 | $5.00 6 July 1900 |
| Bush | J. J., Mrs. | not able to work | none | good | none | 8 | 28 | Apr. | 1917 | $11.00 2 May 1917 |
| Butler | A. M. | sick & unable to work for more than 5 weeks | none | good | none | 12 | 10 | Feb. | 1916 | $12.00 16 Feb. 1916 |
| Butler | Bettie | sick; dau. seriously ill | | | | 8 | 27 | Mar. | 1891 | $8.00 6 Apr. 1891 |
| Butler | Mr. & Mrs. | sick & unable to work | none | good | none | 8 | 28 | Dec. | 1906 | |
| Butts | John W. | unable to work; wife confined to bed; he must take care of her & children | | sober | | | 2 | Mar. | 1891 | $6.00 3 Mar. 1891 |
| Byrnes | Jennie | poor health | none | good | none | 10 | 17 | Nov. | 1916 | |
| Cadd | Edwin | invalid | none | good | $100 per | 10 | | Apr. | 1914 | $10.00 5 May 1914 |

| 1 SURNAME | 2 GIVEN NAME | 15 REASON FOR REQUEST | 16 PROPERTY | 17 SOBRIETY | 18 SOURCE OF INCOME | 19 R $ | 20 | 21 DATE OF REQUEST | 22 | 23 AMOUNT AWARDED/ COMMENTS |
|---|---|---|---|---|---|---|---|---|---|---|
| | | | | | year | | | | | |
| Cadden | Thomas | old age & sickness | none | good | none | 20 | 1 | May | 1912 | $8.00 1912 |
| Cain | Robert M. | too old & feeble to work | none | good | none | 10 | | | | $10.00 11 May 1916 |
| Camario | Fernando | unable to work; feeble | none | sober | none | 8 | 20 | Nov. | 1916 | $8.00 12 Dec. 1916 |
| Cambra | M. J. & family | injured at work; carpenter | | | father's work | | | | | $10.00 8 Sept. 1891 |
| Camenzina | Joseph | sickness of self & wife | none | good | none | 8 | 22 | Sept. | 1916 | $8.00 11 Oct. 1916 |
| Cameron | Douglas | nearly blind and in bad health | none | good | $12.00 per month | 12 | 14 | Nov. | 1910 | $8.00 14 Nov. 1910 |
| Cameron | Mary | sickness | no | temperence | $12.00 per month from Civil War | 12 | 14 | Mar. | 1913 | |
| Campbell | Mary E. | destitute | | | small pension | | 3 | Nov. | 1891 | $5.00 3 Nov. 1891; widow of L. L. Campbell |
| Campbell | T. T., Mrs. | worthy of support | | | | | 5 | July | 1890 | $5.00 7 July 1890 |
| Capell | Susan Francis | invalid | about ½ acre with small house | good | none | 8 | 31 | May | 1900 | $5.00 5 June 1900 |
| Capell | Susan Francis | invalid; unable to work | ½ acre with small house | sober | proceeds of a few chickens | 8 | | | | $5.00 3 July 1899 |
| Capponi | Elena | not able to earn living | | | $20.00 board | | 17 | Nov. | 1917 | |
| Capponi | Elena | old age & infirm | none | good | none | | | | | not recommended 15 Jan. 1917 |

-108-

| 1 | 2 | 15 | 16 | 17 | 18 | 19 | 20 | 21 | 22 | 23 |
|---|---|---|---|---|---|---|---|---|---|---|
| SURNAME | GIVEN NAME | REASON FOR REQUEST | PROPERTY | SOBRIETY | SOURCE OF INCOME | R $ | | DATE OF REQUEST | | AMOUNT AWARDED/ COMMENTS |
| Capponi | Enrico & wife | Enrico pharbaseid (sic); Elena rheumatism | none | good | none | 10 | | | | $10.00 12 July 1916 |
| Capri | Rosa | sick from change of life | none | good | none | | 12 | Nov. | 1912 | $6.00 10 Dec. 1912 |
| Capri | Rosa | son an invalid; unable to work | small cabin in Healdsburg | good | | | | | 1919 | $5.00 25 Feb. 1919 for 3 months only |
| Capucci | Marie Gianpietri | sickness | none | good | none | 6 | | | 1913 | $6.00 6 May 1913 |
| Capucci | Mary | husband left | none | good | | | 2 | July | 1909 | $5.00 July 1909 |
| Capucci | Mary, Mrs. | ill health; unable to work | none | sober | none | 8 | | | | rejected 6 Mar. 1916 |
| Caretto | Peter | bronchitis & lungs | none | good | none | 8 | | | | |
| Carillo | Vincento | getting old | none | good | none | 8 | 24 | Mar. | 1900 | $6.00 26 Mar. 1900 |
| Carlson | John | almost blind | none | sober | none | 6 | 20 | Mar. | 1910 | $6.00 4 Apr. 1910 |
| Carlson | John | old age; unable to work | none | good | none | 8 | | | | |
| Carr | James | ill health & old age | none | good | none | 10 | 26 | Sept. | 1890 | |
| Carrell | Ethel, Mrs. | husband in jail? | | good | | 30 | 8 | Apr. | 1916 | $25.00 11 Apr. 1916 |
| Carriger | Elizabeth, Mrs. | disabled; back trouble; destitute; no friends | | | 16 yr. old works half-time | | | | | |
| Carrillo | Joaquin | old & not able to feed family | little house and lot | | none | | 2 | July | 1888 | |
| Carrillo | Joaquin | in poor health; unable to work | | | | | | | | $15.00 3 Mar. 1890 |
| Carstensen | Henry | ill health & sick wife | none | good | none | 10 | 23 | May | 1912 | $10.00 4 June 1912 |
| Carstensen | Henry & wife | invalids | none | good | none | 10 | 22 | Mar. | 1913 | |
| Casares | Laura, Mrs. | no means of support; caring for children and aged father | none | | none | | 5 | May | 1890 | |

| 1 | 2 | 15 | 16 | 17 | 18 | 19 | 20 | 21 | 22 | 23 |
|---|---|---|---|---|---|---|---|---|---|---|
| SURNAME | GIVEN NAME | REASON FOR REQUEST | PROPERTY | SOBRIETY | SOURCE OF INCOME | R $ | | DATE OF REQUEST | | AMOUNT AWARDED/ COMMENTS |
| Caton | Anna | | none | | | | | | | $5.00 6 July 1900 |
| Cavalli | Irene, Mrs. | separated from husband; unable to work and care for children | | | $25/mo. | | 30 | Jan. | 1915 | |
| Chaffee | Homer H. | sick | none | none | none | 8 | 1 | Apr. | 1915 | $8.00 13 Apr. 1915 |
| Chaffee | Jarvis | sick & unable to work | none | good | none | 8 | 29 | Mar. | 1900 | $5.00 2 Apr. 1900 |
| Charity | John | sick | none | good | none | 10 | 4 | Feb. | 1909 | $6.00 5 Feb. 1909 |
| Charles | M. L. | infirmities of old age | none | good | little | | 25 | Apr. | 1893 | b. Guilford Co., NC |
| Charles | M. L. | feeble | | | | | | | | $ 10.00 12 Sept. 1892; carpenter |
| Charles | Martin Luther | old age, ill health | none | good | none | 8 | 23 | Mar. | 1900 | $7.00 27 Mar. 1900 |
| Chase | N. G., Mrs. | sick; can't work | none | good | none | 8 | 8 | Aug. | 1911 | $6.00 4 Oct. 1911 |
| Chicca | Americo | broken leg | | good | none | 8 | 16 | May | 1914 | $8.00 4 June 1914 |
| Childres | Ruann, Mrs. | to support clothes, school gr-gr-granddau. | own home | good | none | 8 | 23 | Feb. | 1916 | rejected |
| Christensen | Anna M. | father burned home at Preston; in county jail awaiting trial | none | good | collection taken up for them | 8 | 7 | Feb. | 1912 | $20.00 4 Mar. 1912 |
| Christensen | C. P. | partial blindness | lot with small cabin & house | | rental house | | 13 | Mar. | 1918 | recommended Mr. Christensen's sons provide for him |
| Clanton | Rose Velmer | unable through affliction to properly care for herself | none | good | none | 10 | 25 | Apr. | 1916 | $10.00 11 May 1916 |
| Clapp | Florence | husband sick; no work | none | sober | none | 10 | 11 | Dec. | 1916 | $10.00 12 Dec. 1916 |
| Clark | Ellena, Mrs. | chronic disease; physically incapacitated | | | | | 1 | Dec. | 1892 | $5.00 7 Dec. 1892 |

| 1 | 2 | 15 | 16 | 17 | 18 | 19 | 20 | 21 | 22 | 23 |
|---|---|---|---|---|---|---|---|---|---|---|
| SURNAME | GIVEN NAME | REASON FOR REQUEST | PROPER-TY | SOBRI-ETY | SOURCE OF INCOME | R $ | | DATE OF REQUEST | | AMOUNT AWARDED/ COMMENTS |
| Clark | J. H., Mr. & Mrs. | right arm & leg broken one year ago | none | good | none | 12 | 25 | Feb. | 1901 | $8.00 6 Mar. 1901 |
| Clay | Ann, Mrs. | destitute | | | | 10 | | | | increased from $5.00 to $10.00 19 Oct. 1891 |
| Clay | Annie, Mrs. | dangerously ill; unable to work | none | | none | 15 | 9 | July | 1891 | |
| Clements | Maria | old age | none | good | none | 8 | 16 | Sept. | 1907 | $7.00 9 Oct. 1907 |
| Clements | Mary | old age; no means of support | none | good | none | 8 | 3 | Mar. | 1913 | |
| Clinesmith | Mary | physical condition prevents working | none | good | none | 10 | 21 | Aug. | 1914 | $10.00 31 Aug. 1914 |
| Cloer | Sarah | | none | good | none | 10 | 21 | Jan. | 1909 | $6.00 6 Feb. 1909 |
| Cloer | Sarah C. | invalid; unable to walk | none | good | pension $12 per month | 10 | 13 | Mar. | 1913 | |
| Coburn | Lulu, Mrs. | not strong enough to work | none | good | none | 5 | 31 | Mar. | 1900 | $5.00 2 Apr. 1900 |
| Cody | Thomas Michle | ill health | none | good | none | 10 | | | | |
| Coffer | E. M., Mrs. | heart trouble | none | good | none | 5 | 5 | Mar. | 1913 | |
| Coffey | Clara Bell - see H. C. Kirpatrick | | none | good | none | | | | | |
| Collins | Charles T. | poor health; unable to work | none | good | none | 30 | 17 | May | 1915 | |
| Combs | Robert R. | unable to work | | good | none | 10 | 12 | Mar. | 1913 | |
| Comstock | B. F. | cripple & ill health | none | good | none | 5 | 2 | Aug. | 1900 | $4.00 3 Aug. 1900 |
| Conklin | I., Mrs. | in poor health | | | supported for last 2 years by | 10 | 26 | Apr. | 1886 | |

| 1 | 2 | 15 | 16 | 17 | 18 | 19 | 20 | 21 | 22 | 23 |
|---|---|---|---|---|---|---|---|---|---|---|
| SURNAME | GIVEN NAME | REASON FOR REQUEST | PROPERTY | SOBRIETY | SOURCE OF INCOME | R $ | | DATE OF REQUEST | | AMOUNT AWARDED/ COMMENTS |
| | | | | | citizens of Forestville | | | | | |
| Conkling | Fannie | bad eyesight | none | good | none | 12 | 20 | Mar. | 1913 | $8.00 7 Nov. 1912 |
| Conners | Thomas | feebleness & old age | none | good | none | 10 | | | | |
| Connor | Thomas | unable to work | none | good | none | 10 | 26 | Mar. | 1913 | $6.00 |
| Cook | Ella | has consumption and not able to earn living | none | good | none | 6 | 15 | July | 1901 | |
| Cook | Ella, Mrs. | unable to work | none | good | | 8 | 24 | Mar. | 1900 | $5.00 3 Apr. 1900 |
| Cook | Jesse | paralyzed; totally disabled; husband deserted her | none | the best | none | 15 | 28 | July | 1914 | $15.00 8 Aug. 1914 |
| Cook | Madelia | father away | none | good | poorly supported by father | 15 | 10 | Dec. | 1911 | $8.00 11 Dec. 1911 |
| Cook | Solome, Mrs. | sick two years | none | | | | | | | $5.00 9 Dec. 1892 |
| Cooper | Robert F. | sick & unable to work | 40x120 ft. lot with small house | good | none | 8 | 4 | Mar. | 1901 | $8.00 |
| Cornett | Agnes, Mrs. | sick & unable to work | none | | none | 20 | 3 | Mar. | 1892 | $10.00 8 Mar. 1892 |
| Cornwall | Henrietta | | | | | 6 | 7 | Jan. | 1907 | |
| Corri | Joquin | heart condition | some chickens | | | | | | 1892 | $8.00 4 Aug. 1892; came to CA 1881 |
| Cotrell | (family) | paralyzed; epileptic fits | none | | | 20 | 4 | Apr. | 1879 | $15.00 8 Apr. 1879 |
| Cottey | Annie L. | husband deserted her; sick; needs money to care for children | none | good | none | 12 | 26 | May | 1910 | $10.00 8 June 1910 |
| Cotty | A., Mrs. | invalid | | | none | 8 | 3 | Mar. | 1914 | $8.00 6 Apr. 1914 |
| Coulson | Lucinda | husband deserted | none | good | none | 12 | | | | $10.00 7 Aug. 1907 |

| 1 | 2 | 15 | 16 | 17 | 18 | 19 | 20 | 21 | 22 | 23 |
|---|---|---|---|---|---|---|---|---|---|---|
| SURNAME | GIVEN NAME | REASON FOR REQUEST | PROPER-TY | SOBRI-ETY | SOURCE OF INCOME | R $ | | DATE OF REQUEST | | AMOUNT AWARDED/ COMMENTS |
| Cox | Ann E. | family | none | | none | 10 | | | | |
| Cox | J. J. | old age; sick | none | sober | none | 8 | 22 | Jan. | 1915 | $8.00 2 Feb. 1915 |
| Cox | William | helpless invalid | none | good | none | 12 | 29 | May | 1907 | $8.00 4 June 1907 |
| Coyle | Michael, Mrs. | husband's illness exhausted all means | | | | | 1 | Feb. | 1876 | petition accepted; husband died 27 Jan. 1876 |
| Crampton | Eugene R. | sickness; crippled with crutches; unable to find work | none | temperate | none | 15 | 11 | Nov. | 1916 | $15.00 14 Nov. 1916; 1920 census living in San Jose, owning a house |
| Crealy | George | failing eyesight | homestead | good | none | 8 | | | | |
| Cromwell | Rebeca, Mrs. | feeble health | | | | 5 | 6 | May | 1900 | $5.00 21 May 1909 |
| Cromwell | William T. | paralyzed | small house & lot | the best | none | | 4 | June | 1892 | $8.00 7 June 1892 |
| Crozier | P. B., Mrs. | unable to earn living | house & lot | good | none | 5 | 21 | Mar. | 1913 | |
| Culbertson | Alex | unable to work | none | good | none | 8 | 13 | Dec. | 1909 | $6.00 |
| Culbertson | Alexander | ill health | none | good | none | 6 | 8 | Nov. | 1900 | $5.00 6 Dec. 1900 |
| Culbertson | Alexander | infirm; unable to work | | good | none | 10 | 6 | Mar. | 1913 | |
| Culken | C. | sickness & disabled; Will has epilepsy fits; cannot be left alone. | none | good | older son gives $13.00 a week | 15 | 13 | Feb. | 1917 | $15.00 13 Feb 1917 |
| Cunningham | Mrs. | unable to work | | | | | 18 | Feb. | 1890 | $6.00 4 Mar. 1890 |
| Cunningham | Nettie | old age | house and lot mortgaged | good | none | 8 | 22 | June | 1910 | $8.00 13 July 1910 |

-113-

| 1 | 2 | 15 | 16 | 17 | 18 | 19 | 20 | 21 | 22 | 23 |
|---|---|---|---|---|---|---|---|---|---|---|
| SURNAME | GIVEN NAME | REASON FOR REQUEST | PROPER-TY | SOBRI-ETY | SOURCE OF INCOME | R $ | | DATE OF REQUEST | | AMOUNT AWARDED/ COMMENTS |
| Cunningham | Nettie | has tremor; unable to work | 2 houses mortgaged for $900 | all right | rent for houses $12 total | 8 | | Mar. | 1913 | $8.00 29 Apr. 1913 |
| Cunningham | W. A. & J. | old and unable to work | none | | none | | 11 | May | 1889 | |
| Curry | Patrick | blind & deserving | | | | 10 | 24 | May | 1883 | |
| Curry | Patrick | he's blind, wife unable to work | house & lot | sober | none | 10 | 8 | Feb. | 1890 | $10.00 3 Mar. 1890 |
| Curry | Patrick | blind | | | | 8 | 28 | Mar. | 1900 | $8.00 2 Apr. 1900 |
| Curry | Patrick | blind | | | | 15 | | | | request allowance be reinstated |
| Curry | Patrick & family | no means to provide | | | | 10 | 5 | May | 1880 | |
| Damerell | Rebecca, Mrs. | unable to support children | none | excellent | none | 8 | 5 | July | 1899 | $6.00 10 July, 1899 |
| Damrell | R., Mrs. | unable to work | none | good | none | 8 | 5 | Apr. | 1900 | $6.00 6 Apr. 1900 |
| Darden | George | unable to work sufficient to support self | none | temperate | none | 6 | 6 | June | 1900 | rejected 6 July 1900 |
| Dart | L., Mrs. | unable to support self | none | good | none | 10 | 6 | July | 1910 | $8.00 8 July 1910 |
| Dart | L., Mrs. | house burned; wife sick | none | good | works when able | 8 | 28 | June | 1913 | $8.00 8 July 1913 |
| Darwell | J. M. | paralyzed; means of support exhausted | | | working on the coast | | 2 | Sept. | 1890? | needs money to replace house for family |
| Davidson | Augustus W. | unable to work | little home encumber-ed | | none | 8 | 1 | Apr. | 1901 | $6.00 4 Apr. 1901 |
| Davis | C. H., Mrs. | children too young to | none | good | none | 15 | | | | $15.00 13 June 1916 |
| Davis | Grace | | none | good | none | 15 | 13 | Mar. | 1916 | $12.00 25 Mar. |

| 1 | 2 | 15 | 16 | 17 | 18 | 19 | 20 | 21 | 22 | 23 |
|---|---|---|---|---|---|---|---|---|---|---|
| SURNAME | GIVEN NAME | REASON FOR REQUEST | PROPERTY | SOBRIETY | SOURCE OF INCOME | R $ | | DATE OF REQUEST | | AMOUNT AWARDED/ COMMENTS |
| | | leave; no means of support | | | | | | | | 1916 |
| Davis | J., Mrs. | no support | | | | | 9 | Jan. | 1879 | $5.00 18 Nov. 1892; resident of state 16 yrs., county 11 yrs. |
| Davis | Manuel | feeble and unable to work | small cabin; 1/4 acre of poor land | good | none | 8 | 7 | Dec. | 1914 | $7.00 8 Jan. 1915 |
| Davis | Mary | unable to support herself & children | none | temperate | none | 12 | | | 1900 | $8.00 5 Sept. 1900 |
| Davis | Minnie | deserted by husband; poor health; unable to work | none | good | none | 6/ ch | 27 | Aug. | 1913 | $12.00 28 Aug. 1913 |
| Davison | H. W. | ill health; old age | none | good | little charity | | 17 | Apr. | 1898 | |
| Davison | Henry W. | | | | | | 24 | Mar. | 1891 | go to farm 6 Apr. 1891 |
| Davison | Henry W. | | | | | | | | | $4.00 Oct 8 1891 |
| Davison | Henry W. | | | | | | | | | "go to farm again" |
| Davison | John William | sickness of children & self; inability to work | none | strictly sober | none | 12 | 3 | Feb. | 1915 | |
| Deal | George | | | | | 15 | | Apr. | 1879 | acted on 14 May 1879; $15.00 was granted Jan. 1879 also |
| Dean | Edwin B. | infirm & old age | none | good | none | 10 | 24 | July | 1916 | $10.00 15 Aug. 1916 |
| de-Bendeleben | Oufried | unable to work | none | good | $5 occasionally | 5 | 17 | Mar. | 1900 | $5.00 17 Mar. 1900 |

| 1 SURNAME | 2 GIVEN NAME | 15 REASON FOR REQUEST | 16 PROPER-TY | 17 SOBRI-ETY | 18 SOURCE OF INCOME | 19 R $ | 20 | 21 DATE OF REQUEST | 22 | 23 AMOUNT AWARDED/ COMMENTS |
|---|---|---|---|---|---|---|---|---|---|---|
| DeCeveness | Nicholas | crippled and unable to work | none | the best | none | 6 | 10 | Apr. | 1916 | $6.00 10 Apr. 1916 |
| deMooy | Ella Palmer, Mrs. | | none | temperate | none | | | | | $15.00 8 Nov. 1915 |
| Denny | C., Mrs. | deserted by husband | none | | | | | | | $5.00 5 Jan. 1892; resident over 5 years |
| Derrickson | J. W. | disability old age; unable to work | none | good | none | 10 | | | | $10.00 1 Apr. 1912 |
| Deskin | E. | disabled; broken leg | none | good | none | 15 | 3 | May | 1910 | |
| Devereaux | R. E. | sickness; unable to secure or do any work | none | total abstainer | none | 8 | 2 | Nov. | 1916 | $8.00 11 Nov. 1916 |
| Devine | Mary E. | old age and unable to earn a living | none | good | none | 12 | 10 | Mar. | 1913 | |
| Dicks | Margaret, Mrs. | unable to work | none | good | none | 8 | 29 | Mar. | 1899 | |
| Dinucci | Isabella | sick | none | good | none | 10 | | | | $10.00 3 Aug. 1915 |
| Divers | Caroline | aged, infirm and unable to work | none | | | | 3 | Mar. | 1890 | $7.50 4 Mar. 1890 |
| Divers | Edward, Mrs. | deaf; old age | none | good | none | 10 | 8 | Oct. | 1907 | $7.00 11 Nov. 1907 |
| Dixon | William | old age; unable to earn a living by manual labor | none | good | none | 8 | 4 | Jan. | 1910 | |
| Dodson | M. J., Mrs. | husband deceased; unable to find enough work | | | | | | | | $2.00 each to children 3 July 1899 |
| Doggett | Vida Mc L. | | none | good | wages only | 10 | | | | $10.00 19 Nov. 1914 |
| Dohrman | Mrs. | unable to earn enough to clothe and feed family | | | | | | | | dropped from list 19 Feb. 1890 |
| Doidge | Mary L. | husband and herself | none | good | none | 8 | | | | $5.00 9 Feb. 1900 |

| SURNAME | GIVEN NAME | REASON FOR REQUEST | PROPERTY | SOBRIETY | SOURCE OF INCOME | R $ | | DATE OF REQUEST | | AMOUNT AWARDED/ COMMENTS |
|---|---|---|---|---|---|---|---|---|---|---|
| 1 | 2 | 15 | 16 | 17 | 18 | 19 | 20 | 21 | 22 | 23 |
| Doidge | | have no means of support | | | | | | | | |
| Doidge | Richard | unable to work | none | good | none | 8 | 11 | Apr. | 1900 | |
| Doidge | Richard | | none | good | none | 8 | 18 | Dec. | 1900 | $5.00 |
| Doidge | Richard | old & crippled | none | good | none | 8 | 26 | May | 1900 | $5.00 5 June 1900 |
| Doidge | Richard | unable to earn living because of age | house they live in | good | none | 8 | 16 | Jan. | 1912 | $8.00 6 Feb. 1912 |
| Doidge | Richard | old and unable to work | none | good | none | 8 | | | | $5.00 6 Feb. 1899 |
| Dolan | Andrew | asthma, rheumatism | none | sober | none | 5 | 21 | Mar. | 1900 | $5.00 2 Apr. 1900 |
| Dolan | Andrew | old age; unable to work | none | sober | none | 10 | 7 | Mar. | 1913 | |
| Dolan | Andrew | old; poor health; unable to work | none | good | none | 10 | 31 | Jan. | 1914 | $10.00 4 Feb. 1914 |
| Donnolly | Bridget | no means of support | none | good | none | 8 | 11 | Apr. | 1900 | $5.00 7 May 1900 |
| Donnolly | M., Mrs. | unable to earn living; widow; Wm. died 1 Jan. 1884 | small house | | county & friends | | 7 | Feb. | 1890 | $10.00 3 Mar. 1890 |
| Dorman | Louise, Mrs. | unable to work | | | | | | | 1884 | $15.00 7 Jan. 1884 |
| Doss | Seth B. | feeble and unable to care for son | none | does not drink at all | none | 10 | | July | 1913 | $10.00 9 July 1913 |
| Dotterer | Minnie | no means of support | | | | | 2 | Dec. | 1890 | both daus. are sick; $5.00 3 Dec. 1890 |
| Dowd | Z. Z., Mr. | shoulder dislocated; cannot work | | | | | 29 | June | 1878 | acted on Nov. 1878 |
| Dower | James | old age & rheumatism | none | fair | none | 5 | 22 | Dec. | 1910 | $5.00 Jan. 1911 |
| Doyle | M., Mrs. | children | none | sober | none | 8 | 26 | Apr. | 1915 | $8.00 12 Apr. 1915; widow by desertion |
| Drake | Mabel Flora | husband has left her | none | good | none | 10 | 4 | Feb. | 1915 | |
| Drake | S. G. | deaf | none | sober | no money | | | | | stamped 29 Apr. |

| 1 | 2 | 15 | 16 | 17 | 18 | 19 | 20 | 21 | 22 | 23 |
|---|---|---|---|---|---|---|---|---|---|---|
| SURNAME | GIVEN NAME | REASON FOR REQUEST | PROPERTY | SOBRIETY | SOURCE OF INCOME | R $ | | DATE OF REQUEST | | AMOUNT AWARDED/ COMMENTS |
| Drake | | | | | formerly Patchett | | | | | 1893; native of Hampton, NH |
| Drake | S. G. | deaf for 20 years | | | | | | | | $5.00 9 Apr 1892 |
| Duarte | Sarah | husband blind; unable to work | none | | none | | 5 | June | 1889 | |
| Duarte | Sarah | husband blind; invalid dau. 5 years old | | | none | | 4 | Dec. | 1890 | $5.00 |
| Dudley | Mrs. | sick; can't walk | | | | 2 | 4 | Mar. | 1889 | |
| Dudley | Nellie, Mrs. | consumptive; not able to work | | | | 8 | 8 | Feb. | 1890 | $5.00 8 Feb. 1890 |
| Dudley | Nellie, Mrs. | infirm | | | | 12 | 25 | Aug. | 1892 | $10.00 & $2.50 |
| Dudley | Nellie, Mrs. | invalid | | | | 10 | | | | increased to $7.50 7 June 1892 |
| Dudly | Mrs. | poor health | | | $5.00 from city $5.00 from county | 10 | 5 | Aug. | 1889 | $5.00 5 Aug. 1889 |
| Duke | Catherine | penniless and unable to work | none | good | some charity | 5 | 28 | Oct. | 1910 | |
| Duke | Catherine | old and infirm | none | sober | none | 6 | 27 | Feb. | 1913 | |
| Dunbar | Haln Killigrew | old and infirm; no relatives | none | sober | small job caring for property | | 4 | Nov. | 1892 | $5.00 18 Nov. 1892; 77 years old 26 Sept. 1892 |
| Dunbar | Haln, K. | feeble and unable to work | none | temperate | none | 5 | 22 | Mar. | 1900 | $5.00 26 Mar. 1900 |
| Duncan | Charlotte, Mrs. | brutal husband in state prison; unable to provide for family | | | | | | | | $5.00 7 June 1892; seeking a divorce |

| 1 | 2 | 15 | 16 | 17 | 18 | 19 | 20 | 21 | 22 | 23 |
|---|---|---|---|---|---|---|---|---|---|---|
| SURNAME | GIVEN NAME | REASON FOR REQUEST | PROPER-TY | SOBRI-ETY | SOURCE OF INCOME | R $ | | DATE OF REQUEST | | AMOUNT AWARDED/ COMMENTS |
| Dunham | Cora | husband refuses to assist her; left husband because of unkind treatment | claim, Mendocino Co. mortgaged for $1000, 12% interest | good | none | 15 | 2 | Mar. | 1912 | $10.00 7 Mar. 1912 |
| Dyer | Louie | old age | none | but little | none | 12 | 6 | Oct. | 1917 | $8.00 14 Nov. 1917 |
| Eby | Sophia Elgin | unable to do physical labor due to several operations | none | good | none | 20 | 3 | Aug. | 1914 | $20.00 5 Aug. 1914 |
| Edwards | L., Mrs. | sick and cannot work | none | good | none | 8 | 3 | Jan. | 1910 | $6.00 3 Jan. 1910 |
| Edwards | Leavina | no means of earning a living | none | good | none | 8 | 13 | Feb. | 1907 | $5.00 7 Mar. 1907 |
| Elkerton | E. D. | crippled | small chicken ranch | good | none | 10 | 5 | Feb. | 1909 | $10.00 6 Feb. 1909 |
| Elliott | Charles, Mrs. | | none | good | none | | | | | |
| Elliott | Chas., Mrs. | father gone | none | good | none | 25 | | | | |
| Elliott | W. N. | unable to work | none | good | none | 8 | 5 | Oct. | 1909 | $8.00 6 Oct. 1909 |
| Elliott | William N. | old age & general disability | none | good | | 10 | | | | |
| Ellis | William J. | unable to make a living; no home | | | | 10 | 5 | Jan. | 1891 | not enough signers |
| Ellison | Minnie, Mrs. | mo. of six children | none | sober | none | 10 | 4 | Aug. | 1899 | $5.00 10 Aug. 1899 |
| Ellison | Minnie, Mrs. | ill health | none | good | school district | 10 | 12 | Mar. | 1913 | $10.00 1913 |
| Elshio | Antonio F. | inability to work; poverty and sickness | none | sober | none | 10 | 10 | Jan. | 1901 | $5.00 |

| 1 SURNAME | 2 GIVEN NAME | 15 REASON FOR REQUEST | 16 PROPERTY | 17 SOBRIETY | 18 SOURCE OF INCOME | 19 R$ | 20 | 21 DATE OF REQUEST | 22 | 23 AMOUNT AWARDED/ COMMENTS |
|---|---|---|---|---|---|---|---|---|---|---|
| Emerson | Henry | old age and illness | none | sober | none | | 10 | Apr. | 1890 | |
| Entrena | Filomena | both sons ill & unable to work | none | good | none | 8 | 12 | Jan. | 1914 | $8.00 2 Feb. 1914 |
| Eprosen | Felix | sick | none | good | none | 10 | 5 | Dec. | 1914 | $10.00 9 Dec. 1914 |
| Evans | James A. | poor health; children cannot earn enough | none | good | none | 15 | | | | |
| Fadigan | Edward | unable to support himself | none | sober | no | 8 | 5 | Feb. | 1901 | |
| Fancher | John A. | death of wife | none | good | own work | 20 | 18 | Jan. | 1909 | rejected |
| Fawcett | Mary | helpless from paralysis | 3 lots & 4 room house | good | none | 12 | 28 | Jan. | 1915 | rejected |
| Faylor | Mary, Mrs. | old age; unable to work | none | good | none | 10 | 3 | May | 1913 | $10.00 6 May 1913 |
| Felitz | Mary | large helpless family; sickness in family | | | none | | | | | |
| Fergeson | Levi | old age | none | excellent | none | 8 | | | | |
| Ferguson | Levi | unable to earn enough to support himself | none | good | none | 8 | 2 | Sept. | 1899 | |
| Fergusson | Levi | unable to support self | none | sober | earns $75 to $80 per year | 5 | 31 | Mar. | 1900 | $5.00 |
| Finley | Carrie Ann | unable to earn sufficient to support children | none | good | none | 30 | 19 | Apr. | 1915 | rejected |
| Finley | N., Mrs. | | none | good | none | 8 | 3 | Dec. | 1910 | $8.00 5 Jan. 1911 |
| Finley | Nancy, Mrs. | no visible means of support | | | | 8 + | 18 | Mar. | 1913 | |
| Fish | Mary, Mrs. | limited strength; no relatives | | | | 15 | | | | $10.00 8 Oct. 1891 |

-120-

| 1 | 2 | 15 | 16 | 17 | 18 | 19 | 20 | 21 | 22 | 23 |
|---|---|---|---|---|---|---|---|---|---|---|
| SURNAME | GIVEN NAME | REASON FOR REQUEST | PROPER-TY | SOBRI-ETY | SOURCE OF INCOME | R $ | | DATE OF REQUEST | | AMOUNT AWARDED/ COMMENTS |
| Fisher | L. F., Mrs. | husband sick in County Hospital | none | good | none | 15 | | | | $15.00 28 Feb. 1910 |
| Fisher | T. L. | fatally afflicted with consumption; unable to work | none | good | none but donations | 15 | 30 | July | 1910 | $15.00 3 Oct. 1910 |
| Fitch | R. J. | tuberculosis | none | good | none | 15 | 29 | Apr. | 1913 | |
| Fitzpatrick | Mrs. | old age | | | | 15 | | Oct. | 1885 | |
| Flanigan | Richard | partially paralyzed | | sober | none | | | | | $12.50 |
| Fletcher | Charles H. | unable to work enough | | | | | 22 | Mar. | 1910 | $6.00 4 Apr. 1910 |
| Fletcher | Charles H. | rheumatism | none | good | none | 6 | 2 | Mar. | 1913 | |
| Fletcher | Chas. H. | rheumatism | none | good | occasional small jobs | 8 | 25 | Aug. | 1916 | $8.00 15 Sept. 1916 |
| Flood | Lena, Mrs. | sickness | little house with small lot encumbered | good | none | 10 | 16 | Sept. | 1916 | $10.00 11 Oct. 1916 |
| Fochetti | Bernardo | sickness since Jan. 1901; inability to earn a livelihood | none | good | none | 8 | 12 | Sept. | 1901 | $5.00 |
| Ford | Benjamin F. | almost severed left hand and unable to work | none | sober | none | 10 | 6 | Mar. | 1915 | |
| Forpeilha | Rosa T. | because of young child she is unable to provide livelihood | none | | friends | 6 | 3 | Sept. | 1901 | $6.00; husband confined in Napa State Insane Asylum |
| Foster | Augusta C., Mrs. | destitute | | | | 10 | | | | $7.00 5 Dec. 1892 |
| Foster | G. H., Mrs. | no means of making living | none | good | none | 8 | | | | |
| Fouder | Elizabeth | destitute | | | | 5 | 30 | Dec. | 1890 | $5.00 6 Jan. 1891 |

| 1 | 2 | 15 | 16 | 17 | 18 | 19 | 20 | 21 | 22 | 23 |
|---|---|---|---|---|---|---|---|---|---|---|
| SURNAME | GIVEN NAME | REASON FOR REQUEST | PROPER-TY | SOBRI-ETY | SOURCE OF INCOME | R $ | | DATE OF REQUEST | | AMOUNT AWARDED/ COMMENTS |
| Fouts | Elizabeth | old age | none | good | none | | 10 | Apr. | 1900 | $5.00 on 9 June 1900 |
| Fowler | Cinfoliana | old; crippled | none | good | none | 5 | 29 | June | 1899 | |
| Fowzer | William J. | accidental fall from RR train nr. Melita Station | | | | | | | | burial of indigent soldier; Rural Cemetery Santa Rosa; d. 11 Oct. 1909 |
| Francisco | A. | physically incapacitated | 26 acres; mortgaged | good | none | 15 | | | | |
| Francisco | Antone | sick & destitute | none | | none | | 7 | Apr. | 1890 | |
| Franklin | Ann, Mrs. | paralysis | | | | | 26 | May | 1887 | |
| Franklin | Ann, Mrs. | old & infirm | | | mo. allowance from county | | 3 | Mar. | 1890 | $10.00 |
| Fraser | A. F. | disabled; double rupture with protruding piles | none | good | none | 8 | 3 | Oct. | 1914 | |
| Frederickson | Annie | husband at Klondike, she is destitute | none | sober | none | 8 | | | | $5.00 3 July 1899 |
| Frediani | Caterina | husband gone out of his mind | none | good | none | 10 | 16 | Feb. | 1915 | $10.00 8 Mar. 1915 |
| Friend | Robert & Carline | old age | none | good | none | 8 | 9 | June | 1909 | $8.00 |
| Frugoli | Francisco | prolonged illness; lack of funds | none | good | | | 8 | Feb. | 1910 | $10.00 9 Feb. 1910 |
| Frugoli | Francisco | crippled; unable to work | none | none | none | | 15 | Mar. | 1913 | |
| Funk | L., Mrs. | not able to work; son out of work | none | good | none | 10 | 19 | Jan. | 1914 | |

| 1 | 2 | 15 | 16 | 17 | 18 | 19 | 20 | 21 | 22 | 23 |
|---|---|---|---|---|---|---|---|---|---|---|
| SURNAME | GIVEN NAME | REASON FOR REQUEST | PROPER-TY | SOBRI-ETY | SOURCE OF INCOME | R $ | | DATE OF REQUEST | | AMOUNT AWARDED/ COMMENTS |
| Funk | Louise, Mrs. | not able to support herself | none | good | none | 7 | 31 | July | 1907 | $5.00 14 Sept. 1907 |
| Furia | Lazzaro | unable to work; doctor certificate, has heart disease | none | sober | none | 12 | 25 | Apr. | 1910 | $10.00 27 Apr. 1910 |
| Furia | Lazzaro | poor health | none | good | none | 15 | 11 | Mar. | 1913 | |
| Furlong | Thos. | | | | | | 3 | Mar. | 1890 | |
| Futterer | Conrad | old age | tailors tools | good | none | 8 | 4 | Mar. | 1909 | $8.00 6 Mar. 1909 |
| Futterer | Conrad | failing eyesight; wife bedridden | none | good | $10.00 from county | 5 | 17 | Oct. | 1910 | |
| Futterer | Conrad & Louisa | old age; continual illness; husband almost totally blind | none | good | none | 20 | 16 | Apr. | 1913 | |
| Gager | George G. | old age; poor eyesight | none | strictly temperate | none | 10 | 6 | Mar. | 1913 | |
| Gallaudett | E. J., Mrs. | sick; senility | none | good | none | 10 | 24 | Mar. | 1913 | |
| Gamboggi | Rosa | | none | good | none | 10 | 3 | Jan. | 1917 | $10.00 3 Jan. 1917 |
| Ganyard | G. L., Mrs. | ill health; unable to work | none | sober | none | 15 | 23 | Jan. | 1915 | |
| Garnero | Mary | husband sick in hospital; invalid | none | good | none | 8 | 27 | Oct. | 1914 | $8.00 1 Nov. 1914 |
| German | Kate | has sick child and cannot work | | | | 8 | 3 | June | 1899 | $5.00 6 June 1899 |
| German | Katie, Mrs. | not able to find work | | | | | | | | |
| Gerrick | Ella | confined to bed with tumor, husband went to Nome | none | good | none | 8 | 9 | Aug. | 1900 | $6.00 10 Aug. 190 |

| 1 | 2 | 15 | 16 | 17 | 18 | 19 | 20 | 21 | 22 | 23 |
|---|---|---|---|---|---|---|---|---|---|---|
| SURNAME | GIVEN NAME | REASON FOR REQUEST | PROPERTY | SOBRIETY | SOURCE OF INCOME | R $ | | DATE OF REQUEST | | AMOUNT AWARDED/ COMMENTS |
| Giauque | Elizabeth | old; rheumatism | house & lot | sober | own work | 6 | 10 | Oct. | 1900 | $5.00 11 Oct. 1900 |
| Giauque | Elizabeth | very old & feeble | a little cabin | good | none | | | | | $5.00 7 Mar. 1907 |
| Gibson | G. W. | nearly blind; unable to get work | none | good | none | 10 | | July | 1914 | |
| Gibson | G. W. | blind | none | good | $5.00 from dau. | 15 | 8 | July | 1915 | rejected |
| Gilcrist | Mrs. | asthma; unable to secure permanent employment | none | good | none | 8 | 4 | Feb. | 1914 | |
| Glidden | Charles & Esther | husband is old & crippled; wife is old & feeble | nothing | good | none | 15 | 11 | Jan. | 1917 | $15.00 11 Jan. 1917 |
| Gober | Elizabeth | deserted by husband, ill health | none | | | 10 | 2 | Apr. | 1900 | $6.00 3 Apr. 1900 |
| Goetjen | C. & wife | sick | none | good | none | 8 | | | | $10.00 4 Feb. 1913 |
| Goetjen | C., Mr. & Mrs. | sickness | none | OK | none | 10 | | | | $10.00 9 Apr. 1913 |
| Golett | Jane | helpless & distressed | none | good | $5.00/mo. | 5 | 20 | Mar. | 1900 | $5.00 24 Mar. 1900 |
| Gould | Mollie B. | disabled | none | good | none | | 21 | Nov. | 1901 | $5.00 7 Jan. 1902 |
| Gounsky | Fannie, Mrs. | husband deserted her two mos. ago; destitute | | | | | 30 | Apr. | 1887 | |
| Gounsky | J., Mrs. | husband in state prison | | | | | 1 | Dec. | 1888 | |
| Gounsky | Mrs. | destitute | | | | | 6 | Feb. | 1890 | $10.00 |
| Grace | Anne | needs money for rent | none | | | 5 | | | | $5.00 3 Mar. 1890 |
| Grace | Annie, Mrs. | unable to work | | | | 8 | 22 | Nov. | 1892 | $5.00 7 Dec. 1892 |
| Gray | Olive | ill and unable to work | | | | 15 | 7 | Nov. | 1892 | $10.00 7 Dec. 1892 |
| Green | Charles | paralyzed; wife unable to work | | | | | 2 | Dec. | 1884 | petitioner died at county hospital |

| 1 | 2 | 15 | 16 | 17 | 18 | 19 | 20 | 21 | 22 | 23 |
|---|---|---|---|---|---|---|---|---|---|---|
| SURNAME | GIVEN NAME | REASON FOR REQUEST | PROPERTY | SOBRIETY | SOURCE OF INCOME | R $ | | DATE OF REQUEST | | AMOUNT AWARDED/ COMMENTS |
| Green | Hannah, Mrs. | | | | | | | | | 9 Dec. 1884 |
| Green | Nellie M. | unable to earn enough to provide for children | none | good | none | 10 | | | | $10.00 29 July 1911 |
| Green | Richard | | none | | none | 12 | 2 | Oct. | 1913 | $10.00 9 Oct. 1913 |
| Greening | S. J., Mrs. | has no income; must stay with daus. | owns home | sober | none | | 4 | Feb. | 1890 | $5.00 |
| Greenleaf | T., Mrs. | husband sick & disabled | none | good | none | 10 | 1 | Dec. | 1899 | |
| Greenleaf | T., Mrs. | husband sick and cannot work | none | temperate | none | 8 | 9 | Apr. | 1900 | $5.00 9 Apr. 1900 |
| Gregory | Charles M. | sick; almost blind | | good | none | 8 | | | | immediate relief $5.00 10 Nov. 1899 |
| Griffin | J. M. | chronic rheumatism; disabled | none | | | 6 | 13 | Mar. | 1913 | asks for assistance or to be admitted to county farm |
| Griggs | Arthur Odell | sickness prevents him from working and earning a living | none | none | none | 20 | 4 | Feb. | 1891 | $12.00 29 Apr. 1910 |
| Grube | Joseph | old and feeble | none | good | none | 6 | 26 | Apr. | 1910 | $6.00 3 Mar. 1914 |
| Guerin | Frank Merritt | old age; crippled hand; half blind; rheumatism | none | temperate | none | 8 | 30 | Oct. | 1916 | $8.00 14 Nov. 1916 |
| Guilfoyle | Mary | old age, rheumatism | none | good | none | 8 | 23 | Mar. | 1900 | $7.00 24 Mar. 1900 |
| Gussman | Santo | unable to work | none | good | none | 8 | 24 | Aug. | 1907 | $5.00 5 Sept. 1907 |
| Gustavsen | Gus | inflammatory rheumatism | none | sober | none | 8 | 13 | Apr. | 1915 | $8.00 27 Apr. 1915 |
| Hale | Ada | crippled with rheumatism; unable to walk | small house | good | none | 10 | | | | $10.00 5 Jan. 1911 |
| Hale | Ada E. | rheumatism; unable to | none | good | none | 10 | | | | |

| 1 | 2 | 15 | 16 | 17 | 18 | 19 | 20 | 21 | 22 | 23 |
|---|---|---|---|---|---|---|---|---|---|---|
| SURNAME | GIVEN NAME | REASON FOR REQUEST | PROPERTY | SOBRIETY | SOURCE OF INCOME | R $ | | DATE OF REQUEST | | AMOUNT AWARDED/ COMMENTS |
| Hall | Roxania | walk and work unable to work | none | strictly sober | no | 7 | 3 | Dec. | 1914 | $7.00 9 Dec. 1914 |
| Hall | William | sick in bed | none | good | none | 10 | 22 | Mar. | 1900 | |
| Hall | William | sick; no means of support | none | | none | 10 | | | | 28 Apr. 1890 |
| Hamele | Anna | unable to work | house | good | none | 10 | 22 | Nov. | 1916 | should be placed on indigent list |
| Hamlin | Chas. J. | sick one year | 4 acres; mortgaged to limit | good | none | 20 | 4 | June | 1915 | |
| Hammele | Anne | old | small house | sober | none | 10 | 13 | Mar. | 1916 | $10.00 13 Mar. 1916 |
| Handfest | George | old age | none | | none | 5 | 9 | May | 1900 | $5.00 4 June 1900 |
| Hanford | John | old age | none | good | none | 8 | 7 | May | 1900 | |
| Hansen | A., Mrs. | old age | none | good | none | | 8 | Nov. | 1901 | $6.00 4 Dec. 1901 |
| Hansen | Erichtho, Mrs. | too old & feeble | none | yes | none | 8 | 30 | Mar. | 1900 | $7.00 5 Apr. 1900 |
| Hansen | Peter | too old to do hard labor; unable to secure enough light work | none | good | none | 15 | 20 | Dec. | 1915 | $15.00 12 Jan. 1916 |
| Hansen | Peter | physically unable to work | none | sober | none | 15 | | | | $15.00 13 Mar. 1917 |
| Happy | J. H., Mrs. | destitute condition | | | | | 31 | Jan. | 1885 | petition filed 2 Feb. 1885 |
| Harbine | Charles | crippled | none | good | from dau. | 5 | | Mar. | 1912 | $5.00 6 Apr. 1912 |
| Harbine | Chas. | aged; crippled | | | | | 29 | Apr. | 1918 | $12.00 7 May 1918 |
| Harbine | Chas. E. | crippled and unable to work | none | good | none | 10 | 14 | Feb. | 1913 | |
| Hardin | Amelia, Mrs. | old & infirm | none | good | none | 8 | 13 | Apr. | 1900 | $5.00 7 May 1900 |

| 1 | 2 | 15 | 16 | 17 | 18 | 19 | 20 | 21 | 22 | 23 |
|---|---|---|---|---|---|---|---|---|---|---|
| SURNAME | GIVEN NAME | REASON FOR REQUEST | PROPER-TY | SOBRI-ETY | SOURCE OF INCOME | R $ | | DATE OF REQUEST | | AMOUNT AWARDED/ COMMENTS |
| Hardin | Mr. & Mrs. | paralyzed with invalid wife | | | donations from neighbors | 15 | 3 | Oct. | 1892 | $10.00 4 Oct. 1892 |
| Harding | Anna M., Mrs. | invalid | none | good | none | 8 | 23 | Mar. | 1900 | $8.00 2 Apr. 1900 |
| Hardt | Augusta, Mrs. | old | none | good | none | 10 | 23 | Oct. | 1915 | $10.00 8 Nov. 1915 |
| Hardy | Rebecca | sick; unable to earn living | none | good | none | 8 | | | | $5.00 3 July 1899 |
| Harman | Albert M. | unable to work | none | temperate | none | 8 | 31 | Mar. | 1900 | $4.00 2 Apr. 1900 |
| Harmon | Charles | catarrh of stomach | none | good | none | 8 | 5 | Mar. | 1915 | |
| Harmon | Lizzie, Mrs. | inability to earn living | one lot S. E St. | sober | none | 10 | 16 | Feb. | 1916 | $10.00 14 Apr. 1916 |
| Harrison | N., Mrs. | ill; unable to work | none | | none | | 3 | Mar. | 1890 | $5.00 |
| Harrison | Nannie, Mrs. | physical disabilities; can't support family | | | | 10 | 5 | Aug. | 1889 | that she may receive renewed assistance 14 July 1890 |
| Hart | Joseph | cancer in one eye | none | sober | none | 8 | | | | |
| Hasting | F. D. | old and cannot work; children will not help | house & 3 lots | good | none | 10 | | | | $8.00 11 Dec. 1911 |
| Hasting(s) | F. D. | old and unable to work; wife 60 years old and sickly | house & 3 lots | strictly temperate | none | 10 | | | | |
| Hastings | Edward & Mary | walked from Hopland; would like help to get home to SF | | | | | 14 | Nov. | 1890 | none awarded |
| Hastings | Emily | unable to earn a living; destitute | none | good | none | 10 | 1 | July | 1914 | $10.00 7 July 1914 |
| Hauser | A., Mrs. | no means of support | none | good | none | 6 | 12 | Mar. | 1913 | |
| Hauskneckt | Henry | | | sober | none | 15 | 1 | May | 1900 | $5.00 10 May 1900 |
| Hawley | Delia Ann | old | none | good | none | 10 | 10 | Mar. | 1913 | |
| Hawley | Delia, Mrs. | old & infirm | none | yes | none | 10 | 4 | Dec. | 1911 | $7.00 11 Dec. 1911 |

| 1 | 2 | 15 | 16 | 17 | 18 | 19 | 20 | 21 | 22 | 23 |
|---|---|---|---|---|---|---|---|---|---|---|
| SURNAME | GIVEN NAME | REASON FOR REQUEST | PROPER-TY | SOBRI-ETY | SOURCE OF INCOME | R $ | | DATE OF REQUEST | | AMOUNT AWARDED/ COMMENTS |
| Hayhurst | William | ill health | none | entirely temperate | none | 15 | 17 | Sept. | 1914 | $10.00 7 Oct. 1914 |
| Haynes | W. R. | crippled; missing 2 fingers on right hand | | | | | 6 | May | 1892 | $8.00 7 May 1892 |
| Heinsen | Maggie | 4 children under 8; no means of support except little earnings | none | sober | none | 8 | 22 | Feb. | 1901 | $8.00 1 Mar 1901 |
| Heiss | Edwin, Mrs. | cannot meet obligations | house | sober industrious | none | 10 | 15 | Feb. | 1917 | $10.00 15 Feb. 1917 |
| Hekeler | Philip H. | old age & infirm | house & lot | good | $5/mo. from co. | 10 | 4 | May | 1915 | |
| Hekeler | Philip Henry | unable to work | small house & lot | good | none | 7 | 29 | May | 1914 | $7.00 4 June 1914 |
| Henderson | J. H. | right arm & hand paralyzed | none | good | none | 8 | 28 | Feb. | 1914 | $8.00 4 Mar. 1914 |
| Henley | Daniel | too old & feeble | none | good | none | 6 | 21 | Mar. | 1900 | $5.00 3 Apr. 1900 |
| Herford | Thomas | old age | none | good | none | 10 | 27 | Feb. | 1913 | |
| Heryford | Nick | left side crippled | none | good | none | | 30 | Jan. | 1899 | |
| Hesse | Louisa, Mrs. | needy | | | | | 29 | Oct. | 1889 | |
| Hesse | Louisa, Mrs. | frequently unable to work | small house | | | | 25 | Feb. | 1890 | $8.00 3 Mar. 1890 |
| Hester | Clara | abandoned by husband | none | good | none | 20 | 11 | Mar. | 1913 | |
| Hester | Clara, Mrs. | husband out of state; fails to provide | none | good | small amount | 20 | 1 | Mar. | 1912 | $12.00 4 Mar. 1912 |
| Hester | Clara, Mrs. | husband fails to provide | | good | small work at home | 20 | 5 | Feb. | 1913 | $10.00 6 Feb. 1913 |
| Hetzel | C. F. | sick | | good | | 20 | 3 | Mar. | 1913 | |

| 1 | 2 | 15 | 16 | 17 | 18 | 19 | 20 | 21 | 22 | 23 |
|---|---|---|---|---|---|---|---|---|---|---|
| SURNAME | GIVEN NAME | REASON FOR REQUEST | PROPERTY | SOBRIETY | SOURCE OF INCOME | R $ | | DATE OF REQUEST | | AMOUNT AWARDED/ COMMENTS |
| Hetzel | C. F. | sick and unable to support family | none | good | none | 20 | 3 | Mar. | 1913 | |
| Hetzel | Carl | sick | none | good | none | 20 | 4 | Mar. | 1912 | $20.00 Mar. 1912 |
| Hevel | E. L. | unable to work; physical deformity of lungs & ribs | none | no bad habits | none | 8 | | | | $8.00 5 May 1914 |
| Hillbrant | Ethel | too hard to make living | 10 acres | good | none | 6 | 31 | Mar. | 1913 | |
| Hinkley | Eleanor | sick | none | good | none | 10 | 1 | Apr. | 1913 | |
| Hinkley | Eleanor, Miss | old; ill; without means | none | good | none | 12 | 6 | Sept. | 1911 | $10.00 8 Sept. 1911 |
| Hinrichsen | John W. | blind; sick | | | | 50 or 60 | 2 | Apr. | 1903 | rejected 2 Apr. 1903 |
| Hinrichsen | Therese | poor health & husband blind | none | good | none | 10 | 12 | Apr. | 1900 | $8.00 27 Apr. 1900 |
| Hofer | George | old age | none | good | none | 10 | | | | $10.00 15 Mar. 1916 |
| Hoffman | E. E., Mrs. | husband left; she is sick | none | good | room rent free | 15 | 4 | Oct. | 1916 | $15.00 14 Nov. 1916 |
| Hofmann | Carl C. | unable to work | lot & house | temperate | none | 5 | 22 | May | 1900 | $5.00 7 July 1900 |
| Holbrock | William | old age; inability to earn a livelihood | | very good habits | none | | 13 | Mar. | 1914 | |
| Holmes | Clara L. | not able to work | none | good | none | 8 | 20 | Oct. | 1913 | |
| Hopper | Harlow | | none | sober | none | 8 | 10 | Feb. | 1915 | |
| Horgan | Kate, Mrs. | husband died | little house | good | none | 10 | 11 | Oct. | 1911 | $10.00 6 Nov. 1911 |
| Horgan | Mrs. | loss of husband | none | good | none | 10 | 25 | Mar. | 1913 | |
| Houx | John W. & wife | old man is an imbecile and wife unable to labor | | | | | | | | 2 Nov. 1883 |

| 1 | 2 | 15 | 16 | 17 | 18 | 19 | 20 | 21 | 22 | 23 |
|---|---|---|---|---|---|---|---|---|---|---|
| SURNAME | GIVEN NAME | REASON FOR REQUEST | PROPERTY | SOBRIETY | SOURCE OF INCOME | R $ | | DATE OF REQUEST | | AMOUNT AWARDED/ COMMENTS |
| Howard | Amy M. | no means of support | none | good | none | 10 | | | | not allowed; son will provide for his mother |
| Howard | Amy, Mrs. | poor health | none | good | none | 10 | 18 | Feb. | 1915 | rejected |
| Howard | J. G. | old age & sickness | none | good | none | | 23 | Nov. | 1911 | $5.00 6 Dec. 1911 |
| Howard | J. G. | unable to work | none | good | none | 5 | | | | |
| Howard | Jas. G. | old | none | good | none | 6 | 10 | June | 1915 | rejected |
| Howard | John C. | unable to work | none | | none | | 3 | Jan. | 1900 | |
| Howard | John C. | palsy; one arm | | | $6.00 for 2 orphan children | | 8 | Jan. | 1900 | hand written letter |
| Howard | John C. | rheumatism | none | sober | none | 10 | | | | |
| Howe | H. | unable to work; malaria | none | sober | none | | 29 | Mar. | 1915 | |
| Howe | Julia | unable to work due to illness | none | perfect | none | 8 | 19 | Feb. | 1915 | $8.00 4 Mar. 1915 |
| Howeth | Mary | serious sickness of several children | | | | 15 | 26 | June | 1891 | |
| Hoyt | Charles | sick & unable to work | small home | good | none | 10 | 22 | May | 1916 | $10.00 13 June 1916 |
| Hughes | David W. | poor health; broken ankle | none | | | | | | | $5.00 12 Jan. 1892; resident of state 18 yrs. |
| Humphreys | W. F. | nearly blind; imbeciles | none | good | none | 8 | 13 | Dec. | 1899 | $5.00 2 Jan. 1900 |
| Humphries | Charles | no means of support | none | | | 8 | 11 | Aug. | 1900 | $8.00 Aug. 1900 |
| Humphries | Emma, Mrs. | unable to work; husband in county hospital | | | | | | | | filed 6 Oct. 1890 |
| Hurd | Marcus | aged, infirm and unable to work | none | temperate | none | | 3 | Mar. | 1890 | $6.00 4 Mar. 1890 |

| 1 | 2 | 15 | 16 | 17 | 18 | 19 | 20 | 21 | 22 | 23 |
|---|---|---|---|---|---|---|---|---|---|---|
| SURNAME | GIVEN NAME | REASON FOR REQUEST | PROPER-TY | SOBRI-ETY | SOURCE OF INCOME | R $ | | DATE OF REQUEST | | AMOUNT AWARDED/ COMMENTS |
| Hurd | Marcus | old & crippled | none | good | none | 8 | 20 | Mar. | 1900 | $8.00 2 Apr. 1900 |
| Ilse | Frederick & wife | husband: paralysis of his limbs; wife: broken arm; unable to work | vacant lot | | none | | 3 | Feb. | 1890 | $5.00 6 Feb. 1890 |
| Ilse | Mary | unable to work | lot & cabin | sober | none | 5 | 25 | Mar. | 1900 | |
| Ilse | Mary, Mrs. | both legs broken | none | good | none | 8 | 7 | Nov. | 1900 | |
| Imfeld | Mary | physical disability; old age | none | good | none | 8 | 21 | Feb. | 1912 | |
| Ingerson | Capt. James | old; infirm; crippled | none | | | 8 | 8 | June | 1909 | $8.00 4 Aug. 1909 |
| Inghan | William | sick | none | good | none | 75 | 5 | Jan. | 1907 | $10.00 7 Jan. 1907 |
| Isaac(k)s | Jessie | old age | | | | | 3 | Feb. | 1880 | filed 3 Feb. 1880 |
| Ives | C. O., Mrs. | sick all the time | none | good | none | 10 | 13 | Feb. | 1913 | |
| Ives | Samson | poor health | small house & lot mortgaged | good | none | 8 | 13 | Feb. | 1913 | |
| Jack | Humbolt | old | none | good | none | 8 | 14 | Oct. | 1913 | |
| Jacobs | C. M. | incapacitated by illness | | | | | 4 | Sept. | 1890 | |
| Jacobs | C. M., Mrs. | aged; sick | | | $10.00 from co. | 15 | | | | |
| Jacobs | Ruth A. | dau. helpless invalid; Mrs. Jacobs in poor health from age | none | sober | none | 8 | 14 | Mar. | 1900 | $7.00 21 Mar. 1900 |
| Jacobsen | Christ | | | | | 10 | | | | |
| Jacobsen | Christ, Mr. & Mrs. | not strong; unable to work | | | none | 10 | | Jan. | 1913 | $10.00 8 Jan. 1913 |
| James | S. F. | has cancer of stomach | | | | | | | | no support; died 10 Sept. 1892 |
| Jarrett | Lola, Mrs. | | none | good | none | 8 | 1 | Apr. | 1913 | $8.00 8 Apr. 1913 |

| 1 | 2 | 15 | 16 | 17 | 18 | 19 | 20 | 21 | 22 | 23 |
|---|---|---|---|---|---|---|---|---|---|---|
| SURNAME | GIVEN NAME | REASON FOR REQUEST | PROPER-TY | SOBRI-ETY | SOURCE OF INCOME | R $ | | DATE OF REQUEST | | AMOUNT AWARDED/ COMMENTS |
| Jensen | J. P., Mrs. | both sick | | good | neighbors | 15 | 20 | May | 1910 | $15.00 8 June 1910 |
| Jewett | Martha, Mrs. | unable to support self & dau. | none | good | none | 5 | 7 | Jan. | 1916 | rejected |
| Jewett | Mattie, Mrs. | unable to support herself & child | none | good | none | 15 | 3 | Aug. | 1915 | rejected and cancelled 15 Oct. 1915 |
| Johnson | Anne | | | good | none | 5 | 21 | Jan. | 1915 | |
| Johnson | Clara | poor health | none | good | Charities Assoc. | 5 | | | | $5.00 5 Apr. 1909 |
| Johnson | Elna | blind in one eye and partial blind in other | none | good | | | 17 | Dec. | 1898 | $3.00 6 Feb. 1899 |
| Johnson | Elna | blind & unable to work | none | yes | none | 5 | 20 | Mar. | 1900 | $5.00 20 Mar. 1900 |
| Johnson | F. J. | been sick for a long time with typhoid fever | | | | | 7 | Apr. | 1890 | |
| Johnson | H. W., Mrs. | husband unable to support family; mother unable to earn enough | no | good | no | 10 | | | | $10.00 7 Dec. 1914 |
| Johnson | Henrietta | unable to work | none | good | none | 8 | | | | $5.00 1 Feb. 1899 |
| Johnson | Magnus | unable to work; left foot crippled | | good | none | 5 | 24 | Mar. | 1900 | $3.00 26 Mar. 1900 |
| Johnson | Magnus & wife | destitute on account of sickness | | | | | 3 | June | 1891 | |
| Johnson | Margaret | destitute | none | sober | none | 8 | | | | $7.00 3 July 1899 |
| Johnson | Marie | inability to earn living | none | sober | none | 8 | | | | $8.00 |
| Johnson | Mary | age and inability to work | none | good | none | 5 | 30 | Mar. | 1900 | $5.00 31 Mar. 1900 |
| Johnson | Mary | husband left her; rheumatism; can't | 2 room shack on | excellent | nothing | 10 | 27 | Mar. | 1914 | $10.00 7 Apr. 1914 |

| 1 | 2 | 15 | 16 | 17 | 18 | 19 | 20 | 21 | 22 | 23 |
|---|---|---|---|---|---|---|---|---|---|---|
| SURNAME | GIVEN NAME | REASON FOR REQUEST | PROPER-TY | SOBRI-ETY | SOURCE OF INCOME | R $ | | DATE OF REQUEST | | AMOUNT AWARDED/ COMMENTS |
| | | work; no money to buy food | lot | | | | | | | |
| Johnson | Mary E., Mrs. | feeble in health; son unable to earn enough to help her | 2 mort-gaged lots; Pippers Addition | | | | 24 | May | 1892 | $6.00 7 June 1892; came to CA 1874 |
| Johnson | William C. | incapacitated | none | good | little | | | | | $10.00 |
| Johnson | Wm. Clifton | rheumatism | none | good | | 25 | 11 | Mar. | 1913 | |
| Johnston | Margaret | old age | none | sober | none | 8 | 19 | Mar. | 1900 | $7.00 31 Mar. 1900 |
| Jones | Nelson | sick | none | good | none | 8 | 11 | May | 1915 | $8.00 12 May 1915 |
| Jose | Sophia | no means of support | pays $6.00 rent | | | | | | | $12.00 8 Feb. 1890 |
| Jose | Sophia, Mrs. | husband deceased; unable to work because of children | none | | $5.00. mo.; $7.50 from co.; rent $6.00 | 12 | 1 | Apr. | 1889 | |
| Judt | John F. | long illness; face cancer | | | | | 6 | Oct. | 1891 | request for transportation to The Dalles, OR.; refused |
| Kaller | Patrick | sick; unable to work | small shack | good | none | 6 | 8 | Dec. | 1900 | $5.00 8 Dec. 1900 |
| Karry | M. A., Mrs. | unable to support myself & children | none | sober | none | 5 | 14 | Mar. | 1900 | |
| Kase | Louise | husband in prison for 12 months | | | | | | Apr. | 1892 | |
| Kelley | Michel | old age | none | medium | none | 8 | 28 | Apr. | 1916 | $8.00 11 May 1916 |
| Keniston | Joseph | lost leg | house | sober | wife does some washing | | 25 | Apr. | 1893 | |

| 1 | 2 | 15 | 16 | 17 | 18 | 19 | 20 | 21 | 22 | 23 |
|---|---|---|---|---|---|---|---|---|---|---|
| SURNAME | GIVEN NAME | REASON FOR REQUEST | PROPER-TY | SOBRI-ETY | SOURCE OF INCOME | R $ | | DATE OF REQUEST | | AMOUNT AWARDED/ COMMENTS |
| Kennedy | Emma | husband invalid; children demented | 50 acres, mortgage $2000 | good | | 20 | 2 | Aug. | 1915 | $20.00 9 Aug. 1915 |
| Kennedy | Maud E. | discharged from Napa State Hospital; mentally incompetent | none | good | none | 10 | 28 | Jan. | 1914 | $10.00 4 Feb. 1914 |
| Kenney | Mary, Mrs. | 1 dau. crippled; mother now confined to bed; old age | none | | none | | 30 | Oct. | 1891 | $10.00 Nov. 1891 |
| Kennisten | (family) | incapacitated | | | | | 4 | Mar. | 1890 | $10.00 |
| Kenniston | Joseph | lost his foot and unable to work | | | | | | | 1883 | |
| Kern | (children) | mother is dead; father lives in Saratoga; very poor & sickly | none | | none | | | Aug. | 1900 | filed 1 Sept. 1900 |
| Ketcham | George | wife & dau. sick | none | good | none | 8 | 18 | Mar. | 1913 | |
| Ketchum | George | old & infirm | none | good | about $6.00 for 7 mos. | 8 | 29 | Nov. | 1911 | $8.00 5 Dec. 1911 |
| Ketchum | Julia | husband & dau. are unable to support her | none | good | none | 8 | 4 | Nov. | 1910 | |
| Kidd | F. A., Mrs. | deserted by husband 2 years ago | none | | her own labor; not able to get steady work | | 5 | Sept. | 1891 | $5.00; husband, Ed G. Kidd; resident of Sonoma Co. 31 years |
| Kidd | F. A., Mrs. | 1 small child, 15, invalid; mother not in good health; husband gone | none | | none | | | | | |

-134-

| 1 | 2 | 15 | 16 | 17 | 18 | 19 | 20 | 21 | 22 | 23 |
|---|---|---|---|---|---|---|---|---|---|---|
| SURNAME | GIVEN NAME | REASON FOR REQUEST | PROPER-TY | SOBRI-ETY | SOURCE OF INCOME | R $ | | DATE OF REQUEST | | AMOUNT AWARDED/ COMMENTS |
| Kilcourse | Bridget, Miss | sick; can't work | none | yes | none | | | | | $6.00 5 Sept. 1911 |
| Kilgore | Catherine | feebleness; unable to work | none | good | none | 8 | 13 | Dec. | 1900 | $5.00 |
| Kill | James M. | out of work | none | good | none | 10 | 28 | Apr. | 1915 | |
| King | J. H. | sick; unable to work | none | good | none | 6 | 15 | Mar. | 1900 | $5.00 15 Mar. 1900 |
| King | Jos. | ulcerated leg | none | good | none | 15 | | | | $15.00 5 Dec. 1913 |
| King | Joseph | | none | good | none | 8 | | | | |
| Kirk | Maggie | | none | good | none | 8 | 22 | June | 1907 | $8.00 6 Aug. 1907 |
| Kirkpatrick | H. C. | Clara Bell unable mentally & physically to work | none | good | none | 8 | 22 | Nov. | 1913 | $8.00 8 Dec. 1913 |
| Kirry | May, Mrs. | children work in Humbolt Co.; unable to help | none | excellent | none except when working out when she can | 10 | 25 | Sept. | 1911 | |
| Kirry | May, Mrs. | no money from ex-husband | none | excellent | none | 10 | 25 | Sept. | 1911 | $8.00 6 Nov. 1911 |
| Kiser | Lena | husband fails to support her; she cannot earn sufficient | none | very good | none | 15 | 25 | July | 1914 | rejected after consultation with probation officer |
| Kleemons #1 | Rosa, Mrs. | unable to earn enough | | | washing & odd jobs | 10 | 24 | Feb. | 1890 | $10.00 25 Feb. 1890 |
| Kleemons #2 | Rose, Mrs. | unable to earn enough | | | daily labor | | 18 | Jan. | 1890 | |
| Knapp | Lewis C. | unable to work | none | good | none | 6 | 29 | Mar. | 1900 | $5.00 29 Mar. 1900 |
| Knighten | Joseph M. | cripple; physically unable to work | none | | none | 10 | 3 | Feb. | 1891 | $5.00 1891 |
| Knox | J. M. | old age | small home | good | none | 20 | | | | $10.00 |

| 1 | 2 | 15 | 16 | 17 | 18 | 19 | 20 | 21 | 22 | 23 |
|---|---|---|---|---|---|---|---|---|---|---|
| SURNAME | GIVEN NAME | REASON FOR REQUEST | PROPERTY | SOBRIETY | SOURCE OF INCOME | R $ | | DATE OF REQUEST | | AMOUNT AWARDED/ COMMENTS |
| Koenig | Ernest | paralyzed for 4 years | none | don't drink | none | 6 | 5 | Oct. | 1914 | $6.00 6 Oct. 1914 |
| Kostenhoschen | Theodore | unable to do hard work | none | good | only what he can earn | 8 | | | | $5.00 10 Mar. 1910 |
| Kriedel | Mrs. | unable to sustain herself | none | | | 5 | 3 | Mar. | 1890 | $5.00 |
| Lake | Helen M. | blind | small house & lot | good | none | 15 | | Mar. | 1913 | |
| Lallamouth | Henry | poor health | | | | 6 | | | | $6.00 12 Mar. 1892; 30 year resident of county |
| Lamb | Geneva M. | too old to work; has no income | none | good | none | 10 | 10 | Nov. | 1915 | $10.00 11 Nov. 1915 |
| Lamb | Genevra M. | old age | none | good | none | 15 | 14 | July | 1915 | rejected |
| Lancaster | William | old & feeble | none | good | small amount occasionally from son | 5 | 19 | Mar. | 1900 | $5.00 19 Mar. 1900 |
| Lander | Margaret E. | poor health; dau. still in H. S. | none | good | none | 10 | | | | |
| Landeway | Anna | sick | none | | | | | | | $6.00 4 Feb. 1892 |
| Lane | E. C., Mrs. | husband killed year ago | 1 acre; small house | | $10.00 allowance | | | Feb. | 1890 | $10.00 3 Mar. 1890 |
| Lane | Elizabeth | because of age & disability | house & lot | good | none | 15 | | | | |
| Lane | Elizabeth C. | unable to earn enough to support herself & | house & 1 acre | good | what she can earn at | 8 | 21 | Mar. | 1900 | $6.00 26 Mar. 1900 |

| 1 | 2 | 15 | 16 | 17 | 18 | 19 | 20 | 21 | 22 | 23 |
|---|---|---|---|---|---|---|---|---|---|---|
| SURNAME | GIVEN NAME | REASON FOR REQUEST | PROPER-TY | SOBRI-ETY | SOURCE OF INCOME | R $ | | DATE OF REQUEST | | AMOUNT AWARDED/ COMMENTS |
| Lane | Elizabeth C. | son totally dependent on her for board & care children | one house & lot | good | odd jobs | 12 | | | | $10.00 15 Oct. 1915 |
| Lane | Mrs. | mentally unbalanced | | | none | 5 | 16 | Jan. | 1900 | $6.00 25 Jan. 1900 to be held by Thomas Silk |
| Langren | Louisa | cannot make enough to support herself and children | | | | | 22 | Sept. | 1890 | filed 6 Oct. 1890 |
| LaPoint | William | gastric cancer | | | | | | | | requested funeral expenses; veteran; burial in Cypress Hill Petaluma |
| Larrison | Seymour | sick and unable to work | none | good | none | 8 | 6 | July | 1910 | |
| Larsen | Anton | | none | good | none | | 8 | Jan. | 1916 | $8.00 17 June 1916 |
| Lavin | Timothy | crippled, lame; unable to work | none | | none | 10 | 29 | Apr. | 1891 | $6.00 4 May 1891 |
| Law | M., Mrs. | unable to give proper support | | | | 10 | | | | $15.00 17 July 1915 |
| Lawrence | Alva Perry | father physically unable to support himself and family | none | good | none | 6 | 29 | Dec. | 1898 | |
| Lawrence | Katie Amanda | father physically unable to support himself and family | none | good | none | 6 | 29 | Dec. | 1898 | |
| Lawrence | Mary J. | husband in county jail; wife unable to work | | | | | 11 | Jan. | 1888 | |
| Lawson | M. H. | sick & confined to bed | none | good | none | 10 | | | | $10.00 12 July 1916 |
| Leander | Charles | indigent | | | | | 16 | Dec. | 1913 | $6.00 5 Jan. 1914 |

| 1 | 2 | 15 | 16 | 17 | 18 | 19 | 20 | 21 | 22 | 23 |
|---|---|---|---|---|---|---|---|---|---|---|
| SURNAME | GIVEN NAME | REASON FOR REQUEST | PROPER-TY | SOBRI-ETY | SOURCE OF INCOME | R $ | | DATE OF REQUEST | | AMOUNT AWARDED/ COMMENTS |
| Lebeouff | Fred | old, mentally incapable | none | quiet old hermit | none | 5 | 20 | Mar. | 1900 | $5.00 2 Apr. 1900 |
| Lee | Dora | husband deserted | none | good | none | 5 | 18 | Mar. | 1900 | $5.00 2 Apr. 1900 |
| Lee | Dora, Mrs. | no means of living | none | good | none | 8 | 8 | Oct. | 1901 | $5.00 2 Jan. 1900 |
| Lee | Lottie | poor health | none | good | none | 10 | 4 | | 1889 | petition rejected filed 4 June 1889 |
| Lelonarn | Celestine | | none | | none | | 29 | Mar. | 1890 | |
| Leluarn | Celestine, Mrs. | cripple; inflammatory rheumatism | | | | | 23 | Feb. | 1889 | |
| Leluarn | John | heart disease; unable to work; wife invalid | none | good | none | 8 | 30 | Apr. | 1910 | |
| LeMoine | John | old, crippled & feeble | none | good | none | 12 | 24 | Oct. | 1912 | $8.00 6 Nov. 1912 |
| Lennox | James W. | infirm | none | good | none | 8 | 6 | Feb. | 1913 | |
| Lennox | Jas. W. | old age; asthma | none | good | none | | 23 | Aug. | 1911 | $6.00 5 Sept. 1911 |
| Leonard | Mary, Mrs. | old | none | excellent | none | 10 | 24 | Apr. | 1901 | $8.00 7 May 1901 |
| Leonard | S. F., Mr. & Mrs. | unable to work | none | good | none | 10 | 20 | Sept. | 1907 | $10.00 9 Oct. 1907 |
| Letcher | Giles, Mr. & Mrs. | refugees from SF earthquake | none | good | none | 10 | 28 | Mar. | 1913 | $10.00 8 Apr. 1913 |
| Letcher | Kate, Mrs. | sick | none | good | none | 10 | 30 | Jan. | 1912 | $8.00 7 Feb. 1912 |
| Lewis | Cora | poor health | none | good | only what children earn | 25 | 16 | Sept. | 1913 | |
| Lewis | Ellen A. | unable to support children | none | good | none | 10 | 18 | Feb. | 1913 | $10.00 |
| Lewis | Elvira | abandoned | none | good | none | 15 | | | | |
| Lewis | Florence, Mrs. | unable to support family | | | | | 5 | Feb. | 1879 | |
| Lewis | G. W. & family | consumption; confined to bed | | | | | | | | |
| Lewis | Harriet | ill health and unable to work | none | good | none | 6 | 29 | Mar. | 1900 | $5.00 May 1900 |

| 1 | 2 | 15 | 16 | 17 | 18 | 19 | 20 | 21 | 22 | 23 |
|---|---|---|---|---|---|---|---|---|---|---|
| SURNAME | GIVEN NAME | REASON FOR REQUEST | PROPERTY | SOBRIETY | SOURCE OF INCOME | R $ | | DATE OF REQUEST | | AMOUNT AWARDED/ COMMENTS |
| Lewis | James H. | broken leg | none | good | none | 8 | | | | no award 8 Aug. 1899 |
| Lewis | Martha J. | partly paralyzed | house & lot allowed by sister | good | | 10 | | | | $10.00 3 Nov. 1913 |
| Lewis | Martha, Mrs. | Miss Bole in hospital | | good | none | 10 | | | | $10.00 6 Dec. 1911 |
| Lewis | Mary | taking care of grandchildren and their invalid mother | | | | | 4 | Jan. | 1883 | |
| Lewis | R. M. | partially paralyzed | | | | | 27 | June | 1910 | |
| Lewis | R. M. | old and unable to work | none | good | none | 8 | | | | $4.00 June 1900 |
| Lewis | Ralph | sick | none | good | $4.90/ mo. | 10 | 30 | Oct. | 1911 | $10.00 6 Dec. 1911 |
| Lewis | Robert | sick | none | good | none | 15 | 11 | Mar. | 1913 | |
| Lightfoot | Eliza | old | none | good | none | 6 | | | | $6.00 2 Nov. 1913 |
| Lingron | Alfred | | none | good | none | | | | | $10.00 14 July 1915 |
| Livingston | Cornelia E. | mother paralytic; Cornelia confirmed invalid; husband gone | none | | | | 25 | Sept. | 1889 | |
| Livingston | Ella | epileptic; husband abandoned her | none | | charity of friends | | | | | $5.00 5 Jan. 1892 |
| Lockerby | Robert | old age & sickness | | good | | 10 | 29 | Dec. | 1915 | $8.00 14 June 1916 |
| Long | Tilly | recently widowed with 4 children | none | good | none | 6 | 1 | July | 1901 | $6.00 3 July 1901 |
| Lottritz | John & Mary | old | | | | | 29 | Mar. | 1890 | son-in-law Shearman, Daniel |
| Lottritz | Mary E., Mrs. | | small home in mountains | excellent | none | 6 | 24 | May | 1900 | $ 5.00 3 May 1900 |
| Louk | Cora L., Mrs. | husband ran away 1899 | none | sober | none | 12 | 5 | Apr. | 1900 | $ 8.00 7 Apr. 1900 |

| 1 SURNAME | 2 GIVEN NAME | 15 REASON FOR REQUEST | 16 PROPERTY | 17 SOBRIETY | 18 SOURCE OF INCOME | 19 R $ | 20 | 21 DATE OF REQUEST | 22 | 23 AMOUNT AWARDED/ COMMENTS |
|---|---|---|---|---|---|---|---|---|---|---|
| Louk | Olive | not physically able to support themselves | none | good | none | 15 | 25 | Apr. | 1914 | $15.00 5 May 1914 |
| Lounibos | Emile P. | tuberculosis; cannot work | 2 lots & bungalow | sober | none | 25 | 13 | Feb. | 1917 | $25.00 13 Feb. 1917 |
| Lueders | Henry & wife | paralyzed; wife crippled | none | | | | | | | $8.00 Nov. 1891 |
| Maclean | Kate & Margaret, Misses | incapacitated by age; bodily infirmity | | | | | 6 | Jan. | 1890 | |
| Maclean #1 | Katherine & Margaret | Katherine old, delicate health; Margaret lame | | | | | 9 | Nov. | 1888 | $8.00 3 Mar. 1890 |
| Maclean #2 | Katherine & Margaret | in delicate health; brother Alexander an invalid | | | none | | 3 | Mar. | 1890 | $8.00 |
| Maclean #3 | Misses | they are old and destitute; one crippled; other in poor health | | | | | 28 | June | 1890 | $10.00 3 July 1890; brother recently died |
| Magetti | Bartolomeo | old age | none | good | none | 8 | 26 | Mar. | 1900 | $5.00 27 Mar. 1900 |
| Maginnis | Thos. | blindness | none | good | none | | 17 | Nov. | 1911 | $6.00 18 Nov. 1911 |
| Mahan | Charles | old and unable to work | none | | charity | 10 | | | | $5.00 2 Dec. 1890 |
| Maloney | Michael | infirm and poor | | | | 10 | 13 | Jan. | 1892 | $10.00 for one mo. 13 Jan. 1892; resident of state 20 yrs. |
| Maloof | Charlie | sick & unable to work; nearly blind; has fits; wife unable to leave him | small house & lot | sober | none | | 13 | Nov. | 1915 | rejected |
| Manning | Mary | husband 64 and unable to work rest of family also sick | | | | 10 | 14 | Feb. | 1899 | $5.00 16 Feb. 1899 |

| 1 | 2 | 15 | 16 | 17 | 18 | 19 | 20 | 21 | 22 | 23 |
|---|---|---|---|---|---|---|---|---|---|---|
| SURNAME | GIVEN NAME | REASON FOR REQUEST | PROPER-TY | SOBRI-ETY | SOURCE OF INCOME | R $ | | DATE OF REQUEST | | AMOUNT AWARDED/ COMMENTS |
| Maren | James | | none | sober | | 8 | 28 | Feb. | 1913 | |
| Maren | James | old age | none | good | none | 8 | | | | $8.00 5 June 1911 |
| Marion | A., Mrs. | husband's injury at work | none | good | none | 30 | 15 | June | 1915 | |
| Markham | Susan | sick | none | good | none | 8 | 14 | Nov. | 1912 | $6.00 5 Dec. 1912 |
| Marsh | Alida L., Mrs. | unable to clothe and provide for 2 minor children | none | | none | 10 | 9 | May | 1916 | $10.00 11 May 1916 |
| Marsh | J. S. | old and feeble | none | good | none | 8 | 27 | May | 1910 | $8.00 9 June 1910 |
| Marsh | J. S. | not able to support self | none | sober | none | | 3 | Apr. | 1916 | rejected |
| Marsh | John Shelby | old & unable to earn living | none | strictly temperate | none | 6 | | | | |
| Marshall | Izoro K., Mrs. | | none | good | none | 5 | | | | $5.00 14 Nov. 1916 |
| Marshall | Martha J. | sick & unable to work; husband nearly blind; children unable to help | none | good | none | 8 | 31 | Aug. | 1916 | $8.00 11 Oct. 1916 |
| Martell | David | wife very sick; unable to work | none | good | none | 10 | 7 | Sept. | 1912 | $10.00 7 Oct. 1912 |
| Marten | Alex | ill health and unable to work for several months | none | good | none | | | | | $7.00 8 Jan. 1913 |
| Martin | Alex | sick & unable to work; no other means of support | | OK | none | 7 | 21 | Mar. | 1913 | |
| Martin | E. J., Mrs. | unable to work | none | good | none | 10 | | | | $5.00 5 Feb. 1890 |
| Martin | Elizabeth J. | old age | none | good | none | 8 | 19 | Sept. | 1900 | $6.00 10 Nov. 1900 |
| Martin | Elizabeth J. | old | none | good | none | 8 | 21 | Mar. | 1913 | |
| Martin | Elizabeth Jane | invalid & unable to support herself; | some furniture | sober habits | none | 5 | | | | $5.00 8 July 1892; husband Geo. W. |

| 1 | 2 | 15 | 16 | 17 | 18 | 19 | 20 | 21 | 22 | 23 |
|---|---|---|---|---|---|---|---|---|---|---|
| SURNAME | GIVEN NAME | REASON FOR REQUEST | PROPER- TY | SOBRI- ETY | SOURCE OF INCOME | R $ | | DATE OF REQUEST | | AMOUNT AWARDED/ COMMENTS |
| | | husband died in 1888 | | | | | | | | Martini came to CA 1870 |
| Martin | G. W., Mr. & Mrs. | wife delicate; husband unable to get around | none | | | | 28 | Sept. | 1886 | $8.00 2 Oct. 1886 |
| Martin | George W., Mrs. | invalid; unable to work | | | | 8 | 6 | Sept. | 1890 | $5.00 1 Oct. 1890 |
| Martz | Samuel | badly crippled with rheumatism | | good | none | 12 | 28 | Dec. | 1911 | $8.00 5 Jan. 1912 |
| Martz | Samuel | old age; rheumatism; general disability | | sober & honest | | 8 | 3 | Mar. | 1913 | |
| Masa | Susanah | sick & unable to work | none | | none | | 5 | June | 1889 | |
| Masa | Susanah, Mrs. | old; sick; unable to work | none | | none | | 3 | Mar. | 1890 | $6.00 |
| Mason | Myrtle, Mrs. | husband deserted them | none | sober | none | 8 | 11 | June | 1915 | $8.00 14 June 1915 |
| Mastrup | Mary | | none | | none | 10 | | Mar. | 1900 | |
| Mastrup | Mary | divorced with 5 small children | none | good | none | 10 | | | | immediate relief $5.00 6 Jan. 1899 |
| Mastrup | Mary, Mrs. | poor health | none | good | none | 10 | | | 1900 | $10.00 5 July 1900 |
| Mathews | Elizabeth | old and crippled | house & lot | good | none | 8 | | | | |
| Matsen | Marie P. | old age; eyesight | none | very best | few chickens | | 3 | Dec. | 1910 | $8.00 6 Dec. 1910 |
| Matsen | Mary P. | old age | none | good | none | 8 | | | | |
| Matthews | Eliza | old age & sick | small house | good | none | 8 | 17 | Jan. | 1910 | |
| Mausera | Antonio Garcia | lost wife 7 Dec. 1912; unable to work | none | sober | none | 8 | 12 | Dec. | 1912 | $8.00 9 Jan 1913 |
| Mausera | Antonio Garcia | lost wife lately; need help until winter is over | none | good | none | | 8 | Mar. | 1913 | |
| Maxwell | Alvina | temporary work as | none | good | $8.00/ | 10 | 5 | Apr. | 1916 | $10.00 11 May |

| 1 | 2 | 15 | 16 | 17 | 18 | 19 | 20 | 21 | 22 | 23 |
|---|---|---|---|---|---|---|---|---|---|---|
| SURNAME | GIVEN NAME | REASON FOR REQUEST | PROPER-TY | SOBRI-ETY | SOURCE OF INCOME | R $ | | DATE OF REQUEST | | AMOUNT AWARDED/ COMMENTS |
| | | saleslady | | | week | | | | | 1916 |
| McBee | Samentha | old age | none | good | none | 8 | 27 | Mar. | 1900 | $8.00 2 Apr. 1900 |
| McCaleb | Dona, Mrs. | unable to support herself & children | house & lot | sober | none | 10 | 9 | Oct. | 1916 | $10.00 11 Dec. 1916 |
| McCarty | L. E., Mrs. | too old | none | good | none | 15 | 7 | Jan. | 1914 | |
| McCarty | L. W., Mrs. | unable to find work | none | good | dau. works in silk factory, mother sells bks. | 10 | 28 | Jun. | 1916 | allowance not granted |
| McCombs | Aaron C. | unable to get work | none | sober | none | 10 | 3 | Feb. | 1916 | $10.00 16 Feb. 1916 |
| McCoy | Alma, Mrs. | 2 children to support; father in Oregon; contributes nothing | none | good | none | 12 | 6 | Sept. | 1913 | $10.00 9 Oct. 1913 |
| McCriston | Silvester C. | too old; unable to make living | none | sober | none | 10 | 27 | June | 1912 | $10.00 2 July 1912 |
| McDaniel | Pearl, Mrs. | not able to support | none | good | none | 8 | 17 | Mar. | 1900 | $6.00 20 Mar. 1900 |
| McDaniels | Pearl, Mrs. | destitute | none | good | none | 8 | 6 | Sept. | 1899 | $6.00 7 Sept. 1899 |
| McDonald | Isabella, Mrs. | old age | none | good | little earned by husband | 8 | 28 | Mar. | 1900 | $6.00 30 Mar. 1900 |
| McElnay | S. C., Mrs. | old age | none | good | none | 10 | 4 | Sept. | 1912 | $8.00 5 Sept. 1912 |
| McElnay | S. C., Mrs. | old age | none | excellent | none | 10 | | | | |
| McFarland | Vina | feeble; no means of support | | good | none | 8 | | | | $7.00 5 Apr. 1900; listed as colored |
| McFarland | Vina, Mrs. | aged and respectable | | | neighbors | | 8 | Nov. | 1890 | |
| McGreavy | Ellen F. | old age; poor health | none | good | none | 8 | 8 | May | 1916 | $8.00 13 May 1916 |
| McGuire | Elizabeth | | | | | | 29 | May | 1891 | $8.00 3 June 1891 |
| McGuire | Neil | dislocated shoulder; | | | | 15 | | Feb. | 1890 | $5.00 |

-143-

| 1 | 2 | 15 | 16 | 17 | 18 | 19 | 20 | 21 | 22 | 23 |
|---|---|---|---|---|---|---|---|---|---|---|
| SURNAME | GIVEN NAME | REASON FOR REQUEST | PROPER-TY | SOBRI-ETY | SOURCE OF INCOME | R $ | | DATE OF REQUEST | | AMOUNT AWARDED/ COMMENTS |
| McLaughlin | Robert | unable to work | | | | | | | | |
| | | feeble and nearly blind | | | | 10 | 9 | Apr. | 1884 | rejected 11 Apr. 1884 |
| McLean | Margaret | husband in jail | | | | | 28 | Mar. | 1892 | $10.00 5 Apr. 1892; husband's name Daniel J. McLean |
| McMillion | Vada | unable to support mother & child | none | good | does some washing | 10 | 7 | Aug. | 1913 | $10.00 7 Aug. 1913 |
| McNally | Ella | sick | none | good | none | 8 | | | | $5.00 9 Feb. 1900 |
| McNally | Ella, Mrs. | no means of support | none | good | none | 5 | 28 | Mar. | 1900 | rejected 6 Apr. 1900 |
| McPeak | Belle, Miss | sick | none | good | none | 8 | 19 | Apr. | 1900 | $8.00 June 1900 |
| McPeak | Peter F. | unable to work enough to live on | none | good | none | 10 | 3 | Mar. | 1913 | |
| Meador | Bell, Mrs. | bed ridden | none | good | one dau. helps | 7 | | | | $7.00 6 June 1911 |
| Meador | Belle, Mrs. | bedridden | none | good | some help from dau. | 10 | 25 | Feb. | 1913 | |
| Means | Lycurgus | physically unable to earn living | none | good | none | 10 | 19 | Oct. | 1912 | $8.00 6 Nov. 1912 |
| Means | Lycurgus | invalid; incapacitated for work | none | good | none | 10 | 13 | Mar. | 1913 | |
| Mecke | Caroline | lack of funds; invalid | none | good | none | 10 | 13 | Feb. | 1917 | $10.00 13 Feb. 1917; letter attached from H. L. Lorentzen, M.D. |
| Mehan | Patrick | unable to work; confined to bed | | | friend | 12 | 14 | July | 1884 | |
| Mell | Mary | old age; unable to work | none | good | none | 10 | 19 | Sept. | 1912 | $7.00 6 Nov. 1912 |
| Mell | Mary | unable to work | none | good | none | 10 | 18 | Mar. | 1913 | |

| 1 | 2 | 15 | 16 | 17 | 18 | 19 | 20 | 21 | 22 | 23 |
|---|---|---|---|---|---|---|---|---|---|---|
| SURNAME | GIVEN NAME | REASON FOR REQUEST | PROPERTY | SOBRIETY | SOURCE OF INCOME | R $ | | DATE OF REQUEST | | AMOUNT AWARDED/ COMMENTS |
| Mello | Amelia | no means of support | 1 ½ acres | good | none | 10 | 4 | Jan. | 1912 | not allowed |
| Mello | Emilia C. (Mrs. Geo.) | now widowed | | | | 8 | 10 | Dec. | 1892 | |
| Mello | Geo. | incapacitated | | | | | 7 | Sept. | 1892 | $8.00 13 Sept. 1892 |
| Merrell | Ellen A. | old | lot & house | good | none except her labor | 10 | | | | $10.00 8 Dec. 1914 |
| Merrit | Edward | crippled from rheumatism | none | good | none | 10 | 31 | Mar. | 1916 | $10.00 13 Apr. 1916 |
| Merrithen | M. G., Mrs. | unable to work but very little; 7 children to support | none | total abstinence | no | 8 | 1 | Nov. | 1901 | $6.00 |
| Merritt | S. J., Mrs. | old age | none | good | none | 10 | 24 | Dec. | 1909 | $10.00 6 Jan. 1910 |
| Merritt | Sarah J. | unable to work | none | good | none | 8 | | | | |
| Merritt | Sarah J. | old age | none | good | none | 12 | | | | $8.00 4 Mar. 1912 |
| Metcalf | Loretta | husband deserted; sick & unable to work | none | good | none | 15 | 10 | June | 1913 | |
| Metcalf | Loretta | no means of support | none | good | none except her labor | 15 | 17 | Sept. | 1915 | rejected |
| Meyer | Lulu | separated from drunken husband | none | good | none | 8 | 30 | Mar. | 1900 | $6.00 30 Mar. 1900 |
| Meyer | M. | old; sick | | sober | | 8 | | | | $8.00 4 May 1914 |
| Meyers | Lula | poor health and unable to support children | none | good | none | 8 | 9 | Dec. | 1899 | |
| Miller | Carl, Mrs. | poor health | none | good | none | 8 | 18 | Mar. | 1913 | |
| Miller | Carl, Mrs. | husband fails to provide for her | none | sober | | 8 | | | | |
| Miller | Louisa | unable to make living | none | good | $8 to $10 | 8 | 3 | Feb. | 1909 | $5.00 5 Feb. 1909 |

| 1 | 2 | 15 | 16 | 17 | 18 | 19 | 20 | 21 | 22 | 23 |
|---|---|---|---|---|---|---|---|---|---|---|
| SURNAME | GIVEN NAME | REASON FOR REQUEST | PROPER-TY | SOBRI-ETY | SOURCE OF INCOME | R $ | | DATE OF REQUEST | | AMOUNT AWARDED/ COMMENTS |
| | | | | | per month | | | | | |
| Miller | Louisa | can't get work | none | good | none | 8 | | | | |
| Miller | Lucy, Mrs. | husband deserted her | | | | 6 | 13 | Aug. | 1891 | $6.00 Sept. 8 Sept. 1891 |
| Minear | Mrs. | 2 sick children; one invalid; unable to work | | | | | | | 1890 | filed 9 July 1890 |
| Mize | Aditha | has consumptive son to care for | non | good | none | 5 | 12 | Jan. | 1899 | |
| Monaco | Paulena | ill health; ulcerated foot | none | good | none | 10 | 21 | Jan. | 1911 | $7.00 8 Feb. 1911 |
| Monotti | Luigi | unable to work because of age | none | sober | none | 15 | 26 | Oct. | 1900 | |
| Moore | E. J., Mrs. | | none | good | two oldest children partly supported by Washoe Co., NV | 8 | 25 | Feb. | 1914 | $8.00 6 Apr. 1914 |
| Moore | Ellen | old age | none | good | none | 15 | 19 | Mar. | 1915 | |
| Moore | Margaret | unable to earn enough | lot on Sebastopol Ave. | good | small wages | 8 | | | | $8.00 Apr. 1914 |
| Moraga | Jospha, Mrs. | rheumatism; unable to work | none | | none | | 17 | July | 1891 | |
| Moraga | Mrs. | son ill and not likely to recover | | | | | | | | $8.00 10 Apr. 1890 |
| Morrill | Dorinda Rilla | | none | good | none | 10 | | | | $8.00 2 June 1913 |
| Morrisey | Kate, Mrs. | unable to earn enough; husband, John, died 2 Mar. 1885 | none | | | 10 | 2 | Mar. | 1885 | resident of Petaluma for 7 years |

| 1 | 2 | 15 | 16 | 17 | 18 | 19 | 20 | 21 | 22 | 23 |
|---|---|---|---|---|---|---|---|---|---|---|
| SURNAME | GIVEN NAME | REASON FOR REQUEST | PROPER-TY | SOBRI-ETY | SOURCE OF INCOME | R $ | | DATE OF REQUEST | | AMOUNT AWARDED/ COMMENTS |
| Morrison | Mrs. | poor health | none | | | 10 | 4 | Apr. | 1892 | |
| Morrow | James H. | old | | | | 10 | 28 | June | 1910 | |
| Morrow | James H. | old age and infirmity | | good | none | 12 | 22 | Mar. | 1913 | |
| Moulton | S. C. | disabled | | | | 28 | Jan. | 1911 | $8.00 6 Feb. 1911 | |
| Muerth | Alice, Mrs. | | none | best sober | none | 10 | | | | $7.00 18 June 1915 |
| Mulford | Mr. & Mrs. J. | old | none | good | none | 20 | 19 | Feb. | 1915 | $10.00 8 Mar. 1915 |
| Muller | Mary | sickly and unable to earn living | small house | excellent | none | 5 | | | | $5.00 10 Feb. 1899; immediate relief |
| Mullin | Delia, Miss | ill and unable to work | | | | | 30 | Sept. | 1891 | $7.00 6 Oct. 1891 |
| Mulvany | R. M., Mrs. | destitute; husband in Alameda sick; can't contribute | | | neighbor's help | 10 | | | | $8.00 9 Jan. 1892; came to state in 1888 |
| Murphy | Mabel | deserted by parents; father in state prison | none | good | none | 8 | 5 | Feb. | 1900 | $5.00 25 Mar. 1900 |
| Murphy | Mabel, Miss | whereabouts of parents unknown | none | good | none | 8 | 27 | Mar. | 1900 | $5.00 |
| Murphy | R. W. | old age | none | sober | none | 8 | | | | |
| Murphy | Richard W. | old age; unable to earn living | none | good | none | 8 | | | | $8.00 8 Nov. 1911 |
| Myers | Henry | orphan | none | | none | 8 | 30 | Apr. | 1900 | petition rejected 5 Sept. 1902 |
| Navoni | Batista | paralyzed | none | good | none | 6 | 19 | Mar. | 1913 | |
| Navoni | Batista | old age; dau. cannot care for him | none | good | none | 6 | 6 | Oct. | 1909 | $6.00 8 Dec. 1909 |
| Neidring-house | Henry | sick | | good | none | 8 | 15 | Mar. | 1913 | |
| Neidring house | Mr. | old and unable to earn a living | none | good | none | 8 | | June | 1911 | $8.00 5 June 1911 |
| Nelan | Marcella, Mrs. | husband killed 8 Aug. | | | | | 19 | Feb. | 1879 | $8.00 10 Apr. 1879 |

-147-

| 1 | 2 | 15 | 16 | 17 | 18 | 19 | 20 | 21 | 22 | 23 |
|---|---|---|---|---|---|---|---|---|---|---|
| SURNAME | GIVEN NAME | REASON FOR REQUEST | PROPERTY | SOBRIETY | SOURCE OF INCOME | R $ | | DATE OF REQUEST | | AMOUNT AWARDED/ COMMENTS |
| Nelson | A. S. | 1878 by log rolling over him | none | temperate | none | 6 | 6 | June | 1901 | $6.00 6 June 1901 |
| Nelson | Cornelia | old and unable to work | | | | 10 | | | | $10.00 12 Sept. 1916 |
| Nelson | Margaret | very old; walks on crutches | | | none | 8 | 5 | Oct. | 1912 | $8.00 9 Oct. 1912 |
| Nelson | Margaret | walking with crutches | | good | none | 8 | 4 | Mar. | 1913 | |
| Nelson | Margaret, Mrs. | crippled | | | | | | | | $6.00 8 Mar. 1892 |
| Neuman | Marie | | none | good | | 10 | | | | |
| Newman | Elizabeth | unable to work | none | good | none | 5 | 9 | Apr. | 1900 | $5.00 10 Apr. 1900 |
| Newman | John Allen | old age | none | good | none | 10 | 12 | June | 1913 | $8.00 4 Aug. 1913 |
| Newman | John Allen | old age; nearly blind | none | good | none | 10 | | | | $7.00 Apr. 1912 |
| Newman | Marie, Mrs. | fell & broke shoulder | none | good | none | 8 | 7 | Apr. | 1909 | $8.00 Apr. 1909 |
| Newman | W. N. | rheumatism & often confined to bed | | sober | receiving $5.00 | | 30 | Jan. | 1890 | $5.00 |
| Newton | Hulda | invalid 7 years; husband in Veterans' Home | none | good | none | 10 | 12 | Mar. | 1913 | |
| Newton | Hulda S. | invalid; no source of income except pension | none | good | pension | 10 | 1 | May | 1910 | $10.00 |
| Noriel | J. C. | left arm disabled | none | good | none | 8 | 2 | May | 1900 | rejected |
| Noriel | Jesse | crippled | none | good | none | 8 | 30 | Dec. | 1912 | $8.00 9 Jan. 1913 |
| Norris | Anna, Mrs. | ill | | | none | 10 | | Mar. | 1913 | |
| Norris | Anna, Mrs. | poor health; unable to work | none | good | none | 6 | | | | $6.00 7 Aug. 1912 |
| Norris | E., Mrs. | no means of support | small amount in Iowa | good | none | 10 | | | | |

| 1 | 2 | 15 | 16 | 17 | 18 | 19 | 20 | 21 | 22 | 23 |
|---|---|---|---|---|---|---|---|---|---|---|
| SURNAME | GIVEN NAME | REASON FOR REQUEST | PROPER-TY | SOBRI-ETY | SOURCE OF INCOME | R $ | | DATE OF REQUEST | | AMOUNT AWARDED/ COMMENTS |
| Norris | Elizabeth, Mrs. | old age | none | good | none | 10 | 18 | May | 1909 | $10.00 10 June 1909 |
| Northway | I. B., Mrs. | husband sick and unable to work | none | good | about $1.50 per week | 15 | 3 | Mar. | 1915 | child is adopted |
| Norton | John, Mrs. | destitute circumstances | | | | | 30 | Dec. | 1886 | |
| Norton | John, Mrs. | in poor health; boy has fits | none | | none | 10 | 8 | Mar. | 1890 | |
| Norton | Philinda | unable to work | small lot | good | none | 8 | 25 | Apr. | 1900 | rejected |
| Nottingham | Mrs. | sick, crippled | | | | | 7 | Nov. | 1883 | |
| O'Bryan | A. L. | paralyzed | none | strictly sober | donations | 12 | | | | $12.00 |
| O'Halleran | Tymothy | infirm & crippled with rheumatism | none | good | none | 12 | 24 | Oct. | 1912 | $8.00 6 Nov. 1912 |
| O'Halloran | Bella Bransteller | unable to work because of gunshot wounds | none | excellent | none | 12 | 30 | Mar. | 1916 | rejected |
| O'Halloran | J. D., Mrs. | wounded from gunshot inflicted by drunken husband; unable to work | none | good | none | 40 | 4 | Oct. | 1915 | rejected |
| O'Halloran | Timothy | rheumatism | none | good | none | 8 | 6 | Feb. | 1913 | |
| Ohlsen | Henry | has an ulcer of leg | none | good | a little work | 8 | 28 | Oct. | 1914 | |
| Olmstead | L. W. | rheumatism | none | good | none | 4 | 1 | Feb. | 1899 | $4.00 8 Feb. 1899 |
| Olmstead | L. W. | rheumatism | small value | good | none | 5 | 22 | Mar. | 1900 | $5.00 2 Apr. 1900 |
| Olmstead | Levy Willis | unable to work | none | good | none | 10 | | | | |
| Ologue | Mary | husband committed to insane asylum; formerly Carrillo | none | sober | none | 8 | 16 | Nov. | 1899 | $6.00 4 Dec. 1899 |

| 1 | 2 | 15 | 16 | 17 | 18 | 19 | 20 | 21 | 22 | 23 |
|---|---|---|---|---|---|---|---|---|---|---|
| SURNAME | GIVEN NAME | REASON FOR REQUEST | PROPER-TY | SOBRI-ETY | SOURCE OF INCOME | R $ | | DATE OF REQUEST | | AMOUNT AWARDED/ COMMENTS |
| Olway | Abby | crippled | none | good | none | 8 | 26 | June | 1912 | $8.00 2 July 1912 |
| O'Neil | Minnie | husband left her; dau. is sick | | good | none | | 5 | Dec. | 1910 | $6.00 7 Dec. 1910 |
| O'Rourke | Mary, Mrs. | recently widowed | none | | friends raised money to purchase lot & build house | | 9 | Sept. | 1882 | |
| Orth | Helene | poor health | none | good | none | 5 | 21 | Mar. | 1900 | |
| Orth | Helene, Mrs. | health poor | none | good | none | 8 | | | | $5.00 4 Dec. 1899 |
| Ouellet | J. C. | eyes are bad | none | good | none | 8 | 6 | Nov. | 1913 | $8.00 5 Jan. 1914 |
| Pahud | Henriette, Mrs. | pregnant; husband died 30 Oct. 1892 | cow & chickens | | none | | 5 | Nov. | 1892 | $10.00 10 Nov. 1892; in state since 1890 (Mr. G. Pahud) |
| Palmer | Thomas B. | mitral disease of heart; funeral expenses | | | | | | | | burial of indigent soldier; Masonic Cemetery Sebastopol; 3 Jan. 1910 |
| Papera | Arseda | blind; crippled 5 yrs. | none | good | none | 6 | 27 | Feb. | 1909 | $6.00 1 Mar. 1909 |
| Park | Elizabeth, Mrs. | husband left | none | good | none | 15 | 10 | May | 1909 | $15.00 May 1909 |
| Parker | Frederick | old age | none | good | | 8 | 26 | Sept. | 1916 | $8.00 11 Oct. 1916 |
| Parker | Joseph P. | totally blind from gunshot wound; unable to work | none | good | none | 8 | 11 | Apr. | 1916 | $8.00 11 Apr. 1916 |
| Patrick | Jesse | sick in bed with no means of support | none | good | none | 8 | | | | $8.00 7 Jan. 1899; immediate relief |
| Patterson | J. T. | housework prevents | none | good | none | 5 | 27 | Mar. | 1900 | $5.00 2 Apr. 1900 |

| 1 | 2 | 15 | 16 | 17 | 18 | 19 | 20 | 21 | 22 | 23 |
|---|---|---|---|---|---|---|---|---|---|---|
| SURNAME | GIVEN NAME | REASON FOR REQUEST | PROPER-TY | SOBRI-ETY | SOURCE OF INCOME | R $ | | DATE OF REQUEST | | AMOUNT AWARDED/ COMMENTS |
| Patterson | Mary, Mrs. | him from working old age | none | good | none | | 14 | July | 1909 | $7.00 Aug 1909 |
| Patterson | Pearl & Rosa | orphans | none | | none | 8 | 9 | Aug. | 1900 | |
| Paula | George, Mrs. | | 4 room house | | | 8 or 10 | | | | $8.00 or $10.00 1915 |
| Pearse | Mary, Mrs. | no other means of support | small home; mortgaged | good | none | 10 | 14 | July | 1914 | |
| Pedro | John | old & feeble | none | good | none | 5 | 10 | Apr. | 1900 | $5.00 10 Apr. 1900 |
| Pelizzari | Carlo | continued sickness of husband & wife | none | good | none | 20 | 21 | Aug. | 1912 | $15.00 5 Sept. 1912 |
| Pelizzari | Carlo | continuous sickness in family | | good | none | 15 | 29 | Mar. | 1913 | |
| Pellow | Angelina | husband abandoned her | none | good | working in cannery; about to close | 15 | 12 | Nov. | 1912 | $10.00 13 Nov. 1912 |
| Pellow | Angelina | abandoned by husband | none | good | none | 15 | 15 | Mar. | 1913 | |
| Perey | Joe | crippled in both feet | none | sober | few days work each month | 6 | 19 | Mar. | 1900 | $5.00 |
| Perkins | Blanche | under age | none | good | none | 10 | 26 | Oct. | 1909 | $10.00 Nov. 1909 |
| Perkins | Blanche | invalid | none | good | none | 10 | 1 | July | 1910 | $10.00 6 July 1910 |
| Perrot | E. | old age & poor | none | sober | none | 5 | 28 | Apr. | 1913 | |
| Perry | Agnes | has consumption; unable to work | | | | 8 | | | | $8.00 1 Sept. 1890 |
| Perry | Elizabeth | old age | none | good | none | 10 | 14 | Mar. | 1913 | |
| Perry | Margaret Agnes, | husband left her; has | none | | none | | 15 | Nov. | 1888 | |

| 1 | 2 | 15 | 16 | 17 | 18 | 19 | 20 | 21 | 22 | 23 |
|---|---|---|---|---|---|---|---|---|---|---|
| SURNAME | GIVEN NAME | REASON FOR REQUEST | PROPER-TY | SOBRI-ETY | SOURCE OF INCOME | R $ | | DATE OF REQUEST | | AMOUNT AWARDED/ COMMENTS |
| Perry | Mrs. Mary | consumption; destitute has to care for children; Frank lame arm | none | good | none | 20 | 20 | Sept. | 1909 | $10.00 23 Sept. 1909 |
| Peterson | C. D. | no means of support | none | good | none | 6 | 20 | July | 1914 | $6.00 11 Sept. 1914 |
| Peterson | John | old | none | good | none | 8 | 25 | Aug. | 1907 | $8.00 9 Oct. 1907 |
| Peterson | John | old age | none | good | none | 8 | 28 | Feb. | 1913 | |
| Pettis | Lula A. | | none | | | 20 | | | | $20.00 8 Nov. 1915 |
| Petty | James | physically incapable | | | | | | | | |
| Petty | James Ervin | general disability | | good | | 8 | 4 | Aug. | 1913 | $8.00 3 Jan. 1910 |
| Phelan | Jennie, Miss | cripple | none | yes | none | 10 | 14 | July | 1913 | $10.00 4 Sept. 1913 |
| Phelan | Lucinda, Mrs. | helpless | no | yes | no | 10 | 14 | July | 1913 | |
| Phillips | Mariah, Mrs. | unable to earn livelihood | | | | | | | | $6.00 7 July 1890 |
| Philpott | Sarah M. | sickness | none | good | none | 10 | | | | |
| Phinney | Grace M. | abandoned | none | | none | 10 | 2 | Apr. | 1909 | |
| Pickrell | Nellie, L. | husband sick | none | good | none except taking in washing | 10 | 27 | Jan. | 1915 | |
| Piezzi | Leonard | unable to work; lost a leg | none | good | none | | 2 | Nov. | 1916 | $5.00 11 Nov. 1916 |
| Piezzi(e) | Leonardo | broken leg; not repairable; 6 mos. in county hospital | | | | | 7 | Oct. | 1879 | |
| Poggi | G. B. | totally unable to work | | | | | 6 | Feb. | 1899 | $5.00 10 Feb. 1899 |
| Poggi | G. B. | unable to earn living | house & lot, mortgaged | sober | none | 5 | 7 | May | 1900 | $5.00 8 May 1900 |
| Poggi | G. B., Mr. | seriously hurt; no | | | | | | | | filed 7 May 1890 |

-152-

| 1 SURNAME | 2 GIVEN NAME | 15 REASON FOR REQUEST | 16 PROPERTY | 17 SOBRIETY | 18 SOURCE OF INCOME | 19 R $ | 20 | 21 DATE OF REQUEST | 22 | 23 AMOUNT AWARDED/ COMMENTS |
|---|---|---|---|---|---|---|---|---|---|---|
| Pollard | Thomas & Elizabeth | means of support during illness cripple; destitute | | good | $12.00 a year | 10 | 9 | Apr. | 1880 | certificate #4 commenced 3 yrs ago; stamped 26 Apr. 1898 |
| Pollard | Thomas & wife | husband has only 1 hand; wife feeble and almost blind | | | | 15 | 8 | Apr. | 1886 | |
| Pomroy | Mr. | paralyzed; cannot raise his hands to mouth | | | | | | | 1885 | filed 6 Oct. 1885 |
| Pool | Lydia | poor health; crippled hands | none | temperence | none | 10 | 4 | Oct. | 1916 | $10.00 13 Dec. 1916 |
| Pope | Jacob | rheumatism and asthma | none | good | none | 8 | 6 | Oct. | 1916 | $8.00 11 Oct. 1916 |
| Porter | Julia | husband left; sends no money | none | sober | none | 8 | 10 | Jan. | 1899 | $6.00 11 Jan. 1899 |
| Porter | Lucy | crippled; leg wound that will not heal; unable to work | small home worth about $400 | | | | | | | $8.00 10 Nov. 1891; resident of Sonoma Co. 28 years |
| Porter | William | invalid; consumption | none | good | none | | 25 | Oct. | 1912 | rejected 28 Oct. 1912 |
| Porter | William | consumption | none | good | | 5 | | | | |
| Porter | Wm. P. | typhoid-pneumonia | none | good | none | 8 | 5 | Aug. | 1907 | $8.00 6 Aug. 1907 |
| Post | Frances, Mrs. | broken hip | none | temperate | none | 10 | | | | |
| Post | J. B. | rheumatism; no relatives | | | | 75 | 15 | June | 1885 | letter from Veteran Home (SF); filed 7 July 1885 |
| Potter | Edmond | old age and unable to work | none | sober | none | 5 | 14 | Mar. | 1900 | $5.00 |

| 1 | 2 | 15 | 16 | 17 | 18 | 19 | 20 | 21 | 22 | 23 |
|---|---|---|---|---|---|---|---|---|---|---|
| SURNAME | GIVEN NAME | REASON FOR REQUEST | PROPER-TY | SOBRI-ETY | SOURCE OF INCOME | R $ | | DATE OF REQUEST | | AMOUNT AWARDED/ COMMENTS |
| Powell | Frank | old age | none | good | none | 6 | 29 | Jan. | 1916 | $6.00 4 Feb. 1916 |
| Powers | L., Mrs. | sick and in indigent circumstances; husband in county jail | | | | | 5 | Jan. | 1892 | $5.00 5 Jan. 1892; wife of D. P. Powers |
| Press[e]y | William H. | old age | none | good | none | 5 | 27 | Mar. | 1900 | $5.00 2 Apr. 1900 |
| Price | William H. | unable to work because of age | none | good | none | 8 | 1 | Aug. | 1914 | $8.00 10 Sept. 1914 |
| Prince | Louis L.; Freddie F. | Mrs. Livingston is in County Hospital | | | | | 12 | Mar. | 1890 | |
| Proctor | Sadie | husband in county jail; unable to support children | none | good | none | 10 | | | | $10.00 7 July 1914 |
| Pucinelli | Ben | invalid | none | good | none | 8 | 7 | Mar. | 1915 | $8.00 11 Mar. 1915 |
| Purdy | George Washington | partly paralyzed | none | good | $8.00 renter | 5 | | | 1899 | not allowed 13 Nov. 1899 |
| Quackenbush | Lettie | husband deserted | | | | | 25 | May | 1892 | $5.00 3 June 1892 |
| Querola | John | old age | none | good | none | 8 | 26 | Mar. | 1900 | $6.00 26 Mar. 1900 |
| Quirk | Margaret | rheumatism | none | yes | none | 8 | 30 | Apr. | 1900 | $4.00 May 1900 |
| Raddel | Mrs. | | | | good wages | | 12 | Jan. | 1892 | |
| Raddle | Ed., Mrs. | | | | | | 13 | Dec. | | letter complaining that people not needy; has son & dau. working |
| Radel | Edward, Mrs. | sick & unable to work; husband deserted her; refuses to help | | | | 10 | 27 | May | 1890 | filed 31 May 1890 |
| Raefael | Pedro | old age | none | drinks when he | none | 7 | 18 | July | 1911 | $7.00 7 Aug. 1911 |

-154-

| 1 | 2 | 15 | 16 | 17 | 18 | 19 | 20 | 21 | 22 | 23 |
|---|---|---|---|---|---|---|---|---|---|---|
| SURNAME | GIVEN NAME | REASON FOR REQUEST | PROPER-TY | SOBRI-ETY | SOURCE OF INCOME | R $ | | DATE OF REQUEST | | AMOUNT AWARDED/ COMMENTS |
| Raineri | Lucia | | | can get some-thing | | | | | 1913 | |
| Ramis | Elliott M. & wife | husband broken rib | none | good | none | 15 | 13 | Sept. | 1916 | $15.00 24 Sept. 1916 |
| Read | William B. | sickness | none | sober | none | 15 | 31 | Aug. | 1899 | $5.00 6 Sept. 1899 |
| Read | William Bowers | cannot earn a living because of old age | none | good | none | 8 | | | | $5.00 26 Mar. 1900 |
| Redmond | Harriet M. | old age | | | $6/mo. | 8 | 14 | Oct. | 1910 | |
| Redmond | Harriett M. | is a cripple; doesn't have enough to pay rent | none | good | $80/yr. | 6 | 15 | Mar. | 1913 | |
| Reed | Laura | not able to earn sufficient funds | none | good | has judg-ment against husband; received nothing | 4 | 5 | Mar. | 1907 | $10.00 8 Mar. 1907 |
| Reed | Laura | unable to support herself & children until fruit season | none | good | only own labor | 12 | 8 | Jan. | 1909 | $8.00 13 Jan. 1909 |
| Reed | Sarah Jane | grass widow | | | $4.95/ mo. | 10 | | | 1909 | $6.00 4 Jan. 1909 |
| Reeder | Alice H. | rheumatism & other ailments | none | good | none | 8 | 17 | Mar. | 1900 | $7.00 19 Mar. 1900 |
| Reeder | Alice H. | crippled | home | good | sons help | 10 | | Apr. | 1913 | |
| Reeder | Daisy | husband abandoned family 3 years ago; cannot support self & child | none | good | what she receives from taking in washing | 8 | 1 | Jan. | 1915 | $8.00 8 Jan. 1915 |

| 1 | 2 | 15 | 16 | 17 | 18 | 19 | 20 | 21 | 22 | 23 |
|---|---|---|---|---|---|---|---|---|---|---|
| SURNAME | GIVEN NAME | REASON FOR REQUEST | PROPERTY | SOBRIETY | SOURCE OF INCOME | R $ | | DATE OF REQUEST | | AMOUNT AWARDED/ COMMENTS |
| Reeder | S. W., Mrs. | no means of support | | | | | 3 | Nov. | 1890 | filed 15 Nov. 1890 |
| Reedy | Mary | ill | none | good | none | 10 | | | | $10.00 11 Oct. 1913 |
| Reedy | Mary, Mrs. | | none | good | none | 10 | | | | $10.00 8 Jan. 1913 |
| Reedy | Mary, Mrs. | | none | good | none | 10 | | | | $10.00 8 Apr. 1913 |
| Renfroe | James | infirm & sick | none | good | none | 7 | 27 | Mar. | 1900 | $7.00 2 Apr. 1900 |
| Renfroe | James F. | unable to work for about 22 months | | | | | 13 | Jan. | 1890 | |
| Renfroe | James F. | sore on his leg for over 2 years | | | | | 6 | Mar. | 1890 | $5.00 |
| Renfroe | James F. | | | | | | 29 | Oct. | 1891 | $5.00 Nov. 1891 |
| Renfroe | James F. | crippled; unable to work | few chickens | good | none | 5 | 9 | Jan. | 1899 | $5.00 |
| Reyburn | W. B. | old age; inability to earn livelihood | none | good | none | 8 | 14 | Jan. | 1901 | $5.00 |
| Reynolds | Daniel B. | right leg amputated above knee | none | temperate | none | 10 | 12 | June | 1899 | $8.00 3 July 1899 |
| Reynolds | Daniel B. | right leg amputated above knee | none | good | none | 10 | 20 | Mar. | 1900 | |
| Reynolds | S. K. | old age | none | good | none | 7 | 24 | June | 1911 | $7.00 7 July 1911 |
| Reynolds | S. K. | ill | none | good | none | 8 | | | | no award 14 Apr. 1910 |
| Reynolds | Smith K. | nearly blind | none | good | none | 9 | 28 | Feb. | 1913 | |
| Ribardiere | Susanne | no means of support | none | good | none | 15 | | | | $15.00 8 Sept. 1909 |
| Rice | D. P. | disabled by accident | none | good | none | 9 | 15 | Mar. | 1913 | |
| Rice | Ernest | sick | none | good | none | 8 | 14 | Apr. | 1914 | $8.00 5 May 1914 |
| Rice | Thomas & wife | both old | none | fair | none | 15 | 27 | Feb. | 1913 | |
| Richards | Eliza, Mrs. | heart disease | | | | | 6 | Dec. | 1892 | $8.00 7 Dec. 1892; in CA 3 yrs; rent $6 |
| Richardson | Eliza C., Mrs. | husband in jail; she is | homestead, | OK | none | 15 | 4 | May | 1910 | $12.00 4 May 1910 |

| 1 | 2 | 15 | 16 | 17 | 18 | 19 | 20 | 21 | 22 | 23 |
|---|---|---|---|---|---|---|---|---|---|---|
| SURNAME | GIVEN NAME | REASON FOR REQUEST | PROPER-TY | SOBRI-ETY | SOURCE OF INCOME | R $ | | DATE OF REQUEST | | AMOUNT AWARDED/ COMMENTS |
| Rickett | (children) | unable to work | encumbered | | | | | | | |
| Riley | Clara & Harry | orphan children of Charles Rickett | | | | | 29 | Apr. | 1911 | |
| Ring | R. G. | mother dead; father if living, residence unknown | none | good | none | | 23 | Oct. | 1899 | $6.00 7 Nov. 1899 |
| Ring | R. G. | lame | none | good | none | 5 | 30 | Mar. | 1900 | $5.00 5 Apr. 1900 |
| Rippetoe | Dora | unable to work | none | fair | none | 5 | | | 1899 | $5.00 5 Apr. 1899 |
| Ritter | J. W. | she is sick; no means of support | none | not a drinking man | none | 10 | 1 | Mar. | 1901 | $8.00 6 Mar. 1901 |
| Roat | Wm. L., Mr. & Mrs. | old and feeble | house & lot | good | none | 8 | 14 | May | 1912 | |
| Roberson | Malvina J. | old age | | | | | 22 | Nov. | 1890 | $7.00 2 Dec. 1890 |
| Roberts | Rose, Mrs. | husband deserted her; confined to bed | | | | | 18 | Oct. | 1886 | |
| Robertson | F. | no means | none | good | none | 8 | | | 1899 | rejected 6 July 1899 |
| Robertson | Robert | old age; destitute | | | | | 27 | June | 1890 | filed 2 July 1890 |
| Robertson | Sydney Henry | old age | none | good | none | | 10 | June | 1915 | |
| Robinson | F. | totally disabled; stroke | | good | none | 15 | | | | $15.00 15 June 1916 |
| Robinson | Mary, Mrs. | unable to work | none | good | none | 10 | 12 | Dec. | 1899 | $5.00 2 Jan. 1900 |
| Robison | Fletchey | husband in jail | | | | | 6 | Feb. | 1888 | |
| Rodd | John | old age | none | good | none | 5 | 14 | Apr. | 1900 | $5.00 6 July 1900 |
| | | confined to bed | none | good | rent paid by Mr. Vincent | 8 | 31 | Oct. | 1900 | |

| 1 | 2 | 15 | 16 | 17 | 18 | 19 | 20 | 21 | 22 | 23 |
|---|---|---|---|---|---|---|---|---|---|---|
| SURNAME | GIVEN NAME | REASON FOR REQUEST | PROPER-TY | SOBRI-ETY | SOURCE OF INCOME | R $ | | DATE OF REQUEST | | AMOUNT AWARDED/ COMMENTS |
| Rogers | Niles V. | epithelioma of lips; burial expenses | | | | | | | | burial of indigent soldier, Healdsburg Cemetery, 25 June 1910 |
| Rogers | Rita Francisca | poor health | | | | | 24 | June | 1887 | |
| Rose | D. E., Mrs. | destitute | | | | | 15 | Oct. | 1892 | $10.00 10 Nov. 1892 |
| Rose | Jane | abandoned; ill | none | good | none | 6 | 27 | Nov. | 1912 | $6.00 9 Jan. 1913 |
| Rose | Mr. & Mrs. | convalescent | | | | | | | | $6.00 filed 2 Jan. 1900 |
| Rossi | Serafina | mother is sick; underwent operation; children trying to work | none | good | none | 20 | 1 | July | 1914 | rejected |
| Roth | A. R. | old age | none | good | none | 5 | 20 | Mar. | 1900 | $5.00 2 Apr. 1900 |
| Roy | Ann, Mrs. | invalid | | | | 10 | 24 | Jan. | 1891 | $10.00 5 Feb. 1891 |
| Roy | Fannie | sick | | | | 10 | 7 | July | 1891 | assistance not granted |
| Rudolfi | Attilio | rheumatism; almost totally blind | none | good | none | 8 | 1 | Aug. | 1899 | $6.00 10 Aug. 1899 |
| Rudolfi | Attilio | inflammatory rheumatism | none | good | none | 8 | 21 | Nov. | 1899 | $5.00 4 Dec. 1899 |
| Rudolfi | Attilio | sick | none | good | none | 8 | 1 | Mar. | 1913 | |
| Rudolfi | Attilio | inflammatory rheumatism and partial blindness | none | good | none | 8 | 9 | Apr. | 1900 | $5.00 11 Apr. 1900 |
| Ruesch | Christof | old | homestead claim | good | none | 6 | 14 | Nov. | 1914 | $6.00 6 Jan. 1915 |
| Runyan | Hattie | husband sick 8 months | | good | none | 15 | 2 | Aug. | 1909 | $7.00 Aug 1909 |
| Russ | Matilda | old age | house & | good | none | 8 | | | 1909 | $8.00 3 Jan. 1910 |

| 1 | 2 | 15 | 16 | 17 | 18 | 19 | 20 | 21 | 22 | 23 |
|---|---|---|---|---|---|---|---|---|---|---|
| SURNAME | GIVEN NAME | REASON FOR REQUEST | PROPERTY | SOBRIETY | SOURCE OF INCOME | R $ | | DATE OF REQUEST | | AMOUNT AWARDED/ COMMENTS |
| Russell | William H. | very feeble | lot value about $7.00 | good | none | 5 | 24 | Mar. | 1900 | $5.00 24 Mar. 1900 |
| Ryerson | William | old age | none | good | none | 10 | 24 | Nov. | 1907 | $8.00 3 Dec. 1907 |
| Sabieni | Mary | husband in hospital | none | good | none | 10 | 23 | July | 1907 | $8.00 31 July 1907 |
| Sales | Henery | too old to work; rheumatism | no | sober | none | 6 | | | | $6.00 11 Sept. 1914 |
| Sales | Luke & family | fever, bedridden | | | | | | | | $6.00 8 Dec. 1892 |
| Salvador | Mr. | old man; totally blind; partially deaf | none | yes | none | 8 | 20 | Sept. | 1913 | $8.00 7 Oct. 1913 |
| Samuels | Anna | chronic appendicitis | none | no drink habits | none | 10 | | | | |
| Samuels | James, Mrs. | sick | none | good | none | 15 | 2 | Mar. | 1891 | $10.00 3 Mar. 1891 |
| Samuels | Jessie M. | father sent to state prison; petitioner sick | | | | | 13 | Oct. | 1915 | rejected |
| Sandusky | Mattie | unable to work | none | good | none | 10 | 1 | Apr. | 1900 | $8.00 2 Apr. 1900 |
| Sansbury | Benjamin Franklin | cancer | none | sober | 5.00/mo. from sister | 10 | 30 | Apr. | 1910 | |
| Santos | Mary, Mrs. | unable to support family | none | good | from neighbors | 10 | 7 | Oct. | 1909 | |
| Santos | Mary, Mrs. | unable to support and care for children | none | good | none | 10 | 5 | Mar. | 1913 | |
| Sawyer | Alice, Mrs. | sick | | | | | | | | $10.00 7 June 1892; allowed to C. W. York |
| Sawyer | Marsden Albert | old; sick; unable to earn living | house where he lives | very good | none | 6 | 9 | July | 1914 | |

| 1 SURNAME | 2 GIVEN NAME | 15 REASON FOR REQUEST | 16 PROPERTY | 17 SOBRIETY | 18 SOURCE OF INCOME | 19 R $ | 20 | 21 DATE OF REQUEST | 22 | 23 AMOUNT AWARDED/ COMMENTS |
|---|---|---|---|---|---|---|---|---|---|---|
| Schefer | Ernest | sick & temporarily unable to support family | one acre of land | good | none | 15 | 20 | Feb. | 1914 | $15.00 3 Mar. 1914 |
| Schell | Frank | crippled and cannot work | none | good | none | 8 | 13 | Mar. | 1913 | |
| Schlobohm | Albert | no means of support | none | good | none | 8 | 10 | Sept. | 1913 | $8.00 8 Aug. 1914 |
| Schrogen | Mary J. | unable to earn living | none | good | none | 8 | | | | request rejected |
| Schuster | James Elgin | blind in one eye; poor sight in other; no use of one arm | none | sober | none | 15 | | | | $15.00 17 July 1915 |
| Sciacca | G. S. | totally blind | none | good | none | 20 | 7 | Feb. | 1910 | $15.00 7 Feb. 1910 |
| Scott | Albert | | none | good | none | 12.5 | 12 | May | 1910 | $6.00 20 May 1910 |
| Scott | J. H. | | | | | 25 | 3 | Jan. | 1905 | $20.00 for care of K. W. Thomas who died 31 Dec. 1904 |
| Seigel | Frank | old & feeble | house & lot | good | none | 15 | 2 | Feb. | 1915 | |
| Shaeffer | Cynthia | not able to work | none | good | none | 8 | 21 | Mar. | 1913 | |
| Shaeffer | Cynthia | failing health; unable to work | house | good | none | 8 | | | | $8.00 7 Nov. 1911 |
| Shaw | O. F., Dr. | poor health & partially blind | none | temperate | none | 5 | 21 | Mar. | 1900 | $5.00 27 Mar. 1900 |
| Sheldon | R. W. | old age | none | good | none | 6 | 1 | July | 1901 | $6.00 3 July 1901 |
| Sheldon | R. W. | old age | none | sober | none | 8 | 18 | Mar. | 1913 | |
| Shepard | Martin | inability to earn living | none | sober | junk business | 5 | 25 | Jan. | 1899 | $4.00 8 Feb. 1899 |
| Shepherd | Morris | crippled | none | good | none | 8 | 16 | Mar. | 1900 | $8.00 22 Mar. 1900 |
| Sherwood | J. C. | troubled with asthma at | | | | | 3 | Feb. | 1890 | |

| 1 | 2 | 15 | 16 | 17 | 18 | 19 | 20 | 21 | 22 | 23 |
|---|---|---|---|---|---|---|---|---|---|---|
| SURNAME | GIVEN NAME | REASON FOR REQUEST | PROPER-TY | SOBRI-ETY | SOURCE OF INCOME | R $ | | DATE OF REQUEST | | AMOUNT AWARDED/ COMMENTS |
| Sherwood | J. C. | troubled with asthma at county farm; feels fine in Cloverdale | | | | | 3 | Feb. | 1890 | |
| Sholes | Martha J. | old age; poor health; | small house & lot | the best | none | 7 | 20 | Aug. | 1914 | $7.00 8 Sept. 1914 |
| Sholes | Martha J., Mrs. | boy 9 or 10 cripple, needs mother's help | | | | | 9 | Mar. | 1882 | |
| Sibley | Rebecca, Mrs. | unable to work | | | | | 5 | May | 1890 | filed 5 May 1890 |
| Silva | D., Mrs. | | small house & lot | good | none | 8 | 18 | Apr. | 1901 | $5.00 6 June 1901 |
| Silva | Mabel | husband deserted her | none | good | none | 6 | 2 | Aug. | 1913 | $6.00 6 Sept. 1913 |
| Silva | Manuel D. | old age | none | sober | none | 15 | 8 | Oct. | 1917 | $10.00 4 Nov. 1917 |
| Silva | Mary M. | husband, Frank, died 14 Dec. 1885; left family in debt & destitute | | | | | 4 | Jan. | 1885 | |
| Silvia | Leonor | | none | good | none | 5 | | | | $5.00 3 July 1899 |
| Silzle | (children) | father deserted them; gives no support | small interest in real estate in IL | | $25/yr. | 10 | | | | no amount given 2 May 1892 |
| Simoni | Natalina | husband died July | equity $300 on house | good | none | 20 | 10 | Aug. | 1916 | note 14 Nov. 1916 |
| Simpson | Zeptha, Mrs. | unfortunate and helpless condition | | | | | 1 | June | 1886 | |
| Small | Mrs. | | | | | 10 | 1 | Jan. | 1892 | $8.00 5 Jan.1892 |
| Smith | D. W. | rheumatism | none | good | none | 6 | 21 | Dec. | 1909 | |

| 1 | 2 | 15 | 16 | 17 | 18 | 19 | 20 | 21 | 22 | 23 |
|---|---|---|---|---|---|---|---|---|---|---|
| SURNAME | GIVEN NAME | REASON FOR REQUEST | PROPER-TY | SOBRI-ETY | SOURCE OF INCOME | R $ | | DATE OF REQUEST | | AMOUNT AWARDED/ COMMENTS |
| Smith | J. Y., Mrs. | reason of infirmity, almost an invalid; husband died a few yrs. ago | | | | 15 | 28 | Oct. | 1885 | 18 year old dau. died 26 Oct. 1885 |
| Smith | Joseph M. | pulmonary tuberculosis; asks burial expenses | | | | | | | | burial of indigent soldier; Stanley Cemetery, Santa Rosa; 13 May 1910 |
| Smith | Nova N. | unable to work enough to support self & children | none | good | none | 20 | 24 | Jan. | 1916 | $20.00 14 Feb. 1916 |
| Smith | S. H. | old age & infirmity | none | temperate | none | 5 | 14 | Nov. | 1900 | |
| Smith | S. L., Mrs. | husband in Bakersfield; failed to provide anything for two months | none | sober | nothing for 2 months | 15 | 8 | Oct. | 1901 | $7.00; DeWitt, age 10, in the country |
| Smith | Samuel H. | helpless | none | good | none | 8 | 31 | Mar. | 1900 | $4.00 2 Apr. 1900 |
| Smith | Samuel H. | | | | | | | | | $4.00 4 Dec. 1899 |
| Smither | W., Mrs. | husband paralyzed; boys cannot make a living for family | none | | oldest sons | 17 .5 | | | | |
| Smithers | W. L. | stroke several months ago | none | good | some help from relatives | 20 | 8 | Dec. | 1909 | $15.00 1909 |
| Smyth | Mary R., Mrs. | bed ridden 15 days | | | | 10 | 16 | Oct. | 1891 | $8.00 3 Nov. 1891 |
| Snow | Rubin A. | paralytic; peddles in summer | | sober | | | 6 | Jan. | 1880 | admitted to county farm for the winter |
| Solorzano | Antonio | old age & infirm | none | temperate | private charity | 8 | 31 | Mar. | 1900 | $5.00 5 Apr. 1900 |
| Sousa | Marion, Mrs. | husband injured | none | good | none | 12 | 7 | Apr. | 1914 | $10.00 8 Apr. 1914 |

| 1 | 2 | 15 | 16 | 17 | 18 | 19 | 20 | 21 | 22 | 23 |
|---|---|---|---|---|---|---|---|---|---|---|
| SURNAME | GIVEN NAME | REASON FOR REQUEST | PROPERTY | SOBRIETY | SOURCE OF INCOME | R $ | | DATE OF REQUEST | | AMOUNT AWARDED/ COMMENTS |
| Souza | Frank | feeble & unable to earn a living | none | good | none | 12 | 27 | Dec. | 1915 | $12.00 14 Feb. 1916 |
| Spaich | Emilia, Mrs. | husband refuses to pay | none | good | none | 20 | 26 | Feb. | 1910 | $15.00 7 Apr. 1910 |
| Spaich | Emilia, Mrs. | sick | none | good | none | 15 | 28 | Mar. | 1913 | |
| Spaulding | Ambrose N. | old; crippled | none | good | none | 8 | 1 | Oct. | 1913 | $7.00 6 Oct 1913 |
| Speller | George | blind & paralyzed; unable to support self | | | | 5 | 6 | June | 1900 | $5.00; hand written letter |
| Sprunck | Henry P. | old age | house & lot | sober | eggs of 50 chickens | 10 | 18 | Aug. | 1917 | $8.00 13 Nov. 1917 |
| Stafford | B., Mrs. | husband in hospital | none | good | none | 15 | 25 | Feb. | 1916 | $15.00 14 Mar. 1916 |
| Stark | H. E, Mrs. | no means of support | none | good | none | | | | | $5.00 9 Feb. 1900 |
| Stark | Harriot E. | broken hip | none | good | none | 10 | 25 | Jan. | 1915 | |
| Stark | Willie | simpleton | | | | 10 | 1 | Feb. | 1890 | $8.00 |
| Starr | Nancy, Mrs. | poor health | 4 un-improved lots nr. Lakeport | good | small sum from sewing | 8 | | Mar. | 1913 | |
| Steinpis | Rosa | sick and unable to support herself and children | none | good | none | 8 | 5 | Feb. | 1901 | $5.00 11 Feb. 1901 |
| Sterling | James A. | crippled; unable to obtain employment | none | industrious & sober | none | 8 | 28 | Nov. | 1913 | |
| Stewart | Lovilla | old; dau. widow with three children | none | good | none | 10 | | | 1913 | $8.00 2 June 1913 |
| Stewart | Lovilla, Mrs. | old | none | good | none | | | | | rejected 10 Aug. 1915 |
| Stochini | Agostino | old age | none | sober | none | 10 | 20 | Oct. | 1900 | $5.00 8 Dec. 1900 |

| 1 | 2 | 15 | 16 | 17 | 18 | 19 | 20 | 21 | 22 | 23 |
|---|---|---|---|---|---|---|---|---|---|---|
| SURNAME | GIVEN NAME | REASON FOR REQUEST | PROPER-TY | SOBRI-ETY | SOURCE OF INCOME | R $ | | DATE OF REQUEST | | AMOUNT AWARDED/ COMMENTS |
| Stodard | Bud | crippled | none | good | none | 15 | 19 | Nov. | 1912 | $15.00 3 Dec. 1912 |
| Storks | Hariet E., Mrs. | broken hip; unable to work | none | | none | 12 | 20 | Nov. | 1915 | $8.00 16 Dec. 1915 |
| Strock | Emma, Mrs. | poor health | none | good | none | 15 | 1 | Aug. | 1916 | $15.00 15 Aug. 1916 |
| Stump | Daniel A. | disabled owing to cancer | none | good | none | 12 | | | | $8.00 May 1907 |
| Sutherland | Ella | | none | good | none | 6 | | | | |
| Sutherland | Ellen | sick | none | sobriety | none | 10 | 15 | June | 1917 | denied 14 Feb 1917 |
| Sutherland | Ellen, Mrs. | old | none | good | none | 6 | 31 | Jan. | 1910 | $6.00 31 Jan. 1909 |
| Suthland | Ellen | old & sick | none | sober | none | 8 | 11 | Mar. | 1916 | rejected |
| Sweet | James | old | none | good | by own labor | 7 | 25 | Feb. | 1909 | $7.00 1 Mar. 1909 |
| Sweet | James | old age | none | good | none | 7 | 12 | Mar. | 1913 | |
| Talbot | Louis F. | blind | none | good | none | 10 | | | | rejected |
| Talbot | Louis F. | blindness | | good | none | 12 | | | | |
| Talbot | Louis Franklin | blind | none | good | none | 8 | 15 | Mar. | 1900 | $5.00 26 Mar. 1900 |
| Tate | George Sidney | old | none | good | none | 8 | 22 | Sept. | 1910 | |
| Tate | George Sidney | old age; ill | none | good | none | 8 | 25 | June | 1913 | |
| Taylor | Ina F. | inability to provide for self | house & lot in San Luis Obispo | good | $4.00/mo. | 13 | 26 | May | 1915 | rejected; son at Salvation Army, Lytton Springs |
| Tew | Clara | not strong; unable to get employment | | good | | 10 | | | | |
| Thatford | Sarah A., Mrs. | old | none | good | none | 6 | 27 | Mar. | 1900 | $6.00 5 Apr. 1900 |
| Thiesen | C. E. C. S. | paralyzed | none | temperate | none | 8 | 3 | Feb. | 1899 | |
| Thomas | D. W. | sick | | | | 10 | 1 | Apr. | 1891 | $8.00 4 Apr. 1891 |
| Thomas | H. R., Mr. & Mrs. | blood poisoning | none | sober | none | 15 | 9 | Dec. | 1916 | $15.00 12 Dec. |

| 1 SURNAME | 2 GIVEN NAME | 15 REASON FOR REQUEST | 16 PROPERTY | 17 SOBRIETY | 18 SOURCE OF INCOME | 19 R $ | 20 | 21 DATE OF REQUEST | 22 | 23 AMOUNT AWARDED/ COMMENTS |
|---|---|---|---|---|---|---|---|---|---|---|
| | | | | | | | | | | 1916 |
| Thompson | Julia E. | sick | none | good | none | 5 | 26 | Mar. | 1900 | rejected |
| Thompson | Julia E. | no means of support | none | good | none | 10 | 6 | Mar. | 1913 | |
| Thompson | Nellie B. | no support | none | good | none | 20 | 6 | Aug. | 1913 | $10.00 9 Aug. 1913 |
| Thompson | William, Mrs. | husband in asylum | none | excellent | | 8 | 9 | Apr. | 1899 | no award 10 Apr. 1899 |
| Thorp | Carlena Anna Marie | old age | none | perfect | none | 10 | 27 | Apr. | 1917 | $10.00 15 May 1917 |
| Thunmillen | Elizabeth, Mrs. | bedridden; husband cares for children and wife | | | county | | | | | filed 7 Feb. 1885 |
| Timmons | H. M. | crippled; unable to work | none | good | none | 10 | 29 | Dec. | 1915 | rejected |
| Tod | Juliet M. & Isabella | both parents dead; income from property interests insufficient | lot with cottage | | $4,200 life insurance | 16 | 8 | July | 1910 | rejected |
| Tojo | Madalena | unable to earn a living; works for board | none | good | none | 8 | 20 | July | 1912 | $8.00 6 Aug. 1912 |
| Tojo | Madalena | old age and inability to work | none | good | none | 8 | 1 | Mar. | 1913 | |
| Toltschin | J., Mrs. | | | | none | | 17 | Oct. | 1917 | $10.00 13 Nov. 1917 |
| Tombs | Henry C. & Mrs. | old | but little | good | none | 12 | 5 | Apr. | 1913 | $12.00 |
| Toombs | G. A. | | none | good | | 10 | 10 | Dec. | 1914 | |
| Toroni | Margherita | old age | house & lot | good | none | 8 | 31 | Aug. | 1911 | $7.00 1 Nov. 1911 |
| Toroni | Margherita | old age | none | good | none | 7 | 2 | June | 1913 | $7.00 8 July 1913 |
| Toschi | Tranquilla | sick with lung trouble | | good | none | | 26 | Mar. | 1913 | |
| Towle | Ida M. | dau. cannot care for | none | good | none | 8 | 3 | Dec. | 1914 | |

| 1 | 2 | 15 | 16 | 17 | 18 | 19 | 20 | 21 | 22 | 23 |
|---|---|---|---|---|---|---|---|---|---|---|
| SURNAME | GIVEN NAME | REASON FOR REQUEST | PROPER-TY | SOBRI-ETY | SOURCE OF INCOME | R $ | | DATE OF REQUEST | | AMOUNT AWARDED/ COMMENTS |
| | | her; cannot care for herself | | | | | | | | |
| Treat | John J., Mrs. | husband away in SF | none | | | 15 | | | 1909 | filed 7 Jan. 1909 |
| Trimble | Patrick J. | crippled; unable to work | none | | none | 8 | | | | not allowed 4 Dec. 1899 |
| Tritchler | Dora | sick | house & lot | good | none | 8 | 28 | Mar. | 1900 | $5.00 2 Apr. 1900 |
| Truett | William | consumption; unable to work | | | | | 28 | May | 1879 | $10.00; filed 18 June 1879 |
| Tuitchlen? | Dora, Mrs. | | | | | 10 | | | | |
| Tuney | J. | wife invalid; sick 7 years | | | | | 1 | Jan. | 1892 | letter |
| Tuney | J. | | | | | | | | | $20.00 4 Feb. 1892 |
| Tunnell | Eliza A., Mrs. | rheumatism | house, block 25 lots 2 & 3 | | | | | | 1918 | $8.00 5 Mar. 1918 |
| Turner | Annie Maria, Mrs. | old age | none | sober | none | 10 | | | | $10.00 11 Dec. 1916 |
| Turner | J. H. | kidney trouble | none | good | none | 8 | 7 | Dec. | 1900 | $5.00 8 Dec. 1900 |
| Turner | J. H. | liver; stomach; kidney trouble | 1 cow; 1 mule; 23 hens | good | none | 10 | | | | $5.00 8 Dec. 1909 |
| Turner | M., Mrs. | old | none | good | none | 10 | | | | $10.00 6 Aug. 1912 |
| Turner | Martha | old and not able to work | none | sober & Christian | none | 10 | | | | |
| Turner | Mary, Mrs. | destitute; husband deserted | | | | | 25 | June | 1891 | granted 7 July 1891 |
| Turner | Peter W. | inability to work because of age | none | sober | none | 8 | 28 | Sept. | 1899 | $6.00 3 Oct. 1899 |

| 1 | 2 | 15 | 16 | 17 | 18 | 19 | 20 | 21 | 22 | 23 |
|---|---|---|---|---|---|---|---|---|---|---|
| SURNAME | GIVEN NAME | REASON FOR REQUEST | PROPER-TY | SOBRI-ETY | SOURCE OF INCOME | R $ | | DATE OF REQUEST | | AMOUNT AWARDED/ COMMENTS |
| Turner | Peter W. | old age | none | sober | none | 8 | 24 | Mar. | 1900 | $5.00 24 Mar. 1900 |
| Turner | S. E., Mrs. | old feeble & helpless | none | sober | none | 10 | 1 | Aug. | 1899 | $6.00 1 Aug. 1899 |
| Turner | Semantha E., Mrs. | sick; separated from husband | none | good | none | 8 | 26 | Mar. | 1900 | $6.00 26 Mar. 1900 |
| Tyler | Clifton | child is legal orphan too small to earn a living | none | | none | 5 | 29 | Apr. | 1901 | $5.00 8 May 1901 |
| Unger | Julia | unable to support herself and children | none | good | none | 12 | | | | $8.00 4 Sept. 1913 |
| Ursin | Ada | husband blind; needs constant care; unable to work outside | 5 acres with $600 mortgage | strictly temperate | none | 10 | 5 | Apr. | 1910 | $10.00 6 Apr. 1910 |
| Ursin | Ada L. | husband blind & sick; wife sick | 5 acres | good | none | 10 | 20 | Feb. | 1913 | $10.00 8 Apr. 1913 |
| Ursin | Ada, Mrs. | husband blind; wife sick | 5 acres heavily mortgaged | good | none | 10 | | | | $10.00 2 Jan. 1912 |
| Valentine | Mary | old age | none | good | none | 8 | 4 | Apr. | 1899 | $8.00 4 May 1899 |
| Van | Mr. & Mrs. | | | | | | 30 | Mar. | 1889 | letter complaining that people not needy |
| Vance | | grandmother in failing health | | | | 8 | | | | |
| Vance | Robin & Stuart | grandmother unable to earn enough to support them | | | | 10 | | | | filed 8 Feb. 1890 |
| VanGeldern | Mathilde | unable to work because of age | none | good | occasional donations of food and clothing | | 25 | Apr. | 1893 | support continues |

| 1 | 2 | 15 | 16 | 17 | 18 | 19 | 20 | 21 | 22 | 23 |
|---|---|---|---|---|---|---|---|---|---|---|
| SURNAME | GIVEN NAME | REASON FOR REQUEST | PROPER-TY | SOBRI-ETY | SOURCE OF INCOME | R $ | | DATE OF REQUEST | | AMOUNT AWARDED/ COMMENTS |
| VanGeldern | Matilda | financial condition is pitiable | | | | 10 | 15 | Aug. | 1887 | |
| VanGeldern | Matilda, Miss | without means; advanced in years; unable to make a living. | | | | | | | | $10.00 1 Feb. 1890 |
| Vann | E. S. | old age | | | | 10 | 4 | Jan. | 1890 | |
| Vann | E. S. | old age | 2 cows; old horse & buggy | | | | 3 | Mar. | 1890 | $8.00 3 Mar. 1890 |
| Vann | E. S. | infirmities of age; wife is sick | none | good | small contribu-tion from stepson | 8 | | | | $5.00 5 June 1900 |
| Vann | E. S. & wife | unable to make a living especially in winter | | | | | 6 | Dec. | 1888 | |
| Vaughan | E. N., Mrs. | unable to work; needs care | | good | none | 10 | 1 | Feb. | 1915 | $10.00 2 Feb. 1915 |
| Vaughn | Casan E., Mrs. | old age | none | good | none | 10 | 5 | Jan. | 1911 | |
| Veatch | Ellen | old; sick | none | good | none | | 2 | May | 1911 | placed in County Hospital |
| Vellulinni | Ermida & Annie | mother dead; father in insane asylum in Ukiah | none | good | none | | 28 | July | 1914 | request rejected |
| Vest | Eli | wife confined to bed since 1891 | none | sober & industri-ous | | | | | | $6.00 4 Feb. 1892; CA resident 11 years; Sonoma Co. 6 mos. |
| Vestal | Jacob | invalid | none | good | none | 5 | 16 | Apr. | 1900 | $8.00 June 1900 |
| Vier(s) | Mrs. | unable to work; one child crippled | none | | none | | 3 | Mar. | 1890 | $10.00 |

| 1 | 2 | 15 | 16 | 17 | 18 | 19 | 20 | 21 | 22 | 23 |
|---|---|---|---|---|---|---|---|---|---|---|
| SURNAME | GIVEN NAME | REASON FOR REQUEST | PROPER-TY | SOBRI-ETY | SOURCE OF INCOME | R $ | | DATE OF REQUEST | | AMOUNT AWARDED/ COMMENTS |
| Vierra | Anna, Mrs. | old & insufficient means for support | | | | | | | | not granted |
| Vineyard | Leone | 12 year old boy; orphan; no means of support | none | | none | 6 | 23 | Dec. | 1914 | $6.00 6 Jan. 1915 |
| Vinsent | John | blind; partially paralyzed | none | good | none except from aged mother | 8 | | | | |
| Vinyard | Leon | no means of support | | | none | | | | | |
| vonGeldern | Matilda | no visible means of support | none | | none | | 12 | July | 1889 | |
| Wagner | Katherine | husband unable to secure employment; letter attached | none | good | only what husband & children get berry picking | 16 | 25 | July | 1914 | $12.00 3 Aug. 1914 |
| Waldvogel | Marie | invalid; not able to work | none | good | none | 10 | 14 | Mar. | | |
| Walk | Lillie Ellen | husband unable to work; I am sole support of family | none | sober | $1/day | | 29 | Sept. | 1915 | $8.00 15 Oct. 1915 |
| Walker | Ada L., Mrs. | old | none | good | none | 8 | 8 | Dec. | 1913 | $8.00 7 Jan. 1914 |
| Walker | B. K. | | | good | none | | | | | |
| Walker | Benjamin K. | crippled | none | good | none | 10 | | | | $8.00 5 Sept. 1912 |
| Walker | Lizzie | feeble and unable to support family; husband left | | | | 10 | 20 | Aug. | 1889 | |
| Walker | Lizzie | husband disappeared; sick | none | | oldest child works | 10 | 8 | Mar. | 1890 | |

-169-

| 1 | 2 | 15 | 16 | 17 | 18 | 19 | 20 | 21 | 22 | 23 |
|---|---|---|---|---|---|---|---|---|---|---|
| SURNAME | GIVEN NAME | REASON FOR REQUEST | PROPER-TY | SOBRI-ETY | SOURCE OF INCOME | R $ | | DATE OF REQUEST | | AMOUNT AWARDED/ COMMENTS |
| Walker | Nancy, Mrs. | | none | sober | some | 8 | 28 | July | 1899 | $5.00 10 Aug. 1899 |
| Wall | Ada | unable to leave children to work; parent unable to help | none | good | none | 10 | | Oct. | 1911 | $10.00 6 Nov. 1911 |
| Wall | Ada, Mrs. | husband deserted her | none | sober | none | 10 | 27 | Feb. | 1913 | $10.00 8 Apr. 1913 |
| Wallace | James | unable to care for himself | | | | | | | | |
| Ward | Laura | 5 small children; pregnant; unable to work; husband deserted her | none | good | none | 15 | 2 | Nov. | 1912 | $15.00 6 Nov. 1912 |
| Ward | Laura | tuberculosis | none | | none | 45 | 27 | Mar. | 1915 | children reside with father; 45 people signed this petition |
| Ward | Laura, Mrs. | has no means of support | none | good | | 15 | | | 1913 | $15.00 8 Apr. 1913 |
| Ward | Lizzie, Mrs. | no support | in WA, mortgaged; no income | good | none | 8 | 2 | Aug. | 1899 | $6.00 4 Oct. 1899 |
| Ward | Thomas | not able to work | none | good | none | 8 | 28 | Mar. | 1900 | $5.00 5 Apr. 1900 |
| Ward | William | unable to labor | none | good | none | 7 | 22 | Mar. | 1913 | |
| Ward | William | old | none | good | none | | | | | $7.00 7 May 1912 |
| Warne | N. E., Mrs. | invalid; husband deserted her | none | good | none | 5 | 9 | Dec. | 1899 | $5.00 3 Jan. 1900 |
| Warne | N. E., Mrs. | sick; husband left | none | good | none | 5 | 4 | Apr. | 1900 | |
| Wassom | Jacob & wife | old age & feeble | | | | | 12 | Mar. | 1879 | |
| Webb | William B. | old age, crippled | none | good | none | 8 | 21 | Oct. | 1916 | |
| Webster | Anthony | in county hospital | | | Mr. Fix | | 8 | Apr. | 1879 | granted 10 Apr. |

| 1 | 2 | 15 | 16 | 17 | 18 | 19 | 20 | 21 | 22 | 23 |
|---|---|---|---|---|---|---|---|---|---|---|
| SURNAME | GIVEN NAME | REASON FOR REQUEST | PROPER-TY | SOBRI-ETY | SOURCE OF INCOME | R $ | | DATE OF REQUEST | | AMOUNT AWARDED/ COMMENTS |
| | | twice; now has pneumonia | | | | | | | | 1879 |
| Welch | Martha | old age; sick; unable to earn living | none | good | none | 12 | 7 | Mar. | 1913 | $12.00 |
| Welch | Martha, Mrs. | nearly blind | | good | | 13 | 2 | Nov. | 1909 | $8.00 Nov. 1909 |
| Welch | Mary, Mrs. | no income of any kind | small house & lot | excellent | none | 10 | 20 | Mar. | 1913 | $6.00 8 Apr. 1913 |
| Welch | Mrs. | old | small lot | good | none | 6 | | | | $6.00 4 Feb. 1907 |
| Welhe | Irene | poor health | none | good | none | 8 | 11 | June | 1900 | $8.00 11 June 1900 |
| Weller | Ada, Mrs. | unable to earn enough money; in poor health | non | sober | none | 20 | 6 | Nov. | 1916 | $20.00 14 Nov. 1916; note attached to application |
| Weller | George | rheumatism | none | good | none | 6 | 26 | Mar. | 1900 | $5.00 27 Mar. 1900 |
| Wells | J. M. | old age; unable to work; confined to bed | none | first class | none | 10 | 29 | Sept. | 1910 | $10.00 5 Oct. 1910 |
| Wells | Oscar J. | old age; unfit to work | none | very good | none | 10 | 28 | Oct. | 1916 | $10.00 14 Nov. 1916 |
| Wellschott | Theodore & wife | broken leg and unable to work | | | | | | | | filed 1884 |
| Welschott | Theodore | poorly set broken leg; rheumatism; wife also disabled | small house | | neighbors | | | | | $15.00 6 Feb. 1890 |
| Welsholt | Theodore | hopeless cripple; wife is confined to bed with rheumatism | | | | 20 | 5 | Dec. | 1887 | |
| Westgate | Charles, Mrs. | sickly and unable to work | none | sober | $6.00 from state | 15 | 2 | Mar. | 1916 | $15.00 15 Mar. 1916 |
| Wheeler | A. | ill health; destitute; | | | | | | | | $10.00 3 June 1891 |

| 1 | 2 | 15 | 16 | 17 | 18 | 19 | 20 | 21 | 22 | 23 |
|---|---|---|---|---|---|---|---|---|---|---|
| SURNAME | GIVEN NAME | REASON FOR REQUEST | PROPER-TY | SOBRI-ETY | SOURCE OF INCOME | R $ | | DATE OF REQUEST | | AMOUNT AWARDED/ COMMENTS |
| Wheeler | A. | wife sick; poor health; invalid wife; unable to work | | | | 6 | | | | $6.00 7 June 1892 |
| Wheeler | Mary | children unable to support her | none | exempla-ry habits | none | 10 | | | | |
| Whitcomb | O., Mr. & Mrs. | no means of support | none | good | none | 15 | 3 | Mar. | 1911 | $10.00 8 Mar. 1911 |
| White | Catherine R. | old age | none | fine | none | 10 | 13 | Mar. | 1917 | $10.00 14 Mar. 1917 |
| White | John | old; unable to work | none | good | none | 5 | 2 | Aug. | 1899 | $5.00 9 Aug. 1899 |
| White | John | | none | good | none | 5 | 20 | Mar. | 1900 | $5.00 2 Apr. 1900 |
| Whitney | Cora, Mrs. | crippled; husband deserted them | none | good | none | 10 | 1 | Mar. | 1915 | $10.00 |
| Whitson | Charlotte | unable to work because of operation | | | | | | | | $10.00 3 Aug. 1914 |
| Wiatt | Martha A. | sick | 1 ½ acres; little home mortgaged | good | just from county | | | | | certificate sworn 18 Apr. 1893 |
| Wiatt | Martha A. | invalid | 1 ½ acres; little home mortgaged | | | | | | | $6.00 8 Mar. 1892 ; 35 year resident |
| Wieberts | Richard | sick; not likely to recover | none | | neighbor | 10 | | | | $10.00 2 Feb. 1892 |
| Wilhite | George A. | wife has cancer and needs to be taken care of | | | | 7 | 6 | Dec. | 1914 | |
| Wilke | Irene | unable to earn a living | none | sober | none | 8 | 28 | Mar. | 1913 | |
| Wilkerson | John F. | partially paralyzed | none | good | none | 7 | 17 | Aug. | 1911 | $7.00 8 Sept. 1911 |
| Willcox | Eliza | not able to work | none | good | none | 8 | | | | $6.00 filed 9 May 1900 |

| 1 | 2 | 15 | 16 | 17 | 18 | 19 | 20 | 21 | 22 | 23 |
|---|---|---|---|---|---|---|---|---|---|---|
| SURNAME | GIVEN NAME | REASON FOR REQUEST | PROPER-TY | SOBRI-ETY | SOURCE OF INCOME | R $ | | DATE OF REQUEST | | AMOUNT AWARDED/ COMMENTS |
| Williams | Cynthia, Mrs. | father abandoned; she is in poor health | none | good | none | 20 | | | | $15.00 3 Nov. 1909 |
| Williams | George W. & Sarah A. | poor health; unable to support themselves | none | good | | | | | | $8.00 16 July 1892; to California in 1887; Sonoma Co. 1 1/2 years |
| Williams | Ira T., Mrs. | no means of support | none | good | none | 10 | 26 | Nov. | 1916 | denied 14 Dec. 1916 |
| Williams | J. W., Mr. & Mrs. | | | | | 30 | | Oct. | 1892 | $30.00 7 Oct. 1892 |
| Williams | Mary | old age and unable to work | none | good | none | 8 | 16 | May | 1900 | $4.00 5 June 1900 |
| Williams | Wm. | badly hurt, thrown from horse | | | | | 12 | Oct. | 1855 | |
| Williams | Mary Ann | too old to work; crippled with rheumatism | none | good | none | 8 | | | | $5.00 |
| Willis (children) | Ada, Mrs. | high cost of living | small house | | $35.00 from husband | | 27 | Nov. | 1917 | not recommended by Social Service Comm. |
| Wilson | Anthony | unable to work | none | | none | 10 | | | | |
| Wilson | Anton | old & feeble | none | good | none | 10 | 7 | Mar. | 1917 | $10.00 12 Mar. 1917 |
| Wilson | Charles K., Mrs. | crippled with rheumatism; no means of support | none | strictly temperate | none | 10 | 5 | Mar. | 1913 | |
| Wilson | Charles Sovrin | advanced age; feeble; inability to earn livelihood | small lot with shanty | good | none | 8 | 17 | Nov. | 1915 | $8.00 13 Dec. 1915 |
| Wilson | Florence, Mrs. | poor health; husband deserted | | | | 10 | 6 | Dec. | 1892 | $7.00 7 Dec. 1892; husband is so. part of state |

| 1 | 2 | 15 | 16 | 17 | 18 | 19 | 20 | 21 | 22 | 23 |
|---|---|---|---|---|---|---|---|---|---|---|
| SURNAME | GIVEN NAME | REASON FOR REQUEST | PROPERTY | SOBRIETY | SOURCE OF INCOME | R $ | | DATE OF REQUEST | | AMOUNT AWARDED/ COMMENTS |
| Wilson | Florence, Mrs. | not strong; separated 5 years | | good | none | 8 | | | 1900 | $5.00 filed 5 Apr. 1900 |
| Wilson | Lillie, Mrs. | | none | good | none except her labor | 10 | 8 | Dec. | 1914 | $10.00 9 Dec. 1914 |
| Wilson | Lilly | has no means of support | none | excellent | $15/mo. from labor | | 23 | Feb. | 1913 | |
| Wilson | Lilly | unable to support herself & children | none | good | none only from work | 15 | 15 | Sept. | 1915 | rejected |
| Wilson | Lilly, Mrs. | unable to earn enough to feed and clothe children | none | excellent | nursing; $20 alimony | 20 | 4 | Dec. | 1912 | $12.00 5 Dec. 1912 |
| Wilson | P. L. | unable to work | none | good | none | 10 | 6 | July | 1916 | $10.00 12 July 1916 |
| Wilson | Sarah, Mrs. | invalid; destitute | | | | | | | | $6.00 7 June 1892 |
| Winslow | John | old & crippled | none | sober | none | | 2 | Oct. | 1917 | $8.00 12 Dec. 1917 |
| Winter | Bernhardt | cripple; unable to work | none | good | none | 10 | 21 | Mar. | 1913 | |
| Winter | Bernhardt | crippled in legs; cannot move out of chair | none | good | none | 10 | | | | $10.00 6 Apr. 1912 |
| Winton | Robert F. | sick | none | good | none | 10 | 8 | June | 1912 | $10.00 8 June 1912 |
| Winton | Robert F. | invalid | none | good | none | 10 | | | 1913 | $10.00 |
| Woldvogel | Mary | not able to work | none | good | none | 5 | 20 | Mar. | 1900 | $5.00 31 Mar. 1900 |
| Wolfe | N. T. | unable to work because of rheumatism | house & lot worth $200.00 | | none | | 1 | Dec. | 1890 | $7.00 2 Dec. 1890 |
| Wolfe | N. T. | | little home | good | none | 10 | | | | $10.00 8 Feb. 1907 |
| Wolfe | N. T. & Catherine | infirmities of age and unable to earn a living | little shanty | good | none | 8 | 16 | Apr. | 1900 | $5.00 10 May 1900 |
| Wood | Jane | unable to work | none | good | occasional charity | 8 | | | | $6.00 21 Mar. 1900 |

| 1 SURNAME | 2 GIVEN NAME | 15 REASON FOR REQUEST | 16 PROPER-TY | 17 SOBRI-ETY | 18 SOURCE OF INCOME | 19 R $ | 20 | 21 DATE OF REQUEST | 22 | 23 AMOUNT AWARDED/ COMMENTS |
|---|---|---|---|---|---|---|---|---|---|---|
| Wood | Jane, Mrs. | feeble; indigent | | | neighbors | 10 | 15 | Sept. | 1891 | $8.00 5 Oct. 1891 |
| Wood | John | old and feeble | | | | 15 | 27 | Jan. | 1886 | receiving $5.00 per month from county now |
| Wood | John | husband unable to work | | | | 15 | 12 | Feb. | 1890 | $11.25 3 Mar. 1890 |
| Wood | John & Mary Jane | old age | | | | | 30 | Oct. | 1882 | in Petaluma since 1873 |
| Wood | W. E., Mrs. | father died 9 Mar. 1904, Rough & Ready; mother in Healdsburg | none | good | none | 18 | 15 | Feb. | 1909 | |
| Woodley | Josie | husband sick | none | good | none | 15 | 28 | May | 1915 | |
| Woods | Katie | does not receive enough money from father to support them | none | good | $20.00/mo. from father | 10 | 27 | June | 1916 | $10.00 29 June 1916 |
| Woods | Katie, Mrs. | young child; husband no employment | none | good | none | 15 | 26 | Jan. | 1916 | $15.00 4 Feb. 1916 |
| Woodward | Martha Jane | old | mortgaged | good | none | 8 | 24 | Mar. | 1914 | $8.00 Apr. 1914 |
| Wooley | Susan | no means of support | none | good | none | 5 | 12 | Aug. | 1899 | $5.00 14 Aug. 1899 |
| Woolf | Buck, Mrs. | sick; destitute | | | | | 6 | June | 1905 | |
| Woolley | Susan | old; unable to work | none | good | none | 5 | | Mar. | 1900 | $5.00 19 Mar. 1900 |
| Worden | William D. | old and unable to work | | | | | 12 | July | 1899 | |
| Wordin | Annie | injured back in earthquake & unable to work | none | good | none | 10 | 21 | Feb. | 1907 | $6.00 7 Mar. 1907 |
| Workman | Nettie | deserted by husband | none | good | none | 5 | 6 | Mar. | 1899 | $5.00 4 Apr. 1899 |
| Wright | Isaac | old | none | good | | | | | 1909 | $10.00 3 May 1909 |
| Wyatt | Mrs. & Aunt Peggy | | house for life | | son $6.00 | | 3 | May | 1881 | Ladies Aid Society letter |
| Yeager | A., Mrs. | husband sick in County | none | good | | | 26 | Apr. | 1901 | $6.00 7 May 1901 |

| 1 | 2 | 15 | 16 | 17 | 18 | 19 | 20 | 21 | 22 | 23 |
|---|---|---|---|---|---|---|---|---|---|---|
| SURNAME | GIVEN NAME | REASON FOR REQUEST | PROPER-TY | SOBRI-ETY | SOURCE OF INCOME | R $ | | DATE OF REQUEST | | AMOUNT AWARDED/ COMMENTS |
| Young | John | Hospital drunken | little place | good | friends $15 | 8 | 3 | Dec. | 1892 | $5.00 7 Dec. 1892; homestead property |
| Young | Minnie A. | physical disability; hurt in earthquake 1906 | | excellent | | 15 | 9 | Sept. | 1914 | $15.00 9 Oct. 1914 |
| Young | Ada, Mrs. | ill; unable to work; arms lame and painful | none | good | none | 10 | 14 | Apr. | 1916 | $10.00 15 Apr. 1916 |
| Zanolini | M., Mrs. | husband blind; children under the age of 10 | none | good | none | 35 | | | | $8.00 3 Apr. 1899 |
| Zanolini | Michael | total blindness | none | good | none | 15 | 29 | Mar. | 1900 | $9.00 2 Apr. 1900 |
| Zappa | Martin | sick | small cabin belongs to wife | sober | none | | 2 | May | 1910 | $8.00 3 May 1910 |

# Part IV
# Demographics

Filing Status
Marital Status
Township
Number of Children
Nationality
Awards

# Demographics

While a total of 1,208 applications were filed, not all applicants completed all the information required on the form. In addition, the earlier applications consisted of statements of need, before forms were developed. For these reasons, not all summarized categories reflect the total of 1,208 applications. Never-the-less, where information is available, it is interesting to describe the population of indigents represented by this report.

## Filing Status
The largest number of applications were filed by women (657), men filed 485 applications, while 53 couples filed jointly. The age of the applicants ranged from six years to 110 years. For underage applicants, an adult filed on their behalf.

## Marital Status
The largest number of applicants were widowed (386), while the next largest number were single (188); 35 were divorced, and three persons said they had been deserted.

## Township
Of the sixteen townships, all were represented in these data roughly in proportion to the population of the township.

## Number of Children
Number of children per household ranged from one to twelve, while the median was between five and six.

## Nationality
Eighty-eight of the applicants were foreign born, with the largest number coming from England, Germany, and Ireland.

## Awards
Not all applicants who filed received support from the county. A total of 737 persons (61%) received some funds for their support.

The data in tabular form are given on the next page.

| Filing Status | No. |
|---|---|
| Females | 657 |
| Males | 485 |
| Couples | 53 |

Age of applicants ranged from 6 years to 110 years.

| Marital Status | No. |
|---|---|
| Widowed | 386 |
| Single | 188 |
| Divorced | 35 |
| Deserted | 3 |

| Townships | No. |
|---|---|
| Santa Rosa | 483 |
| Petaluma | 173 |
| Mendocino | 120 |
| Analy | 115 |
| Sonoma | 60 |
| Redwood | 51 |
| Bodega | 51 |
| Cloverdale | 45 |
| Russian River | 26 |
| Ocean | 19 |
| Washington | 13 |
| Salt Point | 10 |
| Glen Ellen | 9 |
| Knights Valley | 8 |
| Cazadero | 5 |
| Vallejo | 4 |

| No. Children | No. |
|---|---|
| 1 | 127 |
| 2 | 120 |
| 3 | 244 |
| 4 | 209 |
| 5 | 323 |
| 6 | 247 |
| 7 | 340 |
| 8 | 259 |
| 9 | 6 |
| 10 | 1 |
| 11 | 1 |
| 12 | 1 |

| Nationality (Outside USA) | No. |
|---|---|
| Austria | 1 |
| Azores | 2 |
| Chile | 2 |
| Canada | 2 |
| Denmark | 6 |
| England | 16 |
| Finland | 1 |
| French/Canadian | 1 |
| France | 1 |
| Germany | 15 |
| Holland | 1 |
| Ireland | 12 |
| Italian | 7 |
| Mexico | 1 |
| Portugal | 4 |
| Russia | 1 |
| Scotland | 3 |
| Sweden | 3 |
| Switzerland | 9 |